ICONS

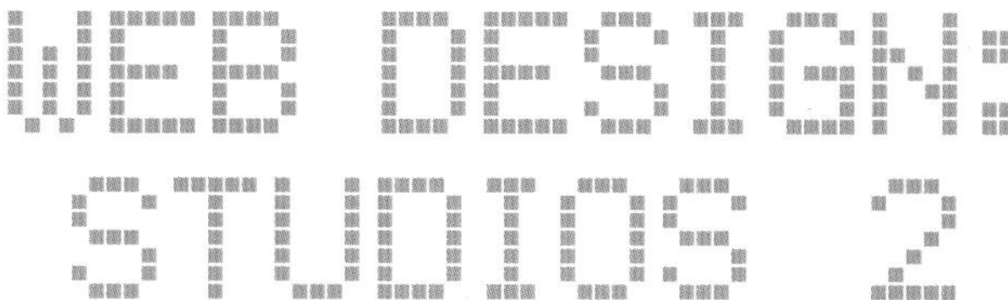

Ed. Julius Wiedemann

TASCHEN

HONG KONG KÖLN LONDON LOS ANGELES MADRID PARIS TOKYO

CONTENTS

Introduction

Jonathan Hills (Domani Studios)

Web design has come a long way since the days of the 216-color web palate and snail's pace connection speeds. Today, interactive designers have more freedom and flexibility than ever before. The tools we use are more robust; target audiences are more savvy; and lush interactive experiences are more possible than we could have imagined even a year ago. The interactive work being created today is more vibrant, textural, and immersive than ever. Creatively, the possibilities seem limitless.

Yet, even with all these rich opportunities at our fingertips, creating immersive online experiences has become increasingly more challenging. As many of the technical barriers and access limitations come down, the way people communicate digitally and perceive interactive messaging is changing dramatically. Interactive designers and web studios are finding that they need to wear more hats to make their projects compelling, keep site visitors engaged, and keep their clients satisfied. We're tasked with playing philosopher, sociologist, and magician as much as designer and technologist because the design process has grown well beyond structuring content or offering a particular service, and is more and more about creating a worthwhile experience where users can share, create, play, or physically interact with a larger group.

On top of all this, online users today expect richer experiences, and are not as likely as they once were to buy into online media simply because they have access to it. Successful interactive designers engage these increasingly shrewd users by finding new ways to build on traditional design principles like typography, layout, identity, and the like. But by adding new layers, such as motion, gaming, 3D design, and social networking, the best web studios are evolving interactive work, and simultaneously the very definition of interactivity.

Client expectations also add to the challenge. Bringing a client's brand message online today often means designing for a handful of separate communication channels. Interactive studios are finding themselves needing to think well beyond a website that houses content and captures email addresses, or a banner campaign that crowds an already chaotic homepage of a popular portal with yet another logo and brand message. A whole new set of questions are surfacing during strategy sessions that are forcing studios to think of interactive as a much broader discipline, one that addresses the myriad ways people are connecting with online content and services, and communicating with each other digitally. The questions we ask when stewarding our clients online often determine how fresh, useful, or viral our projects turn out.

These changes have created a terrifying reality for many who for years have taken the same approach to marketing, used the same channels for communication and the same formulas for messaging. All of these new challenges, however, translate into exciting opportunities for creative thinkers who are eager to deliver a brand's message in a whole new way, and create online destinations that they themselves would enjoy. The interactive studios that stand out are the ones that remain focused on a single compelling idea and push the web to be its most dynamic and collaborative. They do not con or mislead. They engage users on their own terms. They don't just tell a story. They allow users to shape a narrative. They don't just communicate a message; they provide the tools and the spark for users to communicate it for them.

The best designers push themselves to create interactive spaces that are playful, mysterious, and collaborative – no matter the brand or product. Innovative designers are giving users a reason to engage with brands, even brands that lack an inherent online draw on their own, and creating a **destination** that itself becomes the draw. The top web shops know that they need to take their clients to places they have never been, convince them to let go, and give users something they can take more control of. Whether it surfaces within playful, illustrative sensibilities such as those of *JUXT*, the rich physical spaces of *North Kingdom*, or the gaming innovations of *Big Spaceship*, the most engaging online environments foster a sense of play, enable personal expression, and find the delicate balance between a brand's message and what will attract and inspire user interaction.

In fact, facilitating ways in which users share their individual voice is one of the keys to successful interactive these days. When we look deeper into buzz phrases, such as "consumer generated content" and "social networking" we see that a deeper experience centered on community and self-expression is a huge part of how we all live. The wild successes of *YouTube*, *MySpace*, personal blogging, and podcasts are proof of this, and evidence that it is becoming increasingly important that even the smaller branded sites take their users' voices into account.

Indeed, the social networking phenomenon is changing ways designers think about communication. Design has always been about taking a particular message and making it accessible, tasty, or thoughtful. But today, in addition to thinking of design as communication with a particular audience, we as interactive designers are thinking more and more about design as a vehicle for communication laterally **within** that audience. The best web shops find themselves not only delivering a brand message, but also designing online applications and tools that bring users together and interact via a branded experience. Nowadays, innovative strategists, designers and programmers serve as architects of communication as much as they serve to communicate a particular message.

This has been a very complex shift, and it is revolutionizing the very way advertising works. It has been difficult for some traditional designers and agencies to incorporate this approach, but the ones that have embraced it are making stronger connections with their audiences. These connections make parts of the branding process easier, enabling the audience to spread a brand message as well as contribute the content that helps keep a particular site relevant. *AKQA* has done a beautiful job collaborating with users. Its work for *Coke* has made the user an active participant in the marketing process by giving site visitors a voice and encouraging them to create content that helps fuel the brand's vibrant web presence.

And behind the best of the best, even in interactive, there lies the Big Idea. Sure, execution is always a major piece of the puzzle for successful web studios. Beautiful designs, smart interfaces, and Flash wizardry turn heads and get awards. But it is the combination of those pieces with a unifying Big Idea that sets great web studios apart. Studios that hone in on a single compelling idea, align it with the client's brand, and use it as the keystone for interactive design and execution will always stand out.

Interestingly, with consumers less vulnerable to being sidetracked or swayed by peripheral messaging, and more annoyed by larger agencies' screams for attention via loud, overexposed messaging, it is the heightened, Big Idea creativity of the best interactive studios that **is** working. When interactive experiences are creatively compelling and resonate through humor, intrigue, aw-factor, or just because it's meaningful to the user in some powerful way, not only will the audience **embrace** it, they will go out of their way to find it again. Most importantly, they will share that experience with friends.

The interactive studios that stand out today know this and push the web to its most dynamic and collaborative limits. They understand that effective marketing and design is not about communicating a message **to** an audience, but rather embracing digital consumers as active participants who **want** to contribute, who want to become a part of some experience. Their finest works communicate a brand's message within a Big Idea and uniquely immersive experience. Successful studios will continue to create flexible, participatory experiences, but will also continually adapt to users while incorporating new technology and new layers of creativity. The interactive studios featured on the subsequent pages are helping to ensure that from seemingly unrestrained chaosinspiration, beauty, and engaging stories that take people to fresh, collaborative places will rise.

In an alternate reality, **Jonathan Hills** would say he was born in Iceland. He was raised by pandas. He speaks eleven languages. He summited Everest, twice. And he does not place action figures on his computer, as if he were five years old. Unfortunately, Jon is incapable of designing his own life. So he must design other things. To help with this endeavor, Jon started **Domani Studios**, a high-end, interactive design studio in Brooklyn, where he is creative director. Domani Studios creates top-shelf interactive environments and viral marketing experiences for clients such as *Volkswagen*, *Anheuser-Busch*, *Gucci*, and *W Hotels*. Jon has been invited to speak at design seminars across the country, where he enjoys interrupting other panelists and yammering away ad nauseum. When he's not examining the cusp of what is possible in the world of interactive design, Jon can be found playing guitar in NYC's ambient, instrumental duo, *1 Mile North*.

www.domanistudios.com

WORK | SERVICES | STUDIO | CONTACT

Tunnel o' Love
we've got GAME!!
ask about our viral game development skills
Learn More

WHETHER YOU NEED TO CHANGE THE WAY YOUR BUSINESS LOOKS, OR REVOLUTIONIZE THE WAY IT COMMUNICATES, DOMANI STUDIOS CAN PROVIDE POSITIVE AND MEASURABLE ONLINE RESULTS.

Domani Studios has designed brand identities, created comprehensive online marketing campaigns, and developed award winning web sites and eCommerce environments. Please explore our portfolio and services, or contact our business team directly to learn more about our history and design philosophy.

✣ Explore our portfolio ✣ Contact our business team

Domani Studios wins at AIGA 365

Winner of Experience Design category

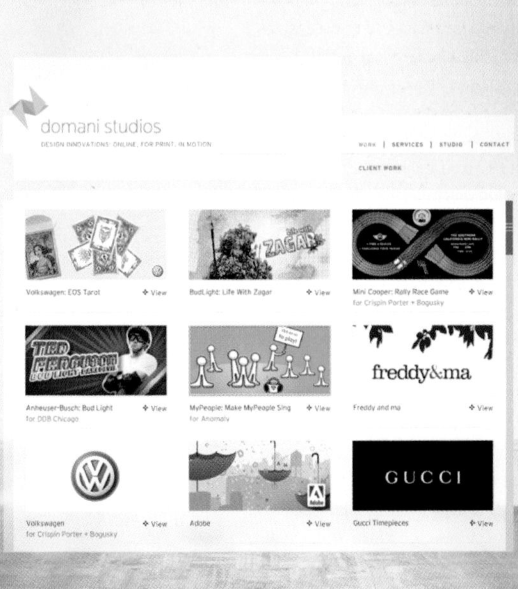

INTRO

Introduction
Jonathan Hills (Domani Studios)

Le design Web a parcouru un long chemin depuis la palette Web de 216 couleurs et une vitesse de connexion digne d'un escargot. À l'heure actuelle, les designers Web disposent d'une plus grande liberté et de davantage de flexibilité. Nous utilisons des outils plus robustes, le public ciblé comprend mieux, et des expériences interactives riches sont beaucoup plus probables que ce que nous aurions pu imaginer il y a un an de cela. Le travail interactif créé à l'heure actuelle est plus dynamique, plus riche en texture et plus immersif que jamais. Les possibilités de création semblent illimitées.

Néanmoins, malgré toutes ces possibilités à portée de main, la création d'expériences Web immersives pose de plus en plus de problèmes. Depuis la disparition de la plupart des obstacles techniques et des limites d'accès, la façon dont les personnes communiquent numériquement et perçoivent la messagerie interactive a considérablement changé. Les designers et les studios Web estiment qu'ils doivent posséder de plus nombreuses compétences pour rendre leurs projets intéressants, conserver l'attention des visiteurs des sites et satisfaire leurs clients. Nous devons ainsi jouer le rôle de philosophes, de sociologues et de magiciens autant que de designers et de technologues, car le processus de conception s'est développé bien au-delà de la structuration du contenu ou de l'offre d'un service particulier. Il devient de plus en plus nécessaire de créer une expérience intéressante permettant aux utilisateurs de partager, créer, jouer ou entrer physiquement en interaction avec un groupe de personnes.

Par ailleurs, les utilisateurs actuels d'Internet s'attendent à vivre des expériences plus enrichissantes et ils ne sont pas aussi enclins qu'ils l'étaient dans le passé à acheter sur Internet simplement parce qu'ils y ont accès. Les designers Web performants parviennent toutefois à intéresser ces utilisateurs de plus en plus astucieux en trouvant de nouvelles façons de créer à partir de principes traditionnels de design tels que la typographie, la présentation, l'identité et des choses de ce genre. Cependant, avec l'ajout de nouvelles couches, telles que le mouvement, le jeu, le design 3D et la mise en réseau sociale, les meilleurs studios Web font évoluer simultanément le travail interactif et la définition même de l'interactivité.

Les attentes des clients représentent également un autre défi à relever. À l'heure actuelle, placer le message de la marque d'un client sur Internet signifie fréquemment qu'il est nécessaire de concevoir pour de nombreux canaux de communication différents. Les studios Web doivent ainsi concevoir bien plus qu'un site Internet hébergeant un contenu et capturant des adresses électroniques, ou qu'une campagne de banderole qui empiète sur la page d'accueil, par elle-même chaotique, d'un portail populaire comportant un autre logo et le message d'une autre marque. Pour répondre aux nouvelles questions qui se posent lors des sessions destinées à la stratégie, les studios Web doivent considérer l'interactivité comme une discipline beaucoup plus vaste pouvant englober les innombrables manières dont les utilisateurs regardent le contenu et les services Web, et dont ils communiquent entre eux de façon numérique. Les questions que nous posons lorsque nous gérons nos clients sur Internet déterminent souvent l'aboutissement de nos projets : nouveaux, utiles ou viraux.

Ces changements ont donné naissance à une terrible réalité pour ceux qui, depuis des années, utilisent la même méthode de marketing, les mêmes canaux de communication et les mêmes formules de messagerie. Tous ces nouveaux défis représentent néanmoins

d'excellentes opportunités pour les créateurs désireux de fournir un message de marque d'une façon entièrement nouvelle et de créer des destinations Internet qu'eux-mêmes apprécieraient. Les meilleurs studios Web sont ceux qui restent centrés sur une seule idée convaincante et font du site Internet leur outil le plus dynamique et collaboratif. Ils n'escroquent pas et n'induisent pas en erreur. Ils intéressent les utilisateurs avec leurs propres termes. Ils ne se contentent pas de raconter une histoire, ils permettent aux utilisateurs de construire un récit. Ils ne se bornent pas à transmettre un message, mais ils fournissent aux utilisateurs les outils et l'intérêt pour le transmettre pour eux.

Les meilleurs designers Web s'efforcent de créer des espaces interactifs amusants, mystérieux et collaboratifs, quels que soient la marque et le produit. Les designers inventifs procurent aux utilisateurs une raison de s'intéresser aux marques, même à celles qui n'ont pas de dessin Internet inhérent, et ils créent une **destination** qui devient elle-même le dessin. Les magasins numéro un sur Internet savent qu'ils doivent emmener leurs clients dans des endroits qu'ils ne connaissent pas, les convaincre et leur proposer quelque chose qu'ils peuvent davantage contrôler. Que leurs sites soient amusants et illustrés, tels celui de *JUXT*, avec de superbes espaces physiques comme *North Kingdom*, ou avec les nouveautés de jeu de *Big Spaceship*, les environnements Web les plus attrayants encouragent le sens du jeu et l'expression personnelle, et trouvent l'équilibre délicat entre le message d'une marque et les éléments pouvant attirer et inspirer l'interaction des utilisateurs.

En réalité, l'une des clés actuelles de succès des sites consiste à fournir aux utilisateurs des moyens de partager leurs opinions personnelles. En observant plus attentivement les phrases à la mode, telles que « contenu généré par les consommateurs » et « mise en réseau sociale », nous constatons qu'une expérience plus profonde, centrée sur la communauté et l'expression personnelle, est une partie importante de notre vie à tous. La preuve en est le succès remporté par des sites tels que *YouTube*, *MySpace*, le blogage personnel et les balados, et il est extrêmement important que tous les sites Web de marques, mêmes les plus petites, prennent en compte l'opinion de leurs utilisateurs.

En effet, le phénomène de mise en réseau sociale modifie la façon dont les designers pensent la communication. Le design consiste depuis toujours à choisir un message déterminé et à le rendre accessible, intéressant ou sérieux. À l'heure actuelle, nous, les designers, devons non seulement considérer le design comme la communication avec un public déterminé, mais également envisager le design comme un véhicule pour la communication latérale **au sein de** ce public. Les meilleurs magasins sur Internet envoient effectivement un message de marque, mais ils conçoivent également des applications et des outils en ligne permettant aux utilisateurs de se regrouper et d'entrer en interaction par le biais d'une expérience de marque. Les stratèges, designers et programmateurs d'aujourd'hui jouent tout autant le rôle d'architectes de la communication que d'expéditeurs d'un message déterminé.

Cette évolution très complexe révolutionne le travail de publicité. Certains designers et agences traditionnels ont rencontré des difficultés pour intégrer cette approche, mais ceux qui sont parvenus à évoluer ont une relation beaucoup plus intense avec leur public. Ce type de relations facilite en partie le processus de stratégie de marque et permet au public de diffuser un message de marque et d'apporter sa contribution au contenu, ce qui permet d'augmenter l'intérêt du site. *AKQA* a réalisé un excellent travail en collaborant avec les utilisateurs. Dans le cadre du travail réalisé pour *Coke*, les visiteurs du site sont devenus des participants actifs du processus de marketing car ils peuvent donner leur avis et sont encouragés à créer un contenu qui alimente la présence dynamique de la marque sur Internet.

Derrière les numéros uns, même dans le monde du Web, nous trouvons la grande idée. Bien évidemment, la réalisation d'un site représente toujours une pièce essentielle du puzzle pour les meilleurs studios, car les magnifiques designs, les interfaces intelligentes et l'assistant Flash attirent l'attention et remportent des prix. Mais c'est la combinaison de tout cela autour d'une grande idée qui permet aux grands studios de se détacher du lot. Les studios qui peaufinent une seule idée intéressante, l'alignent sur la marque du client et l'utilisent comme la pierre angulaire du design et de la réalisation du site sont toujours parmi les plus performants.

Il est intéressant de constater qu'avec des consommateurs moins susceptibles d'être déroutés ou influencés par une messagerie périphérique et plus sollicités par la messagerie massive des grandes agences qui cherchent à attirer leur attention, c'est justement la créativité de la grande idée des meilleurs studios interactifs qui **fonctionne** vraiment. Lorsque les expériences interactives sont intéressantes du point de vue créatif et allient humour, intrigue et surprise, ou lorsqu'elles ont vraiment un sens pour l'utilisateur, le public les **adopte** et va même jusqu'à les rechercher. En outre, et ce qui est encore plus important, les utilisateurs partageront ensuite cette expérience avec des amis.

Les meilleurs studios Web savent bien cela et repoussent les limites de dynamisme et de collaboration des sites Internet. En effet, ils ont compris qu'un marketing et un design efficaces ne visent pas à transmettre un message *à* un public, mais plutôt à considérer les consommateurs numériques comme des utilisateurs actifs **désireux** de participer et de vivre une expérience différente. Leurs meilleurs sites transmettent un message de marque autour d'une grande idée et d'une expérience d'immersion unique. Les studios performants continueront de créer des expériences flexibles et invitant les visiteurs à participer, et ils sauront également s'adapter aux utilisateurs en incorporant de nouvelles technologies et davantage de créativité. Les studios Web présentés dans les pages suivantes travaillent pour faire émerger, de l'inspiration chaotique débridée, la beauté et des histoires intéressantes transportant les utilisateurs vers des endroits nouveaux et collaboratifs.

Dans une autre réalité, **Jonathan Hills** aurait dit qu'il est né en Islande, qu'il a été élevé par des pandas. Il parle onze langues. Il a gravi deux fois l'Everest. Il place des personnages d'action sur son ordinateur, comme s'il avait cinq ans. Malheureusement, Jon est incapable de concevoir sa propre vie. Il doit alors concevoir d'autres choses. Jon a ainsi déployé de grands efforts pour lancer **Domani Studios**, un studio de design Web haut de gamme situé à Brooklyn, dont il est le directeur de la création. Domani Studios crée des environnements interactifs de luxe et des expériences marketing virales pour des clients tels que *Volkswagen*, *Anheuser-Busch*, *Gucci* et *W Hotels*. Jon a été invité comme conférencier à des séminaires sur le design organisés dans de nombreux États des USA, où il prend plaisir à interrompre les autres intervenants et à jacasser sans cesse. Lorsqu'il ne se consacre pas à chercher ce qui est possible dans le secteur du design Web, Jon joue de la guitare dans un duo instrumental de New York, *1 Mile North*.

WORK | SERVICES | STUDIO | CONTACT

DESIGN MARKETING TECHNOLOGY

interactive design & branding

Whether creating an online advertising campaign or developing a fully integrated ecommerce web site, communicating our clients' messaging is always the first priority.

- web design
- CD-ROM development
- video & motion graphics
- brand identity
- print & package design
- and more... (click below)

Click for more information

online marketing & advertising

Domani studios offers a full range of online marketing services including rich media interstitials, road blocks, banners, landing pages, and html email campaigns.

- online advertising
- rich media interstials
- banners
- landing pages
- campaign planning & execution
- and more... (click below)

Click for more information

strategy & technology

From strategy and information architecture through Content Management development and user tracking, DS often serves as a single point of contact for many of our clients' interactive needs.

- e-commerce solutions
- database development
- content management systems
- custom data analysis
- email and web hosting
- and more... (click below)

Click for more information

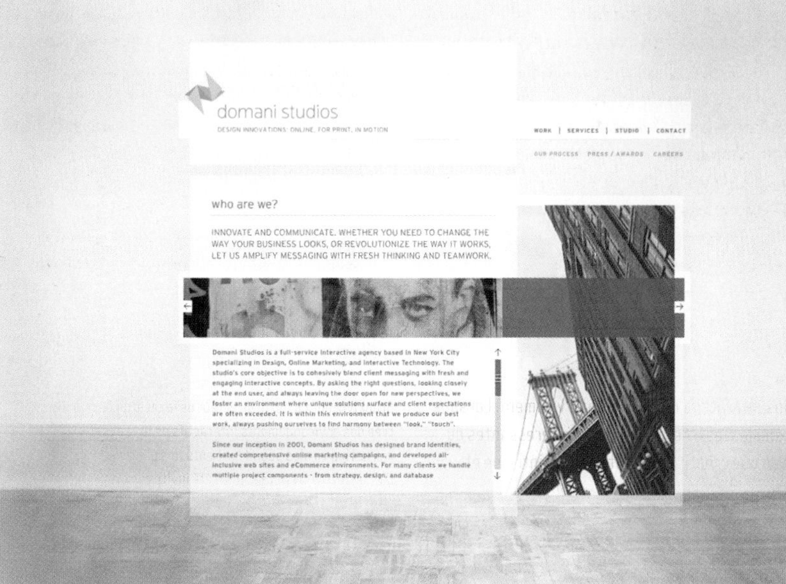

Einfürung

Jonathan Hills (Domani Studios)

Webdesign ist inzwischen zu einer äußerst komplexen Angelegenheit geworden; die 216-Farben-Palette und schleichend langsame Internetverbindungen gehören längst der Vergangenheit an. Für Designer von interaktiven Medien bieten sich heute mehr Möglichkeiten als jemals zuvor. Die inzwischen verwendeten Tools sind robuster, die Zielgruppen kennen sich viel besser als früher mit Internet und Computern aus und zudem sind heute fantastische Kreationen interaktiver Erlebniswelten machbar, die noch vor einem Jahr unvorstellbar schienen. Das interaktive Design von heute ist lebendiger, texturreicher und eindringlicher wie nie zuvor. Den kreativen Möglichkeiten scheinen keine Grenzen gesetzt zu sein.

Die schier unendliche Vielfalt an Gestaltungsalternativen konfrontiert die Webdesigner allerdings auch mit immer größeren Herausforderungen. Technische Hindernisse und Verbindungsprobleme existieren immer seltener, was einerseits die digitale Kommunikation leichter macht, gleichzeitig aber auch das Verhalten und die Erwartungen der Internetnutzer verändert. Interaktive Designer und Webstudios erkennen, dass sie immer tiefer in die Trickkiste greifen müssen, wenn sie bei Onlinenutzern das Interesse an Webseiten wecken oder aufrechterhalten und ihre Kunden auf Dauer zufrieden stellen wollen. Sie müssen nicht nur stets auf dem neuesten Stand der Technik sein, sondern zugleich die Fähigkeiten von Ges ellschaftswissenschaftlern und Zauberkünstlern in sich vereinen, denn beim Webdesign geht es nicht längst nicht mehr nur darum, Content zu strukturieren oder einen bestimmten Service anzubieten: Der Trend geht zunehmend dahin, den Usern reizvolle interaktive Online-Erlebnisse zu bieten, die ihnen ermöglichen, mit anderen Nutzern oder Gruppen direkt zu kommunizieren, Ideen auszutauschen, Games zu spielen oder gemeinsam kreativ zu sein.

Hinzu kommt, dass die Nutzer inzwischen attraktivere Internetangebote erwarten und wählerischer werden: Sie rufen Seiten nicht mehr nur deshalb auf, weil sie auf sie zugreifen können. Eine Webseite muss schon mehr bieten. Erfolgreiche Webdesigner schaffen es, die Aufmerksamkeit dieser immer anspruchsvolleren Nutzer zu fesseln, indem sie neue Wege finden und dabei auf klassische Designprinzipien setzen, wie Typografie, Layout, Identity und dergleichen. Indem sie neue Ebenen wie Motion, Gaming, 3D-Design und Social Networking hinzufügen, entwickeln die besten Webstudios eine neue Dimension der interaktiven Kommunikation und damit gleichzeitig eine neue Definition von Interaktivität.

Die Erwartungen der Kunden stellen eine zusätzliche Hürde dar. Wenn die Markenbotschaft eines Kunden über das Internet vermittelt werden soll, bedeutet das derzeit oft, dass das Design für mehrere separate Kommunikationskanäle gestaltet werden muss. Agenturen für interaktives Design müssen bereit sein umzudenken: Es geht nicht mehr nur um die Einrichtung eine Webseite, die Content und E-Mail-Finder enthält, oder um die Konzeption einer Banner-Kampagne, die die bereits mit Werbung überfüllte Homepage eines populären Portals um ein weiteres Logo mit einer weiteren Markenbotschaft überfrachtet. Im Laufe von Strategiesitzungen taucht eine ganze Reihe neuer Fragen auf, die die Webdesign-Agenturen zwingen, Interaktivität als eine wesentlich breitere Disziplin zu begreifen, die all die verschiedenen Möglichkeiten umfasst, wie die Menschen auf Onlinedienste und -inhalte zugreifen und digital miteinander kommunizieren können. Die Fragen, die

wir im Zusammenhang mit einem Internetprojekt eines Kunden stellen, haben oft einen großen Einfluss darauf, wie effektiv und gewinn-bringend das Ergebnis für den Kunden letztendlich ist.

All diese Veränderungen stellen eine erschreckende Realität für viele dar, die seit Jahren stets denselben Marketingansatz verfolgen, dieselben Kommunikationskanäle nutzen und dieselben Formeln für Botschaften verwenden. Zugleich bedeuten all diese neuen Herausforderungen jedoch aufregende Möglichkeiten für kreative Denker, die es spannend finden, Markenbotschaften auf eine völlig neue Art und Weise zu vermitteln und Onlinewelten zu kreieren, die sie selbst gern erkunden würden. Die erfolgreichsten Agenturen für interaktives Design sind diejenigen, die sich auf eine einzige brillante Idee konzentrieren und das Internet als dynamisches und formbares Medium begreifen und nutzen. Sie machen den Nutzern keine falschen Versprechungen und führen sie nicht auf Irrwege. Sie fesseln die Aufmerksamkeit der Nutzer in dem Maße, wie die Nutzer es zulassen wollen. Sie erzählen den Nutzern nicht einfach nur eine Geschichte. Sie ermöglichen den Nutzern, den Verlauf der Geschichte aktiv zu beeinflussen. Sie vermitteln den Nutzern nicht einfach nur eine Botschaft – stattdessen geben sie den Nutzern die Tools und den Anreiz, die Botschaften an ihrer Stelle zu verbreiten.

Die besten Designer treiben sich selbst zu Höchstleistungen an, um interaktive Welten zu erschaffen, die verspielt, geheimnisvoll und kollaborativ zugleich sind – unabhängig von der Marke oder vom Produkt. Innovative Designer liefern Nutzern einen Grund, sich mit Marken zu beschäftigen, sogar mit den Marken, die gar keine eigene Internetattraktivität besitzen, indem sie eine **Destination** kreieren, die die wahre Attraktion darstellt. Die besten Webdesigner wissen, dass sie ihre Kunden an Orte entführen müssen, die sie nie zuvor gesehen haben und dass sie ihre Kunden überzeugen müssen, Kontrolle abzugeben, damit die Nutzer mehr Kontrolle bekommen. Die attraktivsten Webumgebungen – zum Beispiel die Kreationen von *JUXT*, *North Kingdom* oder *Big Spaceship* – appellieren an die Spielfreude der Nutzer, geben ihnen Möglichkeiten, sich persönlich auszudrücken und sorgen bei der Vermittlung der Markenbotschaft und des Anreizes, der den Nutzer zur Interaktion animieren soll, für die richtige Ausgewogenheit.

Tatsächlich liegt der Schlüssel zum Erfolg interaktiver Webseiten darin, den Nutzern mehr Möglichkeiten zu geben, sich selbst mitzuteilen. An Schlagwörtern wie „Consumer Generated Content" und „Social Networking" können wir erkennen, dass prägende Erlebnisse in Verbindung mit Gemeinschaft und der Möglichkeit, sich selbst auszudrücken, einen wesentlichen Teil unseres Lebens darstellen. Die überwältigenden Siegeszüge von *YouTube*, *MySpace*, persönlichen Blogs und Podcasts illustrieren dies auf beeindruckende Weise und zeigen auch, dass es auch für die Webseiten kleinerer Marken immer wichtiger wird, ihren Nutzern die Möglichkeit zu bieten, sich Gehör zu verschaffen.

Das Phänomen des sozialen Netzwerkens verändert die Art und Weise, wie Designer Kommunikation begreifen. Design erfüllt seit jeher die Aufgabe, eine ganz bestimmte Botschaft zu vermitteln und sie dem Adressaten auf eine ganz bestimmte Weise schmackhaft zu machen. Heute beschränkt sich Design aber nicht mehr nur darauf, mit einer bestimmten Zielgruppe zu kommunizieren. Design wird zunehmend auch auf interaktiver Ebene eingesetzt – als Mittel, um die Kommunikation **innerhalb** dieser Zielgruppe zu fördern. Die besten Webdesigner begnügen sich nicht damit, eine Markenbotschaft zu vermitteln, sondern konzipieren zudem Online-Anwendungen und Tools, die die Nutzer zusammen bringen und ihnen ermöglichen, über eine webbasierte Marken-Erlebniswelt miteinander zu kommunizieren. Die innovativsten Strategen, Designer und Programmierer sehen ihre Aufgabe heute nicht mehr nur darin, eine bestimmte Botschaft zu kommunizieren, sondern begreifen sich auch als Architekten der dazu erforderlichen Kommunikationsstruktur.

Dieser komplexe Wandel, der gerade stattfindet, revolutioniert die Art und Weise, wie Werbung funktioniert. Für manche klassisch arbeitenden Designer und Agenturen ist es schwierig, sich dieser Entwicklung anzupassen, doch diejenigen, die den neuen Ansatz verinnerlichen, werden in der Lage sein, Zielgruppen stärker zu binden. Diese Bindung zur Zielgruppe erleichtert den Branding-Prozess, da die Nutzer die jeweilige Markenbotschaft durch Interaktion mit anderen Nutzern weiter verbreiten und auf diese Weise zugleich dazu beitragen, dass der Content der betreffenden Webseite weiterhin attraktiv bleibt. Die Agentur *AKQA* hat ein schönes Beispiel für die interaktive Einbindung von Nutzern geliefert. In ihrem Projekt für *Coke* hat sie Nutzer zu aktiven Mitgestaltern des Marketingprozesses gemacht, indem sie den Besuchern der Webseite ein Stimme gab und sie dazu ermutigte, selbst Content zu kreieren, um so die lebendige Internetpräsenz der Marke noch mehr aufzuwerten.

Doch auch die Besten der Besten brauchen etwas ganz Wesentliches, wenn sie erfolgreich sein wollen, selbst in der interaktiven Werbung – nämlich die Big Idea. Natürlich stellt die Realisierung eines Internetkonzepts immer eine besonders spannende Herausforderung für erfolgreiche Webstudios dar. Schönes Design, smarte Interfaces und Flash-Zaubereien sorgen für Aufsehen und bringen Preise ein. Doch erst die Kombination all dieser Elemente mit der alles vereinenden brillanten Idee macht die besten Webagenturen so erfolgreich. Studios, die sich auf eine einzige geniale Idee konzentrieren, um sie mit der Marke des Kunden in Einklang zu bringen und als Dreh- und Angelpunkt für das interaktive Design und dessen Realisierung zu nutzen, werden ihren Mitbewerbern immer einen Schritt voraus sein.

Konsumenten achten immer weniger auf periphere Botschaften und sind zunehmend genervt von der Überschwemmung mit den oft aufdringlichen und marktschreierischen Werbebotschaften großer Agenturen. Die Top-Agenturen für interaktives Design setzen stattdessen auf raffinierte Kreativität, die auf einer brillanten Idee basiert – **mit Erfolg**. Interaktive Erlebniswelten, die durch ihre Kreativität faszinieren, die witzig sind, neugierig machen oder aus einem anderen Grund eine ganz besondere Anziehungskraft ausüben, werden die Nutzer so **begeistern**, dass sie sie immer wieder besuchen werden. Und vor allem werden sie den Wunsch haben, dieses Erlebnis mit Freunden zu teilen.

Die besten Studios für interaktives Design wissen das und haben sich der Mission verschrieben, die Möglichkeiten und Grenzen des Internets neu zu definieren und wegweisende dynamische Onlinelösungen mit aktiver Nutzereinbindung zu entwickeln. Sie begreifen, dass Marketing und Design heutzutage nicht mehr effektiv ist, wenn eine Botschaft nur **an** eine Zielgruppe gesendet wird: Es geht darum, digitale

Konsumenten als aktive Teilnehmer in den Kommunikationsprozess zu integrieren, indem man sie dazu motiviert, Teil einer ganz besonderen Erlebniswelt werden zu wollen. Die besten Arbeitsbeispiele kommunizieren die Botschaft einer Marke unter dem Dach einer Big Idea im Rahmen einer einzigartigen und faszinierenden Erlebniswelt. Erfolgreiche Webstudios werden auch weiterhin flexible und partizipatorische Erlebniswelten kreieren, sich aber zugleich ständig an das sich wandelnde Nutzerverhalten anpassen und dabei neue Technologien und neue Kreativitätsebenen einführen. Die interaktiven Designstudios, die auf den folgenden Seiten präsentiert werden, sorgen auf ihre Weise dafür, dass aus einem anscheinend zusammenhanglosen Chaos in kreativer Teamarbeit immer wieder fantastische Erlebniswelten mit fesselnden Geschichten erwachsen – faszinierende Orte der Begegnung, die neugierig machen und zu Entdeckungsreisen inspirieren.

In einer anderen Wirklichkeit würde sich die Biografie von **Jonathan Hills** so lesen: Er wurde in Island geboren und von Pandas aufgezogen. Er spricht elf Sprachen. Er hat den Mount Everest bestiegen, zwei Mal bereits. Und er stellt definitiv keine Action-Figuren auf seinen Computer, schließlich ist er kein fünfjähriger Knirps. Leider kann Jon sein eigenes Leben nur in begrenztem Maße designen. Dieser Umstand zwingt ihn dazu, seine Leidenschaft für Design an anderen Dingen auszuleben. Um das Gelingen seiner Mission zu unterstützen, gründete Jon in Brooklyn, New York ein High-End-Studio für interaktives Design: **Domani Studios**. Jon ist Creative Director von DS. DS gestaltet interaktive Erlebniswelten und virale Marketing-Kampagnen der Spitzenklasse für Kunden wie *Volkswagen*, *Anheuscher-Busch*, *Gucci* und *W Hotels*. Jon wird häufig eingeladen, Vorträge auf Design-Seminaren in ganz USA zu halten. Dort macht es ihm besonders viel Spaß, andere Diskussionsteilnehmer zu unterbrechen und gnadenlos zuzutexten. Wenn Jon nicht gerade damit beschäftigt ist, die Machbarkeitsgrenzen interaktiven Designs zu erforschen, spielt er Gitarre bei *1 Mile North*, einem New Yorker Ambient-Instrumental-Duo.

CASE:01

The illusive creative process

Fred Flade (de-construct)

Ever since we started **de-construct** in 2001 we have been asked by clients, peers and journalists to describe – sometimes in detail – our creative process. To explain and clearly define our process seemed to be something we had to be able to do. It almost seemed that the existence of the companies "magic formula" which ensures creativity and innovation every time, was a fundamental building block in the success of the company. The promise was that our creative process would serve as the ultimate reassurance to anybody that we work with.

Needless to say we never managed to bolt down what the crucial bits between start and finish of a project really are and how they come about. Creativity by nature is such a random and chaotic process that it can't be pressed into a formula or a set of steps. It seemed to work much better to simply keep the expectations in our own work at the highest level and let the project shape the process organically with the parameters of each project varying greatly. Different clients, different target audience, different personalities etc. ensure that the dynamics of the creative process change completely every time. We found soon that a free undefined creative process had a big advantage; it avoids repetitiveness, ensuring variation every time we work on a new project.

Based on the ethos of letting the project itself shape the process it became clear quite quickly that we needed to ensure we work on projects of varying sizes, because the scale of a project has the biggest single impact on how the creative process evolves. The bigger the project the bigger the need to control and plan, which means it can be more difficult to make creativity an intrinsic part of the project.

It has been interesting to experience many different projects, each grown out of a very unique creative journey. One of the most unusual project in terms of how it evolved has been the website for designer Vince Frost **<www.frostdesign.co.uk>**. The project was more an intuitive reaction to the problem based on conversations and collaborations with Vince, rather than a formal process of any kind. For example, the doodle created in one of the first meetings with Vince formed the basis for the core interactive model of a navigable landscape. The whole project was shaped by a very playful and collaborative creative approach, which felt more like a fun experimental project. I'm convinced it's one of the reasons it became a multi award winning website. The challenge of course is to instill as much of this very open and creative approach into large more complex projects, which aren't naturally suited for intuitive, emotional and spontaneous reactions.

Another advantage of having no clearly defined process is the fact that it offers a large amount of flexibility should there be a dramatic shift in the industry. Through the increase in broadband uptake we are experiencing such a shift. The possibilities in terms of story telling online have changed completely and with that expectations of clients as well as users change accordingly.

Most projects we worked on this year demanded a very different creative process, which included script writing, filming, editing and post-producing of video content. A website we created for *Panasonic*, promoting 3 of their new *Lumix* cameras, featured three different stories in three different cities telling the stories of people using their cameras. Each story involved a two day shoot on location with a fairly large crew. Content creation on that scale would have been unthinkable just a few years ago.

The impact on the creation process is immense of course. It used to be the case that some of the best ideas arise out of "happy accidents" during the production process. There was always room to try out a few different possibilities and experiment right up to the last minute. This changes of course when a site features video content. More complex and costly content means there is less room for spontaneous experimentation. Shoots have to be planned much more accurately with time literally meaning money.

This is not to say that rich content immediately means less creativity, it just means creativity has to be managed more consciously before the project enters the production phase. Main concepts and key creative ideas need to be completely locked down before the realization process kicks in.

This is of course a small price to pay considering how the developments of online technologies have increased the creative possibilities. Rich content and interaction is now truly enabling us to engage with the audience through high impacting narratives; websites that are more software applications than simply information distributors. It certainly feels like an amazing time to be working in the digital design industry.

In hindsight it actually was an advantage for **de-construct** not to set in stone "our creative process" but remain flexible. Looking ahead it seems also clear that the necessity to be flexible has never been greater. Surely ongoing developments such as – for example – the separation of content from media, enabling it to be consumed by people wherever and whenever they want, will yet again fundamentally change the way the creative process needs to work to deliver powerful solutions.

Fred Flade is creative director and founding partner of creative digital agency **de-construct**. He is responsible for visual communication and graphic and interactive design for clients such as Panasonic and the Barbican Centre in London.
During his 10 years working in the industry he managed to win 18 international awards. His characteristically strong graphic and seamless interactive design work led to award-winning projects such as the Onemusic website for the BBC, Panasonic's european internet guidelines and the Barbican website, as well as the highly acclaimed website for designer Vince Frost.
Fred gave talks at the Fresh Conference in Hong Kong and various D&AD events. Over the last year he was also invited to judge the D&AD (British Design & Art Direction) Award and ISTD (International Society of Typographic Designers) Award. Prior to founding "de-construct", Fred Flade was a design director of "Deepend London". Fred has studied Marketing Communication and holds a degree in Visual Communication Design from Ravensbourne College.

Le processus de création illusoire

Fred Flade (de-construct)

Depuis la fondation de « **de-construct** » en 2001, des clients, collègues et journalistes nous demandent de décrire – parfois dans le détail – notre processus de création, car ils estiment que nous pourrions être en mesure de l'expliquer et de le définir clairement. Il semble presque que l'existence de sociétés à « formule magique », qui assurent à tout moment créativité et innovation, est une unité élémentaire de structure dans la réussite de notre entreprise. En outre, il paraît certain que notre processus de création pourrait représenter une garantie définitive pour toutes les personnes avec lesquelles nous travaillons.

Inutile de dire que nous ne sommes jamais parvenus à déterminer avec exactitude les parties cruciales entre le début et la fin d'un projet et la façon dont elles sont réalisées. Par nature, la créativité est un processus si aléatoire et chaotique qu'elle ne peut pas être réduite à une formule ou une suite de phases. Il semble beaucoup plus efficace d'avoir des attentes très élevées et de laisser le projet former organiquement le processus, en laissant la place à une variation des paramètres de chaque projet. Avec différents clients, différents publics visés et différentes personnalités, la dynamique du processus de création est complètement différente pour chaque projet. Nous nous sommes rapidement rendu compte qu'un processus de création libre et non défini présente un avantage considérable : il évite de se répéter et permet des variations à chaque nouveau projet.

En se fondant sur la philosophie de laisser le projet former le processus, il devient assez rapidement évident que nous devons travailler sur des projets de tailles différentes, car l'échelle d'un projet est l'aspect qui a le plus de répercussions sur l'évolution du processus de création. Plus le projet est important, plus il est nécessaire de le contrôler et de le planifier, ce qui signifie qu'il est plus difficile que la créativité constitue une partie intrinsèque du projet.

Il est très intéressant de réaliser plusieurs projets différents, chacun évoluant à partir d'un parcours de création unique. L'un des projets les plus inhabituels pour ce qui est de son évolution a été le site Internet créé pour le designer Vince Frost **<www.frostdesign.co.uk>**. Plus qu'un processus officiel, ce projet a davantage été une réaction intuitive au problème ayant surgi lors des conversations et des collaborations avec Vince. Par exemple, le griffonnage créé pendant l'une des premières réunions avec Vince a constitué la base du principal modèle interactif d'un paysage navigable. L'ensemble du projet a été modelé avec une approche créatrice de jeu et de travail en commun, ce qui s'apparente davantage à un amusant projet expérimental. Je suis convaincu que c'est l'une des raisons pour lesquelles ce site a remporté de nombreux prix. Dans des cas comme celui-ci, le défi consiste à intégrer cette approche ouverte et créative, dans la plus large mesure possible, dans de grands projets beaucoup plus complexes ne convenant naturellement pas à des réactions intuitives, émotionnelles et spontanées.

Un autre avantage que présentent les processus non définis clairement est de permettre une marge de manœuvre importante en cas de bouleversement dans l'industrie, et l'augmentation de la disponibilité de large bande entraîne un tel changement. En ce qui concerne les histoires pouvant être racontées sur le Web, les possibilités ont complètement changé, de même que les attentes des clients et des utilisateurs.

La plupart des projets sur lesquels nous avons travaillé cette année requéraient des processus de

création très différents comprenant la rédaction de scripts, le tournage, le montage et la postproduction de vidéos. Le site que nous avons créé pour *Panasonic* pour la promotion de trois de leurs nouvelles caméras *Lumix* comporte trois histoires différentes, tournées dans trois villes différentes, de personnes qui utilisent leurs caméras. Pour chaque histoire, nous avons réalisé un tournage de deux jours sur place avec une équipe assez importante. La création de contenu à cette échelle aurait été impensable il y a quelques années.

Bien sûr, les répercussions du processus de création sont énormes. Il arrive souvent que certaines des meilleures idées proviennent d'« accidents heureux » survenus lors du processus de production. Il est toujours possible d'essayer diverses possibilités et de faire des expériences jusqu'au tout dernier moment. Cela n'est pas le cas lorsqu'un site Web comporte une vidéo. Plus un projet est complexe et coûteux, moins il laisse de marge pour des expériences spontanées. Les tournages doivent être planifiés de façon beaucoup plus précise, car le temps est littéralement de l'argent.

Je ne veux pas dire pour autant qu'un contenu plus élaboré implique moins de créativité, mais simplement que cette dernière doit être gérée plus consciemment avant que le projet n'entre dans la phase de production. La plupart des concepts et des idées créatives doivent être entièrement bouclés avant le démarrage du processus de réalisation.

Cela n'est qu'un prix minime à payer si l'on pense que les progrès des technologies Web ont permis d'augmenter les possibilités de création. Grâce à un contenu plus riche et à l'interaction, nous pouvons vraiment impliquer le public au moyen d'histoires impressionnantes et de sites Web qui sont davantage des applications logicielles que de simples distributeurs d'informations. Il est vraiment surprenant de travailler dans l'industrie du design numérique.

Avec du recul, je pense que le fait de ne pas avoir gravé dans le marbre « notre processus de création » mais d'être restés flexibles a représenté un véritable avantage pour **de-construct**. En se tournant vers l'avenir, il semble évident que le besoin de flexibilité jouera aussi un rôle très important. Les développements continus, par exemple la séparation du contenu et du média qui permettra aux utilisateurs de le consulter où et quand ils le souhaitent, contribueront à changer fondamentalement la façon dont le processus de création doit être mis en œuvre pour fournir des solutions puissantes.

Fred Flade est le directeur artistique et le co-fondateur de l'agence numérique de création « **de-construct** ». Il est chargé de la communication visuelle et du design Web et graphique pour des clients tels que Panasonic et le Barbican Centre de Londres.
Au cours de sa carrière de 10 années dans l'industrie, il a remporté 18 prix internationaux. Son travail de design harmonieux caractérisé par d'excellents graphiques a permis de réaliser des projets primés, par exemple le site Web Onemusic pour la BBC, les recommandations Internet européennes de Panasonic, le site Web de Barbican et le site Internet du designer Vince Frost, qui a reçu un accueil élogieux.
Fred a donné des conférences dans le cadre de la Fresh Conference à Hong Kong et de plusieurs événements de la D&AD (direction britannique du design et de l'art). L'année dernière, il a été invité comme jury des prix D&AD et ISTD (Société internationale des Designers typographiques). Avant de fonder l'agence de-construct, Fred Flade était directeur de design de la société Deepend London. Il a suivi des études de communication en marketing et a obtenu un diplôme en design de communication visuelle au Ravensbourne College.

CASE:01

Für kreative Prozesse gibt es keine Formel

Fred Flade (de-construct)

Seit der Gründung von **de-construct** in 2001 werden wir von Kunden, Kollegen und Journalisten oft gebeten, unseren Kreativprozess zu erklären, manchmal im Detail. Man scheint von Agenturen zu erwarten, dass sie ihre kreative Arbeit ganz selbstverständlich definieren können. Diese „magische Formel" scheint jedes Mal der Garant für Kreativität und Innovation zu sein, also ein grundlegender Baustein für den Erfolg der Agentur und auch eine Art ultimative Rückversicherung für die Zusammenarbeit mit uns.

Natürlich ist es uns nie gelungen, ein Schema zu erstellen, das die entscheidenden Punkte eines Projektes auflistet und den Ablauf des kreativen Prozesses festlegt. Kreativität ist naturgemäß ein sehr spontaner und chaotischer Prozess, der sich einfach nicht in Formeln oder Schemata pressen lässt. Für uns war es besser, auch weiterhin höchste Anforderungen an unsere eigene Arbeit zu stellen, die organische Entwicklung des Kreativprozesses jedoch vom jeweiligen Projekt abhängig zu machen, zumal die Parameter bei jedem einzelnen Projekt stark variierten. Da es bei Projekten große Unterschiede in Bezug auf Kunden, Zielgruppen, Persönlichkeiten usw. gibt, verläuft der kreative Prozess jedes Mal anders. Ein freier, undefinierter Kreativprozess bietet zudem einen großen Vorteil: Er minimiert die Gefahr von Routine, denn wir können bei jedem neuen Projekt mit frischen Ideen ans Werk gehen.

Der Ansatz, dass die Entwicklung des Kreativprozesses durch das Projekt selbst geprägt werden sollte, ließ uns schnell erkennen, dass es wichtig war, an Projekten verschiedenen Umfangs zu arbeiten, denn die Größe eines Projektes beeinflusst die Entwicklung des Kreativprozesses enorm. Je größer ein Projekt ist, desto mehr Steuerung und Planung ist nötig, was es unter Umständen schwieriger macht, der Kreativität innerhalb des Projektes genug Raum zu geben.

Es ist noch immer sehr interessant und inspirierend, an vielen unterschiedlichen Projekten mitzuwirken, denn jedes Projekt führt uns auf eine einzigartige kreative Reise. Eines der außergewöhnlichsten Projekte in punkto Kreativprozess war die Gestaltung der Webseite des Designers Vince Frost **<www.frostdesign.co.uk>**. Bei diesem Projekt gingen wir bei der Aufgabenstellung eher intuitiv vor, auf Basis von Gesprächen mit Vince, statt uns nach einem bestimmten formalen Prozess zu richten. Zum Beispiel bildete das Gekritzel aus einem der ersten Meetings mit Vince die Basis für das grundlegende interaktive Modell einer navigierbaren Landschaft. Das gesamte Projekt war von einem sehr spielerischen kreativen Ansatz in Teamarbeit geprägt, wobei mit sehr viel Spaß experimentiert wurde. Dies war mit Sicherheit einer der Gründe dafür, warum diese Webseite so viele Preise erhielt. Die Herausforderung besteht natürlich darin, soviel wie möglich von diesem sehr offenen kreativen Ansatz in große komplexere Projekte einzubringen, die naturgemäß nicht so viel Spielraum für eine intuitive, emotionale und spontane Herangehensweise lassen.

Ein weiterer Vorteil des undefinierten Kreativprozesses besteht darin, dass das kreative Team flexibler arbeiten kann und dadurch nah an der Marktentwicklung bleibt. Der Siegeszug der Breitbandtechnologie ist ein aktuelles Beispiel dafür, wie wichtig Flexibilität und Marktnähe sind. Die Möglichkeiten für das erzählerische Vermitteln von Online-Inhalten haben sich stark weiter entwickelt und die Erwartungen von Kunden und Benutzern ändern sich entsprechend.

Die meisten unserer Projekte der letzten Monate

erforderten einen ganz neuen kreativen Ansatz, einschließlich Scriptentwicklung, Filmdrehs, Schnitt und Postproduktion für Videoinhalte. Auf einer Webseite, die wir im Auftrag von *Panasonic* im Rahmen der Werbekampagne für die neuen *Lumix* Digitalkameras gestalteten, wurden drei verschiedene Geschichten in drei verschiedenen Städten erzählt, mit drei verschiedenen Personen, die diese Kameras benutzten. Jede Geschichte erforderte einen zweitägigen Dreh vor Ort mit einer ziemlich großen Filmcrew. Die Kreation von Inhalten dieser Größenordnung wäre vor einigen Jahren noch undenkbar gewesen.

Die Auswirkungen auf den Kreativprozess sind natürlich immens. Früher entstanden einige der besten Ideen oft durch „glückliche Zufälle" im Verlauf der Produktion. Es gab immer Raum, bis zur letzten Minute mehrere verschiedene Alternativen auszuprobieren. Das ändert sich natürlich, wenn eine Webseite Videoinhalte umfassen soll. Komplexere und kostenintensivere Inhalte bedeuten, dass es weniger Raum für spontane Experimente gibt. Drehs müssen viel präziser geplant werden, denn Zeit bedeutet jetzt wirklich Geld.

Das soll nicht heißen, dass komplexe und kostenintensive Inhalte die Kreativität einschränken – doch die Kreativität muss nun gezielter eingesetzt werden, schon bevor ein Projekt die Produktionsphase erreicht. Hauptkonzept und kreative Hauptidee müssen bereits komplett fest stehen, bevor der Realisierungsprozess startet.

Dieses Zugeständnis an die kreative Freiheit lässt sich natürlich leicht verschmerzen, wenn man sich klar macht, dass die Entwicklung von Online-Technologien die kreativen Möglichkeiten stark erweitert hat. Komplexe Inhalte und interaktive Elemente machen es jetzt möglich, Internetnutzer mit spannenden Geschichten zu fesseln, mit Webseiten, die nicht mehr nur der reinen Informationsvermittlung dienen und mehr in Richtung Softwareanwendung gehen. Digitales Design ist wirklich ein faszinierendes und aufregendes Arbeitsfeld.

Im Nachhinein war es für **de-construct** von Vorteil, dass wir „unseren Kreativprozess" nicht in Stein gemeißelt haben, sondern flexibel geblieben sind. Und der Blick in die Zukunft zeigt, dass die Fähigkeit zur Flexibilität wichtiger ist als je zuvor. Mit Sicherheit werden aktuelle Entwicklungen – wie derzeit etwa der Trend zur Trennung von Inhalten und Medien, damit Nutzer jederzeit und überall auf Inhalte zugreifen können – weiterhin dazu führen, dass der Ablauf von kreativen Prozessen angepasst wird mit dem Ziel, den Kunden optimale Lösungen zu bieten.

Fred Flade ist Creative Director und Gründungspartner der digitalen Kreativagentur **de-construct**. Er ist verantwortlich für visuelle Kommunikation und für grafisches und interaktives Design. Er betreut Kunden wie Panasonic und das Londoner Barbican Centre.
In seiner 10jährigen Designerkarriere hat er bereits 18 internationale Preise gewonnen. Typisch für seine Arbeit ist ein stark grafikbetontes und nahtloses interaktives Design. Zu seinen preisgekrönten Projekten zählen die Onemusic-Webseite für die BBC, die europäischen Internetrichtlinien von Panasonic, die Internet-seite von Barbican und die viel gelobte Webseite für den Designer Vince Frost.
Fred hielt bereits zahlreiche Vorträge auf der Fresh Conference in Hong Kong und auf verschiedenen Veranstaltungen der D&AD (British Design & Art Direction). Zudem wurde er in die Award-Jurys des D&AD und des ISTD (International Society of Typographic Designers) berufen. Vor der Gründung von de-construct war Fred Design Director bei Deepend London. Fred studierte Marketingkommunikation und graduierte am Ravensbourne College mit einem Abschluss in Visual Communication Design.

Creating for the Web

Roger Stighäll (North Kingdom)

Interactive agency North Kingdom is probably best known for its work with *Vodafone* on **<www.vodafone.com/futurevision>** and **<www.vodafonejourney.com>**. These days they are also doing work for a number of leading advertising agencies, which actually could be seen as both a partner as well as a competitor. Many people in the marketing world are curious as to how it is possible to both own your client's brand and sometimes support advertising agencies in their interactive work.

To a large extent, this is a choice driven by the organizational structure of our clients. Some brands have all their brands' communication going through one head advertising agency. In these cases, challenging projects come to us through that agency. In other cases and organizations, we can work directly with the brand, because they have a strong internal communications team that coordinates everything around the brand and its communication, and hence can hold relationships with multiple agencies.

But it can also be attributed to the choices we have made, owing to the current organizational structure in our agency. Work for regular clients, such as *Vodafone* and *ABSOLUT*, demands more on the client services side and work with agencies is often shorter and more intense, with projects focusing more on the creative and production side. North Kingdom has always been on the look out for those right projects, the ones in which we believe we can make a difference. And this is independent of whether it is our own clients/brands or if it has been an agency approaching us with an early idea.

One example of a good working relationship has been that of Swedish ad agency *SWE* and the project launch of the car *Toyota Aygo*. The ad agency and the client approached us with a project brief. The unique aspect about this car was that you could NOT buy it you subscribed to it. In Sweden, a subscription is something you normally do with a newspaper or magazine so that you receive it through your mailbox. We had a creative discussion internally and explained to the agency that if we were to take this car launch on, it would need to have a different feel and not resemble that of a classic car site at all!!!! (I believe this has been one of our main reasons for success, we strive to do things differently and pay attention to details).

As you can see in the pictures (below?), we proposed a solution in which the *Toyota* magazine transformed into a car as it came through the mail slot. Both the ad agency and the client liked our concept. The ad agency helped out by writing the copy, supplying content and pictures and supporting us throughout the process, as they have a greater knowledge about the brand than we do.

To us, this mutual respect is the key to success between interactive agencies and traditional ad agencies. We need to respect and understand that ad agencies know the brand much better than we do through the history they often have with the brand. At the same time they have to respect us as online experts who know what works online and what does not. Unfortunately, not all of our agency relationships have been based on that kind of mutual respect and understanding, leading to a boring process. When none of the expertise you provide is utilized, the end effect of the campaign results in a solution that does not serve the client as well as it could have.

We try to keep an open mind towards our relationships with other agencies, and if it proves that the chemistry in the relationship is there, we do not see a problem in creating amazing things in conjunction with ad agencies instead of going solo with the brand/client directly.

In the end, the goal at North Kingdom is to create engaging interactive communication. As long as we are given the opportunity to work together with these kinds of challenging brands and projects, our focus will remain on continuing to deliver world-class experiences.

After growing up near the Arctic Circle, in the north of Sweden, **Roger Stighäll** decided at age 20 to move to the tropics and Florida. After 7 years, he decided to return back to the cold and to join childhood friend Robert Lindström and work for *Paregos*. Succeeding in making *Paregos* (today part of *Framfab*) known internationally, the two friends decided to move onto the next level and **North Kingdom** was founded in 2003. After the incredibly successful *Vodafone Future Vision* launched in 2004, the international advertising world opened up their eyes to North Kingdom. Here are the highlights of actually both Robert's and Roger's career so far: 4 Gold Cannes Cyber Lions, and was Jury Chairman – Interactive – at the largest Swedish advertising awards "Guldägget" (Golden Egg).

CASE:02

Crée pour le Web

Roger Stighäll (North Kingdom)

L'agence interactive North Kingdom est probablement connue pour son travail avec *Vodafone* sur **<www.vodafone.com/futurevision>** et **<www.vodafonejourney.com>**. À l'heure actuelle, elle travaille également avec de nombreuses grandes agences de publicité, qui pourraient en réalité être perçues à la fois comme des partenaires et des concurrents. De nombreuses personnes du monde du marketing sont curieuses de savoir comment il est possible de travailler avec les marques de ses propres clients et de collaborer de temps à autre avec le travail interactif d'agences de publicité.

Ce choix est dans une large mesure guidé par la structure de l'entreprise de nos clients. En effet, certaines entreprises choisissent de confier toutes les communications de leur marque à une seule agence de publicité. Dans ce cas, les projets intéressants nous parviennent par le biais de cette agence. Dans d'autres cas et avec d'autres entreprises, nous pouvons travailler directement avec le client, car il dispose d'une solide équipe interne de communication qui coordonne tous les aspects relatifs à la marque et à sa communication, et peut ainsi gérer des relations avec plusieurs agences.

Ce choix peut également être attribué aux décisions que nous avons prises en fonction de la structure de notre agence. Le travail avec des clients réguliers, tels que *Vodafone* et *ABSOLUT*, requiert davantage des services du côté du client, et le travail avec les agences est souvent plus réduit et plus intense, avec des projets centrés la créativité et la production. North Kingdom a toujours recherché ce type de projets appropriés, ceux pour lesquels nous pensons pouvoir faire la différence, que le projet provienne de l'un de nos clients/marques ou qu'une agence nous ait contactés en nous faisant part d'une idée.

Un exemple de bonne relation de travail a été celui de l'agence de publicité suédoise *SWE* et du lancement du projet pour la voiture *Toyota Aygo*. L'agence et le client nous ont contactés en nous présentant le dossier d'un projet. L'aspect exceptionnel de cette voiture était que le consommateur ne pouvait pas l'acheter mais devait y souscrire. En Suède, une souscription se fait généralement pour un journal ou un magazine qui est envoyé par la poste. Après une discussion créative en interne, nous avons expliqué à l'agence que si nous acceptions de nous charger du lancement de cette voiture, le site devrait dégager quelque chose de différent et ne pas ressembler du tout à un site classique de voitures (je pense que la clé de notre réussite réside dans le fait que nous nous efforçons de faire les choses de façon différente et que nous nous soucions des détails).

Comme vous pouvez le voir sur les images (ci-dessous), nous avons proposé une solution dans laquelle le magazine *Toyota* se transformait en voiture à mesure qu'il approchait de l'ouverture de la boîte aux lettres. Notre concept a plu à l'agence et au client, et l'agence a collaboré en rédigeant le script, en fournissant le contenu et les images et en nous apportant son aide pendant toute la durée du processus, car elle connaît beaucoup mieux la marque que nous.

À notre avis, ce respect mutuel entre les agences interactives et les agences de publicité traditionnelles est un facteur essentiel de réussite. Nous devons respecter et comprendre que les agences de publicité connaissent beaucoup mieux que nous la marque car elles travaillent depuis plus longtemps avec elles. Les agences doivent également nous respecter en tant qu'experts Web qui savent ce qui peut fonctionner sur

Internet et ce qui n'aura aucun succès. Malheureusement, toutes nos relations avec des agences ne sont pas fondées sur ce type de respect et de compréhension mutuels, et le processus est souvent ennuyeux. Lorsqu'aucune des expertises que vous fournissez n'est utilisée, le résultat final de la campagne est une solution qui n'est pas aussi utile pour le client que ce qu'elle aurait dû être.

Nous tentons de garder un esprit ouvert dans le cadre de nos relations avec d'autres agences et, si le courant passe, nous pouvons sans problème créer des choses étonnantes en collaboration avec des agences de publicité au lieu de travailler en solo directement avec la marque/le client.

En résumé, l'objectif de North Kingdom consiste à créer une communication interactive attrayante. Tant que nous aurons la possibilité de travailler en collaboration avec ce type de marques et de projets passionnants, nous continuerons à élaborer des expériences incomparables.

Après avoir grandi près du cercle polaire arctique, au nord de la Suède, **Roger Stighäll** a décidé, à l'âge de 20 ans, de partir vivre dans les tropiques, en Floride. Environ 7 plus tard, il est reparti vivre dans le froid pour rejoindre son ami d'enfance Robert Lindström et travailler pour *Paregos*. Les deux amis, ayant réussi à faire conférer à la société *Paregos* (qui fait aujourd'hui partie de *Framfab*) un statut international, ont décidé de passer à un niveau supérieur et de fonder **North Kingdom** en 2003. À la suite du retentissant succès de *Future Vision de Vodafone* lancé en 2004, le monde de la publicité a découvert North Kingdom. Jusqu'à présent, la carrière de Robert et Roger a été récompensée par les prix suivants : 4 Cyber Lions d'or à Cannes, présidence du jury – section Web – pour la prestigieuse compétition de publicité suédoise *Guldägget* (Golden Egg).

CASE.02

Die Gestaltung von Kampagnen fürs Internet

Roger Stighäll (North Kingdom)

North Kingdom ist eine in Nordschweden beheimatete Agentur für interaktive Medien, die vor allem durch die Gestaltung von Online-Auftritten für *Vodafone* auf **<www.vodafone.com/futurevision>** und **<www.vodafonejourney.com>** bekannt wurde. In letzter Zeit arbeitet sie auch verstärkt für einige führende Werbeagenturen, also für Kunden, die Partner und Mitbewerber zugleich sind. Viele Marketingleute fragen sich, wie es eigentlich sein kann, dass wir einerseits direkt für eine Marke arbeiten und andererseits Werbeagenturen, die ja eigentlich unsere Konkurrenten sind, bei der Gestaltung von interaktiven Kampagnen unterstützen.

Dass wir dies tun, liegt vor allem an der organisatorischen Struktur unserer Kunden. Manche Marken legen die Koordination ihrer Markenkommunikation in die Hände einer einzigen Werbeagentur. In diesen Fällen ist es dann diese Werbeagentur, die uns mit einem Projekt beauftragt. In anderen Fällen ist die Organisationsstruktur anders und wir können direkt mit der Marke zusammen arbeiten, weil sie intern über ein starkes Kommunikationsteam verfügt, welches die gesamte Markenkommunikation koordiniert und aus diesem Grund selbst Kontakte zu vielen verschiedenen Agenturen hat.

Es kann aber auch auf Entscheidungen zurückzuführen sein, die wir aufgrund der aktuellen Organisationsstruktur in unserer eigenen Agentur getroffen haben. Die direkte Zusammenarbeit mit Kunden oder Marken wie *Vodafone* und *ABSOLUT* ist häufig langfristig angelegt und erfordert daher ein höheres Maß an Kundenbetreuung. Dagegen ist die Arbeit für Agenturkunden oft von kürzerer Dauer, dafür aber intensiver, wobei die Projektschwerpunkte eher auf kreativen und produktionsbezogenen Aspekten liegen. North Kingdom sucht seit jeher gezielt nach den richtigen Projekten, das heißt nach Projekten, bei denen wir davon überzeugt sind, wirklich etwas bewegen zu können. Diese Zielsetzung hat nichts damit zu tun, ob es sich um das Projekt einer von uns direkt betreuten Marke handelt oder ob wir von einer Werbeagentur kontaktiert werden.

Ein Beispiel für eine gut funktionierende Arbeitsbeziehung war die Zusammenarbeit mit der schwedischen Werbeagentur *SWE* für den Launch des neuen *Toyota Aygo*. Die Werbeagentur und der Kunde schickten uns ein Projektbriefing. Der einzigartige Aspekt an diesem Auto war, dass man es NICHT kaufen, sondern abonnieren konnte. In Schweden kennt man Abonnements normalerweise nur in Verbindung mit Zeitungen oder Zeitschriften, die einem dann mit der Post zugeschickt werden. Nach einem internen Brainstorming erklärten wir der Agentur, dass die Übernahme des Projektes für uns nur dann Sinn macht, wenn die Internetseite völlig neu gestaltet werden würde und nicht mehr aussähe wie eine klassische Auto-Internetseite. (Ich glaube, dass einer der Hauptgründe für unseren Erfolg darin liegt, dass wir die Dinge anders machen wollen und sehr auf Details achten.)

Wie auf den (unten stehenden?) Bildern zu sehen ist, schlugen wir eine Lösung vor, bei der sich das Toyota-Magazin in dem Moment, wo es durch den Briefschlitz kommt, in ein Auto verwandelt. Unser Konzept gefiel sowohl der Werbeagentur wie auch dem Kunden. Die Werbeagentur unterstützte uns dann im weiteren Verlauf des Prozesses, etwa durch das Verfassen von Texten und die Lieferung von Content und Bildmaterial, da sie über mehr Hintergrundinformationen über die Marke verfügte als wir.

Dieser gegenseitige Respekt ist unserer Meinung

nach der Schlüssel zu einer erfolgreichen Zusammenarbeit zwischen Agenturen, die auf interaktive Medien spezialisiert sind, und klassischen Werbeagenturen. Wir müssen begreifen und respektieren, dass Werbeagenturen aufgrund ihrer oft schon sehr langen Zusammenarbeit mit der Marke diese natürlich viel besser kennen als wir. Zugleich müssen die Werbeagenturen uns als Internetexperten respektieren und akzeptieren, dass wir am besten wissen, was online machbar ist und was nicht. Leider basieren nicht alle unsere Geschäftsbeziehungen mit Werbeagenturen auf dieser Art von gegenseitigem Respekt und Verständnis, was sich letzten Endes negativ auf das Projekt auswirkt. Wenn das Fachwissen, das wir zur Verfügung stellen, nicht genutzt wird, resultiert das Projekt schließlich in einer Lösung, die dem Kunden nicht den maximalen Nutzen bietet, den sie ihm ansonsten hätte bieten können.

Wir versuchen immer, unvoreingenommen mit anderen Agenturen zusammen zu arbeiten und wenn sich zeigt, dass die gegenseitige Chemie stimmt, haben wir überhaupt kein Problem damit, im Team mit einer Werbeagentur eine tolle Kampagne für einen Endkunden zu entwickeln, statt direkt mit der Marke/dem Kunden zusammenzuarbeiten.

Letzten Endes besteht das Ziel von North Kingdom darin, spannende interaktive Kommunikation zu gestalten. Solange wir die Chance bekommen, an aufregenden Projekten für interessante Marken mitzuwirken, werden wir uns auch weiterhin einfach nur darauf konzentrieren, interaktive Weltklasse-Kampagnen zu liefern.

Roger Stighäll wuchs in Nordschweden am Rande der Arktis auf. Mit 20 entschloss er sich, ins tropische Florida umzusiedeln. Sieben Jahre später kehrte er wieder in die Kälte zurück, um gemeinsam mit seinem alten Kumpel Robert Lindström für *Paregos* zu arbeiten. Nachdem es ihnen gelungen war, *Paregos* (gehört heute zu *Framfab*) international bekannt zu machen, beschlossen die beiden Freunde, die nächste Ebene zu erklimmen. 2003 hoben sie **North Kingdom** aus der Taufe. Durch den riesigen Erfolg von *Vodafone Future Vision* in 2004 wurde die internationale Werbeszene auf North Kingdom aufmerksam. Vier Goldene Cyber-Löwen von Cannes sind die bisherigen Höhepunkte der gemein-samen Karriere von Roger und Robert. Zudem war Roger Jury-Vorsitzender der Kategorie „Interaktiv" bei „Guldägget" (Goldenes Ei), der wichtigsten schwedischen Werbepreisverleihung.

CASE:03

Design in Japan

Hideki Ogino (FICC inc.)

The Japanese are probably the biggest consumers of technology on the planet. Mobile phones are marketed towards children from a very young age, with video conferencing and GPS capabilities (not to mention VGA screens and JAVA browsers!). 85% of the population are online, 1/2 of them (40 million) have connections above ADSL, and diffusion of FTTH connections are at the highest levels in the world.

Thus, when designing websites for Japanese viewers we must keep in mind their somewhat unique profiles. Most viewers will tend to have very high bandwidth and large LC Displays. Many are very computer literate and are constantly bombarded with endless images of advertising wherever they go (most of the advertising are quite BIG, compared to computer displays). For them, beautiful designs and images are a part of the everyday scenery and any information they need (or feel they need) is always available at their fingertips. Their supercharged mobile phones provide them with any service imaginable, the Japanese call this the "ubiquitous" society, where anything is available anywhere and at any time.

This overwhelming amount of image and information creates users with very different patterns of action depending on the type of contents viewed. As one can imagine, the Japanese are very skilled when actively searching for real information that they need, but are very inactive when viewing content as a passive user. They are too accustomed to the television (now digital with even more information going back and forth) that they simply will not "click" and make choices out of interest. "Why bother?" when everything you need is fed to you in such enormous amounts? We have actually found that when viewing such image-oriented-websites, most Japanese people will just sit in front of their displays and wait, to see what happens...

Since most of our work at FICC is about creating these image-oriented-websites (for such passive viewers), this causes us to design and create websites in certain ways:

1) MINIMUM interaction
2) BIG images
3) CLEAR guidance

Like television, some of our works don't require the user to click anything. After arriving at the URL, they can simply "sit back" and enjoy. *GORAKADAN* **<www.gorakadan.com>** is a renowned spa & hotel, famous for their hospitality. We hoped to illustrate such hospitality through the website by not requiring the viewer to do anything upon their arrival. The viewer does not need to click anything to discover *GORAKADAN*, they can simply wait and watch for the animation to illustrate the relaxing world of this hotel. When that's done, the website will automatically move on to a slideshow of the facilities that can be found there.

For *Seven Salotti* **<www.sevensalotti.jp>**, a brand of luxury sofas, we created a website where once the viewer has selected their sofa, they can enjoy the images at full screen. The images will load and change as a slideshow automatically. Detailed specs and information are available on the screen, but we felt it was most important to have the user first sit back and relax, before considering these luxury items. After all, stress from navigating through small images on a computer screen is not a feeling we would like to associate with luxury sofas.

Educated in Paris, France, **Hideki Ogino** worked as a photographer assistant from 1998 to 2000. He joined a software development company in Malaysia later that year as a Flash content designer. Upon his return to Japan, he took up the position of Art Director at *ANTEPRIMA Ltd.* and set up a design office in Tokyo, working mainly in the field of fashion. In 2004, Ogino set up **FICC inc.**, a company offering web development and branding consultation services to a wide range of clientele.

CASE:03

Le design au Japon

Hideki Ogino (FICC inc.)

Les Japonais sont probablement les plus grands consommateurs de technologie de la planète. En effet, les téléphones portables, avec des fonctions de visioconférence et de GPS (sans parler des écrans VGA et des navigateurs Java) sont commercialisés à des enfants très jeunes. Environ 85 % de la population dispose d'une connexion à Internet, la moitié (40 millions) ayant des connexions ADSL et supérieures, et la diffusion de connexions par fibre optique est la plus élevée du monde.

Ainsi, lorsque nous créons des sites Web pour des visiteurs japonais, nous devons garder à l'esprit leurs caractéristiques particulières. La plupart des visiteurs japonais disposent d'une très large bande passante et d'écrans à cristaux liquides de grande taille, et nombre d'entre eux possèdent d'excellentes connaissances en informatique et sont constamment bombardés, où qu'ils se trouvent, par des images publicitaires (la plupart des publicités ont une taille importante par rapport aux écrans). Pour ces utilisateurs, les beaux designs et les magnifiques images font partie du décor et toutes les informations dont ils ont besoin (ou pensent avoir besoin) sont à portée de leur main. En outre, leurs téléphones portables surdoués leurs proposent tous les services imaginables. Les Japonais appellent cela la société « omniprésente », où tout est disponible partout et à tout moment.

Cet impressionnant volume d'images et d'informations crée chez les utilisateurs différents modèles d'action en fonction du type de contenu regardé. Comme l'on pourrait s'y attendre, les Japonais sont extrêmement compétents lorsqu'il s'agit de rechercher activement les informations dont ils ont besoin, mais ils ont une attitude inactive lorsqu'ils regardent un contenu en tant qu'utilisateurs passifs. Ils sont tellement habitués à la télévision (qui est à présent numérique et diffuse un plus grand volume d'informations) qu'il ne leur vient pas à l'idée de « cliquer » et de faire des choix utiles. Pourquoi « se donner la peine » lorsque tout ce que vous voulez vous est fourni dans des quantités gigantesques ? Nous nous sommes rendu compte que lorsque des sites Internet avec des images apparaissent à l'écran, la plupart des Japonais se contentent de s'asseoir devant leur écran et d'attendre, pour voir ce qui va se passer...

À FICC, la plus grande partie de notre travail étant centrée sur la création de ces sites Internet à images (s'adressant à des visiteurs passifs), nous devons donc concevoir et créer les sites Web en respectant certains critères :

1) Interaction MINIMUM
2) GRANDES images
3) Indications CLAIRES

Comme lorsqu'ils sont devant leur écran de télévision, les utilisateurs n'ont pas besoin de cliquer lorsqu'ils visitent la plupart de nos sites. Après avoir saisi ou trouvé l'adresse URL, ils peuvent tout simplement se caler dans leur chaise et passer un bon moment. *GORAKADAN* **<www.gorakadan.com>** est un hôtel avec station thermale très connu et réputé pour son hospitalité. Nous avons créé pour cet hôtel un site Internet qui reflète parfaitement ce sens de l'hospitalité, car le visiteur n'a rien à faire lorsque le site s'affiche sur son écran. Il n'a pas besoin de cliquer sur un élément pour découvrir *GORAKADAN*, il suffit d'attendre et de regarder l'animation qui recrée le monde de détente proposé par cet hôtel. Lorsque l'animation est terminée, le site passe automatiquement en mode diaporama pour présenter les services et les chambres de l'hôtel.

Pour *Seven Salotti* <**www.sevensalotti.jp**>, marque de canapés de luxe, nous avons créé un site Internet sur lequel, une fois que le visiteur a sélectionné le canapé qui lui plaît, les images s'affichent en mode plein écran. Les images sont chargées et affichées automatiquement, comme des diapositives. Des spécifications et des informations détaillées peuvent également être affichées, mais nous avons pensé qu'il était plus important que l'utilisateur commence par s'asseoir confortablement et se détendre avant d'examiner le produit proposé. En effet, le stress entraîné par la navigation entre des images de petite taille sur un écran d'ordinateur n'est pas une sensation que nous aimerions associer à des canapés de luxe.

Après avoir terminé ses études à Paris, **Hideki Ogino** a travaillé comme assistant photographe de 1998 à 2000. Il est ensuite parti rejoindre une société de développement de logiciels en Malaisie en tant que designer des contenus Flash. À son retour au Japon, il est devenu directeur artistique chez *ANTEPRIMA Ltd.* et a mis en place un bureau de design à Tokyo, qui travaille principalement dans le domaine de la mode. En 2004, Ogino a créé la société **FICC inc.**, qui propose des développements Web et des services de consultation en stratégie de marque pour de nombreux clients de divers secteurs.

CASE:03

Design in Japan

Hideki Ogino (FICC inc.)

Die Japaner schlagen als Technologiekonsumenten vermutlich alle Rekorde auf diesem Planeten. Schon für Kleinkinder werden Mobiltelefone angeboten, die über Videokonferenz- und GPS-Funktionen verfügen (ganz zu schweigen von VGA-Screens und JAVA-Browsern!). 85% aller Japaner haben einen Internetzugang, die Hälfte davon (40 Millionen) nutzen dabei Leitungen, die noch leistungsfähiger sind als ADSL, und die Zahl der FTTH-Nutzer zählt zu den höchsten der Welt.

Wenn man also Webseiten für japanische Internetnutzer gestaltet, muss man dabei deren besonderen Gewohnheiten, Vorlieben sowie ihre technische Ausstattung berücksichtigen. Die meisten japanischen Internetnutzer verfügen über sehr schnelle Breitbandanschlüsse und große LC-Displays. Viele kennen sich sehr gut mit Computern aus und sind zudem daran gewöhnt, beim Surfen ständig mit Werbung bombardiert zu werden (die Werbebanner sind im Verhältnis zu den Computerdisplays häufig geradezu RIESIG). Für die Japaner gehören schönes Design und schöne Bilder zum Internet-Alltag und sie sind daran gewöhnt, auf alle Informationen, die sie brauchen (oder haben möchten), sehr schnell zugreifen können. Ihre megaleistungsstarken Mobiltelefone bieten ihnen jeden auch nur erdenklichen Service. Die Japaner nennen das „allgegenwärtige Gesellschaft" – eine Gesellschaft, in der alles jederzeit und überall zu haben ist.

Bedingt durch diese überwältigende Anzahl an Bildern und Informationen gibt es Nutzer mit sehr unterschiedlichen Aktionsmustern, die jeweils von der Art des betrachteten Inhalts abhängen. Die Japaner sind sehr geschickt darin, wenn es um die aktive Suche nach real benötigten Informationen geht. Bei der Betrachtung von Inhalten als passive Nutzer tendieren sie jedoch stark dazu, untätig zu bleiben. Sie sind einfach zu sehr ans Fernsehen gewöhnt (das jetzt digital ist und ihnen eine noch größere Informations- und Bilderflut als zuvor bietet) und „klicken" nicht einfach von selbst weiter, um aus Neugier mehr Informationen aufzurufen. „Warum sich die Mühe machen?", wenn alles, was man braucht, einem in so riesiger Menge auf dem Silbertablett serviert wird?

Wir haben festgestellt, dass die meisten Japaner beim Anblick von bildorientierten Webseiten einfach vor ihrem Bildschirm sitzen und abwarten, was passiert. Da bei FICC der Großteil unserer Arbeit darin besteht, solche bildorientierten Webseiten zu programmieren (für diese passiven Nutzer), sind wir dazu übergegangen, bei Design und Gestaltung von Webseite nach bestimmten Schemata vorzugehen:

1) MINIMUM an Interaktionen
2) GROSSE Bilder
3) KLARE Führung

Es ist wie beim Fernsehen – einige der von uns gestalteten Webseiten erfordern sogar überhaupt keine Klicks vom Nutzer. Sobald sie die URL aufgerufen haben, brauchen sie nichts weiter zu tun als sich „zurückzulehnen" und das zu genießen, was ihnen sodann präsentiert wird.

GORAKADAN **<www.gorakadan.com>** ist ein in Japan sehr bekanntes Spa & Hotel, das für seine Gastfreundlichkeit berühmt ist. Unser Ziel bestand darin, diese Gastfreundlichkeit über die Webseite zu vermitteln, indem der Internetnutzer sich wie ein Gast des Hotels fühlen kann, der bei seiner Ankunft dort in Empfang genommen wird und nichts mehr selbst tun muss. Der Internetbesucher braucht überhaupt keinen Finger zu rühren, um *GORAKADAN* zu entdecken – er kann sich einfach zurücklehnen und den Anblick der ihm gebotenen Präsentation genießen, die ihm die entspannende Atmosphäre dieses Hotels vermitteln soll. Sobald diese Präsentation beendet ist, führt die Webseite den Betrachter automatisch zu einer Diashow, die ihm die verschiedenen Einrichtungen des Hotels zeigt.

Für *Seven Salotti* **<www.sevensalotti.jp>**, eine Luxussofa-Marke, haben wir eine Webseite gestaltet, die so funktioniert: Sobald der Nutzer ein Sofamodell ausgewählt hat, erscheinen sofort Bilder dieses Modells in voller Größe auf dem Bildschirm. Die Bilder wechseln von selbst wie bei einer automatischen Diashow. Auf dem Bildschirm sind auch Detailansichten und weitere Informationen verfügbar, doch wir fanden es wichtig, dass der Nutzer sich zuerst zurücklehnen und entspannen kann, bevor er sich näher mit diesen Luxusobjekten beschäftigt. Wenn der Nutzer sich auf seinem Computerbildschirm durch eine Reihe kleiner Bilder klicken muss, fühlt er sich gestresst – und Stress ist unserer Ansicht nach das letzte aller Gefühle, das mit Luxussofas assoziiert werden sollte.

Nach seiner Ausbildung in Paris arbeitete **Hideki Ogino** von 1998 bis 2000 als fotografischer Assistent. Dann zog er nach Malaysia um, wo er für eine Softwareentwicklungsfirma Flash Content designte. Schließlich kehrte er nach Japan zurück, um als Art Director bei *ANTEPRIMA Ltd.* einzusteigen und ein Designbüro in Tokio aufzubauen, das hauptsächlich für die Modebranche tätig ist. 2004 gründete Ogino **FICC inc.** Das Unternehmen macht Webentwicklung und Branding-Beratung für viele unterschiedliche Kunden.

20:20 LONDON

UK

www.2020london.co.uk

since 2002

Mission

Tell them and they'll forget; show them and they'll remember; but INVOLVE them and they'll UNDERSTAND. /// Dites-leur et ils oublieront. Montrez-leur et ils se souviendront. Impliquez-les et ils comprendront. /// Sag ihnen etwas und sie werden es vergessen, zeig ihnen etwas und sie werden sich erinnern, doch erst wenn du sie in etwas EINBINDEST, werden sie es BEGREIFEN.

www.nickthediamond.com

Location

20:20 London
Augustine Hall, Yorkton Street
London, E2 8NH
United Kingdom
<peter.riley@2020london.co.uk>

Team

1 Creative Director, 4 Copywriters, 4 Art Directors, 4 Programmers.

www.audi-elements.com

Clients EA Games, Five, Audi Cars, Jaguar, Sony PlayStation, Procter & Gamble, Pernod Ricard, Sony BMG.

Awards Cannes Lions (3 Gold/3 Silver/Bronze).

3INDESIGN MEDIA SOLUTIONS MEXICO

www.3indesign.com since 2000

Mission

Being a highly competitive multimedia agency and improving our work daily. /// Agence multimédia très compétitive qui ne cesse de s'améliorer. /// Eine der besten Multimedia-Agenturen der Branche zu sein und unsere Arbeit jeden Tag noch besser zu machen.

www.enriquecovarrubias.com

Location

3indesign Media Solutions
Calzada de los corceles #110 Colinas del Sur
Delegación älvaro Obregón
Mexico – DF cp 01430
<info@3indesign.com>

Team

2 Creative Director, 1 Art Director, 4 Designers, 1 Programmer, 1 Editor.

www.pascalarquitectos.com

Clients HSBC, IUSACELL, TV Azteca, Promeco Boehringer Ingelheim, Contempo International Management Models, Pascal Arquitectos, Enrique Covarrubias.

Awards a! Diseño International Prize, Quorum, and mentions of publications online.

AGENCYNET INTERACTIVE

USA

www.agencynet.com

since 1996

Mission

AgencyNet is an award winning full-service Strategic Interactive Agency providing forward-thinking clients with innovative solutions under one roof. Our dedicated team of talented designers, tactical developers, programmers, video production experts, strategic-planners, usability experts, and marketing professionals generate award-winning projects that maximize return on investment.

www.ownyourC.com

Location

AgencyNet Interactive
Las Olas Riverfront, 300 SW 1st Ave, Suite 155
Fort Lauderdale, Florida 33301
USA
<rlent@agencynet.com>

Team

6 Executives, 1 Creative Director, 9 Designers, 7 Programmers, 5 Project Managers.

AgencyNet est une agence Web stratégique primée à service complet. Elle fournit aux clients de nouvelles solutions en un seul endroit. Notre équipe dédiée de designers talentueux, de développeurs tactiques, de programmateurs, d'experts en production vidéo, de planificateurs stratégiques, d'experts en convivialité et de professionnels en marketing peut donner naissance à des projets primés permettant de maximiser le rendement du capital investi. /// AgencyNet ist eine preisgekrönte Full-Service-Agentur für strategisches interaktives Marketing, die zukunftsorientierten Kunden innovative und maßgeschneiderte Lösungspakete bietet. Unser engagiertes Team aus talentierten Designern, taktischen Entwicklern, Programmierern, Experten für Videoproduktion, strategischen Planern, Usability-Experten und Marketingprofis liefert höchst rentable Lösungen, die schon mit vielen Preisen ausgezeichnet wurden.

www.bacardidj.com

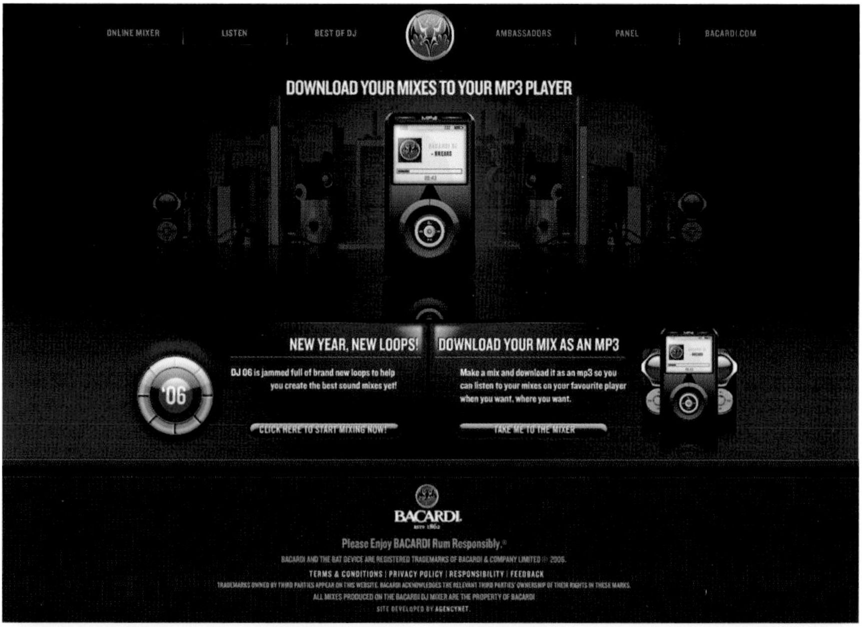

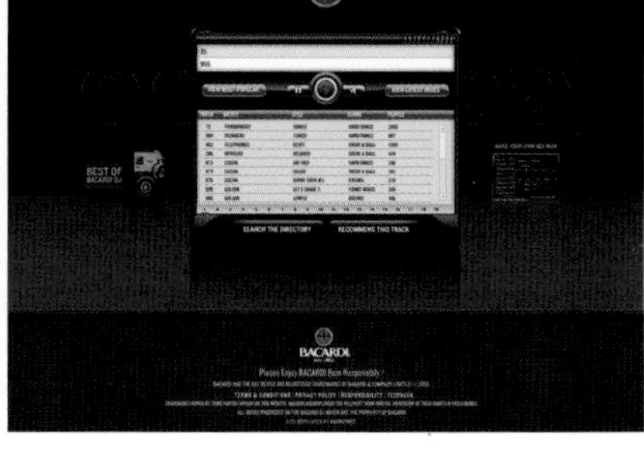

Clients

Bacardi, Bombay Sapphire, Oxygen, The Golf Channel, Ford, BBC America, Howard Stern, Nascar, MLB, OLN, InDemand Television Networks, Motorola.

Awards

FWA (Site of the Day/Site of the Month/Top 20 agency sites in history), Interactive Emmy, OMMA Award (Best Viral Campaign), Cannes Cyber Lion (Shortlist), American Graphic Design Awards, Interactive Media Awards, Ultrashock Bombshock, Flash Forward (Finalist).

AKQA

UK/WORLDWIDE

www.akqa.com

since 1995

Mission

AKQA was founded on four core values: Innovation, Service, Quality and Thought. Everything we do revolves around these values and in addition takes into account the principles of outstanding thinking, outstanding execution and outstanding client service.

www.coke.com

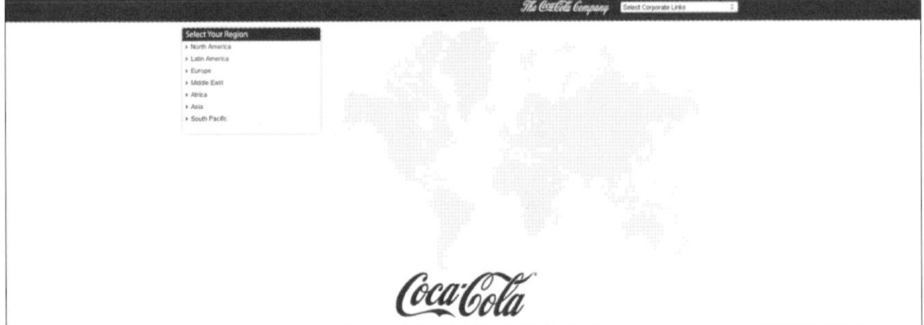

Location

AKQA
1 St John's Lane, 4th floor. London, EC1M 4BL, United Kingdom
Other locations:
San Francisco, Washington D.C., New York, Singapore, Shanghai
<info@akqa.com>

Team

470+ Designers, Programmers, Art Directors, Account Executives, and Architects worldwide.

L'agence AKQA a été fondée sur la base de valeurs essentielles : innovation, service, qualité et pensée. Tout notre travail est axé autour de ces valeurs et tient compte des principes d'une réflexion, d'une réalisation et d'un service remarquables. /// **AKQA wurde auf der Basis von vier Kernwerten gegründet: Innovation, Service, Qualität und Konzept. Unsere gesamte Arbeit ist von diesen vier Werten inspiriert und zeichnet sich zusätzlich durch hervorragende Ideen, hervorragende Ausführung und hervorragenden Kundenservice aus.**

www.clickmore.com

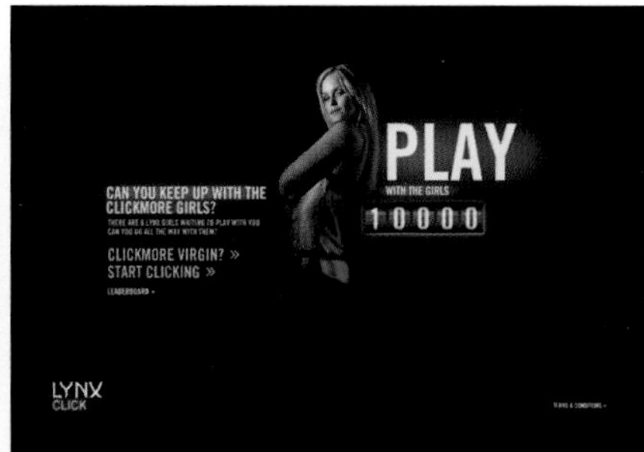

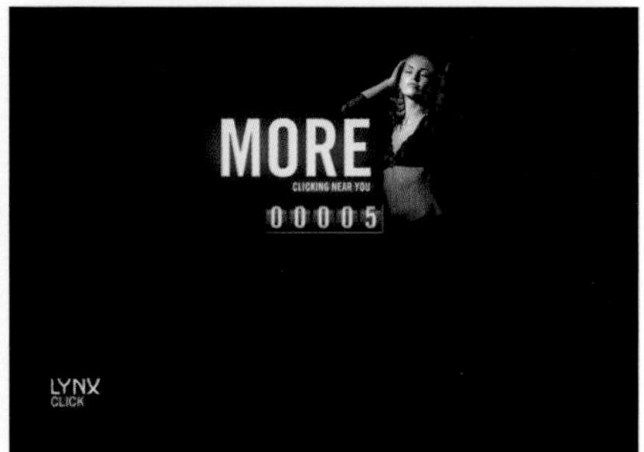

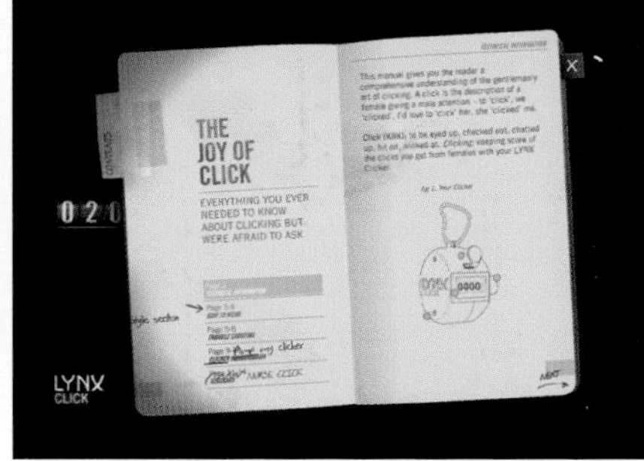

Clients

The Coca-Cola Company, Diageo, ESPN, McDonald's, Microsoft, Nike, Norwich Union, Orange, Sainsbury's, Sky TV, Target Corp, Unilever, USPS, Visa USA, Xbox, Yell.com.

Awards

2006: London International Advertising Awards (Winner), Podcast of the Week, Revolution Magazine, CNET Technology Awards, MSN Creative Awards, Campaign Digital Awards, IAB Creative Showcase (Gold), FAB Awards, One Show Interactive (Silver/Bronze), Revolution Awards, Creativity Magazine, OMMA Awards.

ALMAPBBDO

BRAZIL

www.almapbbdo.com.br

since 1993

Mission

Relevant strategic planning combined with creative ideas. Almap's priority has always been to create a differentiated perspective for our customer's brands and to conquer the market through a unique technological approach on the internet.

www.spacefox.com.br

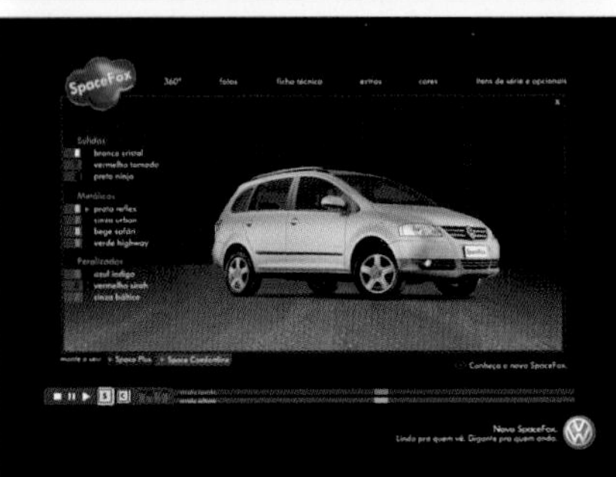

Location

AlmapBBDO
Av. Roque Petroni Jr., 999
São Paulo, 04707-905
Brazil
<mugnaini@almapbbdo.com.br>

Team

1 Creative Director, 4 Art Directors, 2 Copywriters, 1 Designer, 5 Programmers.

Planification stratégique adéquate associée à des idées créatives. La priorité d'Almap a toujours été de créer une perspective différenciée pour les marques de ses clients et de conquérir le marché au moyen d'une solution technologique unique sur Internet. /// **Zielorientierte strategische Planung in Kombination mit kreativen Ideen. Almap gibt die oberste Priorität seit jeher dem Ziel, für die Marken unserer Kunden eine differenzierte Perspektive zu kreieren und den Markt durch einzigartige Internetkampagnen auf Basis modernster Technologien zu erobern.**

Greenpeace Brazil (Hotsite)

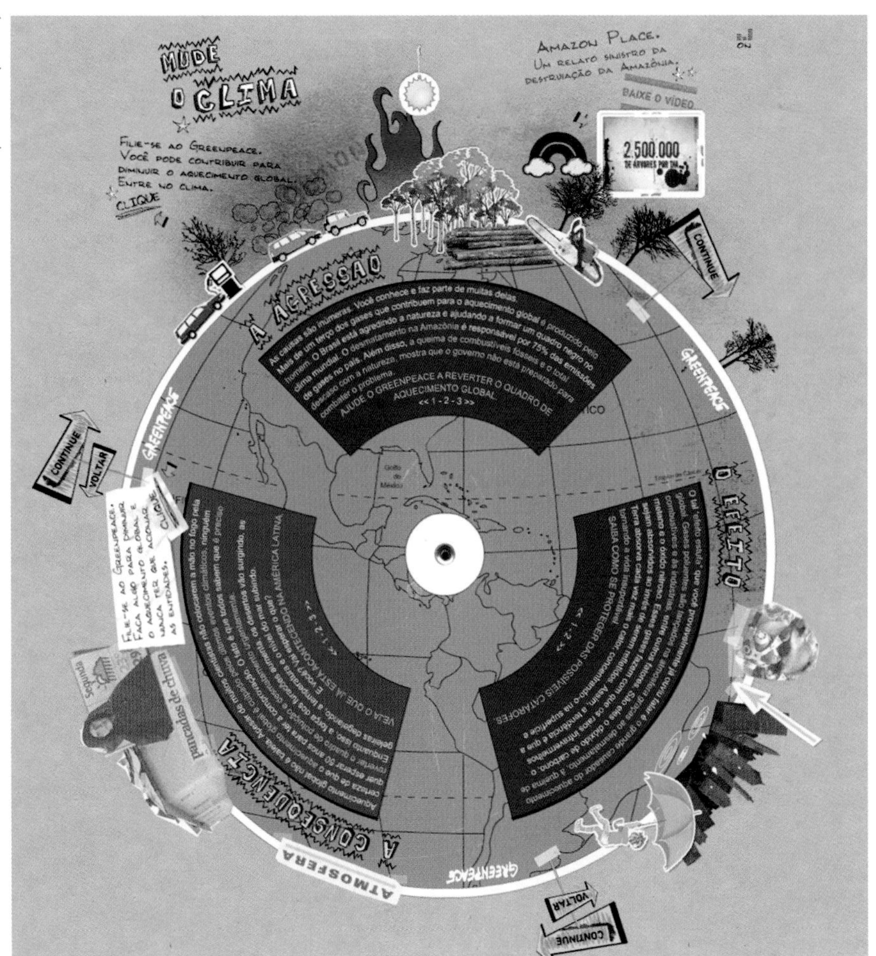

Clients

Antarctica, Audi, Bauducco, Bayer, Carrefour, Claro, Companhia das Letras, Editora Abril, Elma Chips, Embratel, Forum, Gatorade, Gol Linhas Aéreas, Greenpeace, Havaianas, Liz, Master Foods, Miller, Mizuno, Escola Panamerica de Artes, Pepsi, Quaker, Super Interessante, Veja.

Awards

Flash Forward (Gold), Art Directors Club (Merit), Communications Arts (Gold), One Show Interactive (Merit), D&AD (Shortlist), FIAP (Gold/Silver/Bronze), CCSP (Silver/Bronze), Ibest (Gold), El Sol (Silver), Premio Abril (Finalist/Gran Prix), Cannes Lions (Shortlist), El Ojo Iberoamerica, London Festivals (Gold).

AMBERFLY

SCOTLAND

www.amberfly.com

since 2004

Mission

Every individual, project, or business has a unique personality. Amberfly does whatever it takes to ensure that the online presence has this character and always shows its best side. /// Chaque personne, projet ou activité possède sa propre personnalité. Amberfly déploie tous ses efforts pour s'assurer que chaque site Internet ait son propre caractère et montre son meilleur aspect. /// Jeder Mensch, jedes Projekt und jede Marke ist einzigartig. Amberfly stellt seine Kunden mit einer einzigartigen Onlinepräsenz ins rechte Licht und zeigt sie von ihrer besten Seite.

www.sologourmet.ca

Location

Amberfly
22 Forth Street
Edinburgh, EH1 3LH
Scotland
<hello@amberfly.com>

Team

1 Creative Director, 1 Techical Director.

www.move-me.com

www.f1play.com

Clients

Age Concern Scotland, Artation, Computer Cabs, Field and Lawn, F1Play, American Learning Resources, Pulp and Fiber, Goat Media.

Awards

FWA (Site of the Day), American Design Awards, Netscape (Cool Site of the Day), Internet TINY Awards (Site of the Week), Flash Loaded (Site of the Month), TAXI (Site of the Day).

ANALOGUE

CANADA

www.analogue.ca

since 2005

Mission

Analogue has always prided itself on being unique by offering our clients custom solutions that would be next to impossible to find elsewhere. We keep things as simple as possible and focus on making our creations feel like experiences, regardless of the technology used.

www.dipnahorra.com

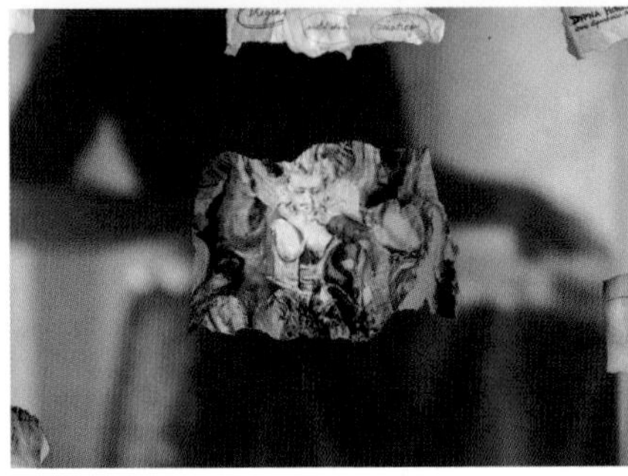

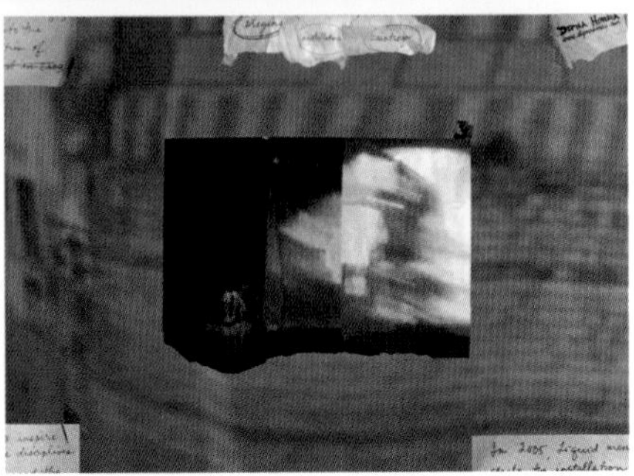

Location

Analogue
418 Richmond Rd, Suite 1
Ottawa, K2A 0G2
Canada
<info@analogue.ca>

Team

2 Founding Partners/Designers.

L'agence Analogue s'est toujours montrée fière d'être unique en proposant à ses clients des solutions personnalisées qu'il serait pratiquement impossible de trouver ailleurs. Nous nous efforçons de faire les choses aussi simplement que possible et de transformer nos créations en expériences, quelle que soit la technologie utilisée. /// **Analogue ist bekannt dafür, seinen Kunden einzigartige maßgeschneiderte Lösungen zu bieten, die sie woanders kaum bekommen würden. Wir halten die Dinge so einfach wie möglich und konzentrieren uns darauf, echte Erlebniswelten zu kreieren, unabhängig von den verwendeten Technologien.**

www.yogaschelter.com

Clients

Max Graham, Rebrand Records, Dipna Horra, Miv Photography, Kate Schelter, Cady McClain, Gary Andrew Poole, Yoga Schelter.

Awards

FWA (Site of the Day), Netdiver (Best of the Year 2005).

ARC WORLDWIDE

CANADA

www.arcww.com

since 2004

Mission

Our mission is to deliver Practical Magic (TM) – inspired marketing solutions that fuse Creativity and Accountability. We aim for highly creative, big ideas that are grounded in clear insights about our clients' brands, channels and consumers and drive measurable growth.

www.leoburnett.ca

Location

Arc Worldwide, Canada - a Leo Burnett Company
175 Bloor Street East, North Tower, 12th Floor
Toronto, Ontario M4W 3R9, Canada
Shirley Ward-Taggart <shirley.ward-taggart@arcww.ca>
Richard Bernstein <richard.bernstein@arcww.ca>

Team

1 Creative Director, 5 Art Directors, 7 Web Designer/Developer/Production, 3 Writers, 4 Creative Technology.

Notre mission : Fournir Practical Magic (TM), des solutions de marketing mêlant la créativité et la responsabilité. Nous aspirons à de grandes idées très créatives fondées sur une perception claire des marques, canaux et consommateurs de nos clients et à une croissance mesurable. /// **Wir bieten unseren Kunden Practical Magic (TM) – inspirierte Marketinglösungen, die auf magische Weise Kreativität und Pragmatik verbinden. Wir streben nach brillanten kreativen Ideen, die auf einem klaren Verständnis der Marken, Kanäle und Konsumenten unserer Kunden basieren und messbares Wachstum erzeugen.**

www.munchemsmagic.com

www.frootloops.com

Clients

Allstate Canada, Conagra Foods, Kellogg Canada, Kellogg USA, Minute Maid, Moosehead Breweries, P&G, Norman Hardie Winery, Smuckers Canada, The Score, Tourism Toronto, Visa Canada, Wrigley Canada.

Awards

ADC of Toronto, ANDY, Applied Arts, Campaign Digital, Cannes Cyber Lions, Clio, CMA, Comm Arts, D&AD, EFFIE, Flashforward, FWA, Golden Drum, London International Advertising, New York Festivals, OneShow Interactive, P&G Fusion, Shots Grand Prix 06 - World's Most Awarded Interactive Agency, Webby Awards.

B-REEL

SWEDEN

www.b-reel.com

since 1999

Mission

B-Reel is an advertising agency's best creative friend especially when it comes to the production of commercials, web and motion graphics. We put positive energy and life into every single project.

www.travelersinsynch.com

Location

B-Reel
Tjärhovsgatan 4
116 21 Stockholm
Sweden
<Hello@b-reel.com>

Team

2 Key Account Managers, 3 Producers, 1 Creative Director, 5 Art Directors, 2 Asst. Art Directors, 4 Flash Animation/Programming, 3 2d/3d Animators, 1 CEO.

B-Reel est le meilleur allié créatif des agences de publicité, en particulier en matière de production de messages publicitaires et de graphiques Internet et en mouvement. Nous insufflons de l'énergie positive et de la vie dans chacun de nos projets. /// **B-Reel ist der beste Kreativpartner für Werbeagenturen, insbesondere bei der Produktion von Werbespots und Grafikanimationen für das Web. Wir füllen jedes einzelne Projekt mit Leben und positiver Energie.**

www.statoil.se/sammapris

www.vingflex.se

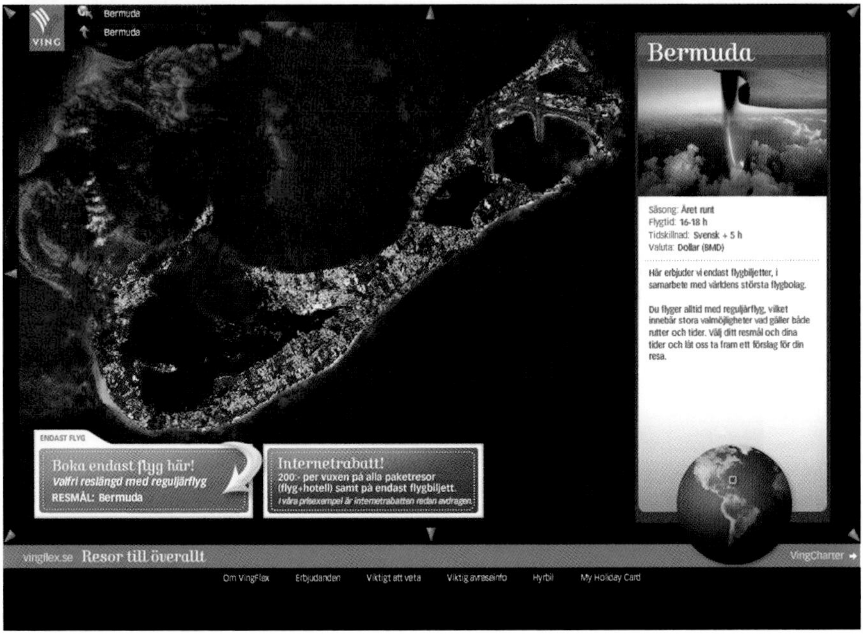

Clients HM, IKEA, MTV, Forsman & Bodenfors, Åkestam.Holst, Fallon Worldwide.

Awards FWA (Most Influential Site of 2006/Site of the month/ Site of the Day), New York Festivals (Silver/Bronze), Epica (Silver/Bronze), London International Advertising Awards (Winner), Eurobest (Silver), ANDY Awards (winner), Cannes Cyber Lion (Bronze).
* Job for Advertising Agency.

BEE-CREATIONS

ISRAEL

www.bee-creations.com

since 2003

Mission

Bee-Creations goal is to provide visual solutions on multiple platforms for a wide variety of clients. We believe that the concepts we use should be adjusted separately for each media format, so as to find a unique way to present our work on every platform.

www.imagebank.org.il

Location

Bee-Creations
19 Rotschield Blvd
Tel-Aviv, 66881
Israel
<info@bee-creations.com>

Team

2 Creative Directors, 2 Designers, 2 Webmaster, 1 Project Manager.

L'objectif de Bee-Creations : fournir des solutions visuelles sur plusieurs plates-formes pour de nombreux clients. Nous pensons que les concepts que nous utilisons doivent être adaptés séparément à chaque format de média afin de présenter de façon unique notre travail sur chacune des plates-formes. /// Bee-Creations bietet visuelle Lösungen auf einer Vielzahl von Plattformen für Kunden aus allen Branchen. Unser Ansatz besteht darin, die von uns erarbeiteten Konzepte individuell an jedes Medienformat anzupassen und für jede Plattform eine einzigartige Präsentation zu inszenieren.

www.eyalbartov.co.il

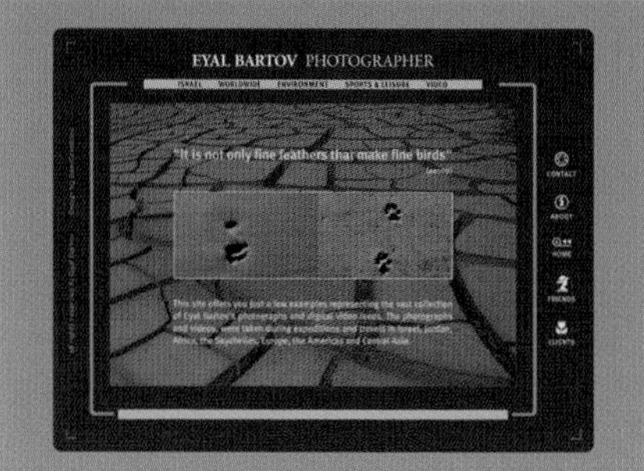

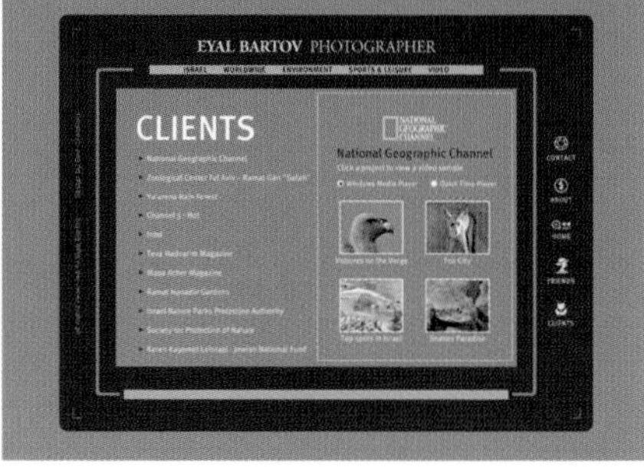

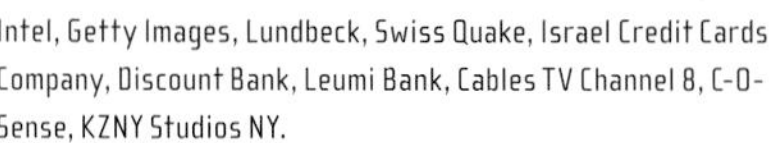

Clients Intel, Getty Images, Lundbeck, Swiss Quake, Israel Credit Cards Company, Discount Bank, Leumi Bank, Cables TV Channel 8, C-O-Sense, KZNY Studios NY.

Awards American Design Awards, How Design Magazine (Top 5), Plasticpilots, NewWebPick, DOPE, Netdiver, Cool Homepages, Pixelmakers (Site of the Day).

BIG SPACESHIP

USA

www.bigspaceship.com

since 2000

Mission

We are addicted to popular culture and obsessed with emerging technology. It shows in the brands that we work with, the award-winning campaigns we build across disciplines, and in the way our entire crew collaborates in the creative process. More than anything, though, we love to tell a good story.

www.nikeair.com

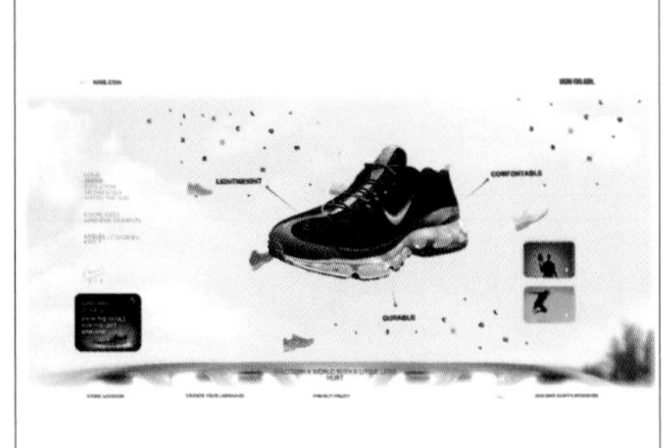

Location

Big Spaceship
45 Main Street, Suite 716
Brooklyn, NY 11201
USA
Michael Lebowitz <m.lebowitz@bigspaceship.com>

Team

50 creative collaborators.

Nous avons une passion pour la culture populaire et la technologie émergente. Cela se reflète dans les marques pour lesquelles nous travaillons, les campagnes primées que nous réalisons dans diverses disciplines et dans la façon dont toute notre équipe participe au processus de création. Et, plus que tout, nous aimons raconter une bonne histoire. /// **Zu unseren wichtigsten Inspirationsquellen zählen Popkultur und die neuesten Technologien. Dies zeigt sich an den Marken, für die wir arbeiten und an unseren preisgekrönten Kampagnen, die das Ergebnis unserer einzigartigen kreativen und interdisziplinären Teamarbeit sind. Am meisten lieben wir es jedoch, spannende Geschichten zu erzählen.**

www.sodarktheconofman.com

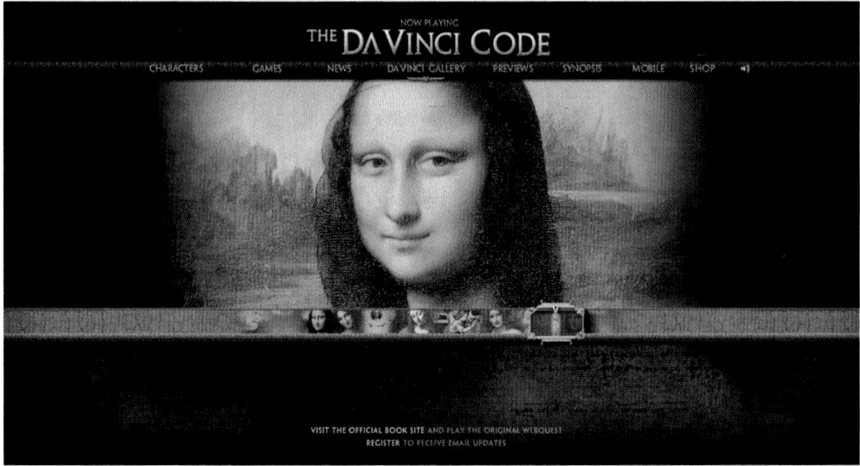

Clients

Nike, Sony, Coca-Cola, Google, Adobe, Moma, Gucci, and ABC, among others.

Awards

Cannes Cyber Lions, One Show Pencils, Webby, Clio, Web Award (Best in Show), Key Art Award, among many others.

BKWLD

USA

www.bkwld.com

since 2001

Mission

A lot of people like to put things in boxes and label it so they know exactly what it is. We hate labels. We are more than just an Internet design company. And we do much more than develop websites. We are an idea company. A collective of people who can't stop thinking of ways to solve problems.

www.thebeachboys.com

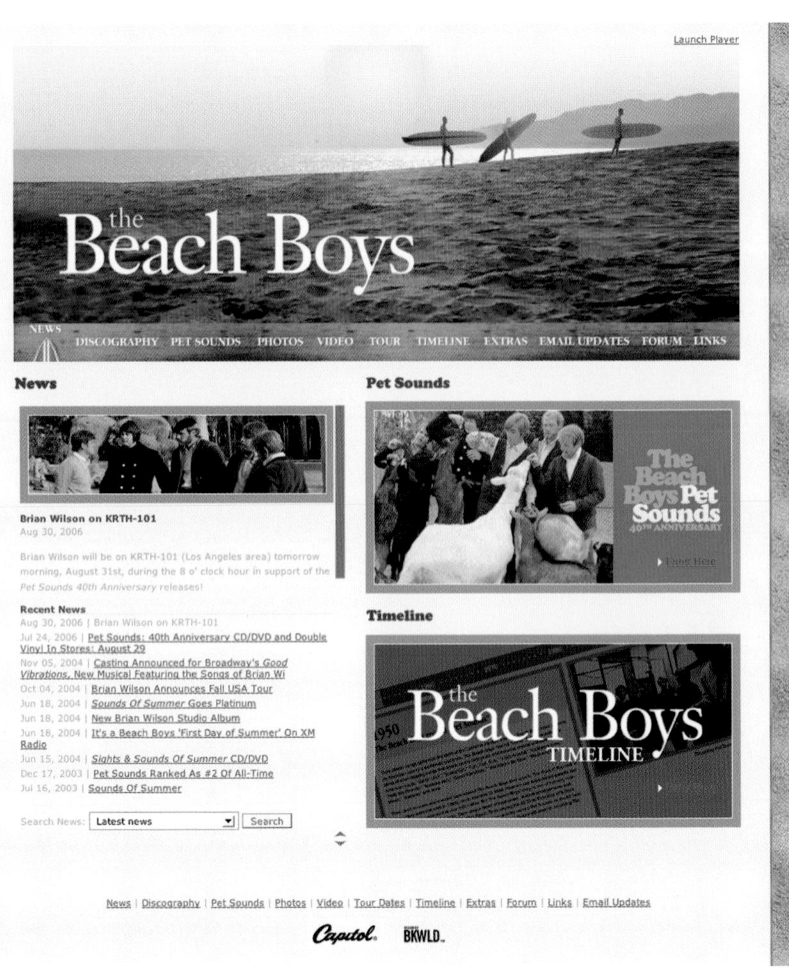

Location

BKWLD
Sacramento: 1901A Del Paso Blvd. Sacramento, CA 95815
Seattle: 219 First Ave. South Ste. 401 Seattle, WA 98104
USA
Ryan Vanni <ryan.vanni@bkwld.com>

Team

1 Studio Director, 1 Development Director, 1 Lead Programmer, 2 Flash Programmers, 2 Art Directors, 1 Designer, 3 Account Service.

La plupart des personnes aiment mettre les choses dans des boîtes avec des étiquettes, pour savoir exactement ce qu'il y a dedans. Nous n'aimons pas les étiquettes. Nous sommes bien plus qu'une société de design Internet et notre travail va au-delà du développement de sites. Nous sommes une société d'idées, un groupe de personnes qui ne peut cesser de penser aux manières de résoudre des problèmes. /// Viele Leute stecken Dinge gern in Schubladen und verpassen ihnen ein Etikett, damit sie einen genauen Begriff davon haben. Wir lehnen Etiketten und Schubladen ab. Wir sind weit mehr als eine Agentur für Internetdesign. Unsere Arbeit geht weit über das Entwickeln von Webseiten hinaus. Wir sind eine Ideenfabrik. Unser unermüdliches Team kennt nur eine Mission: Optimale Lösungen für unsere Kunden zu finden.

www.electricvisual.com

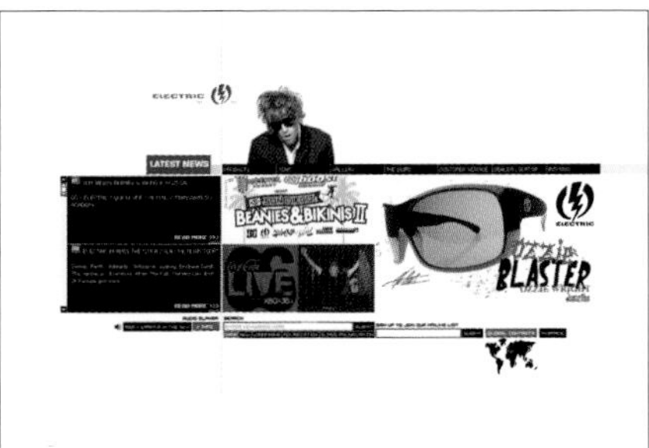

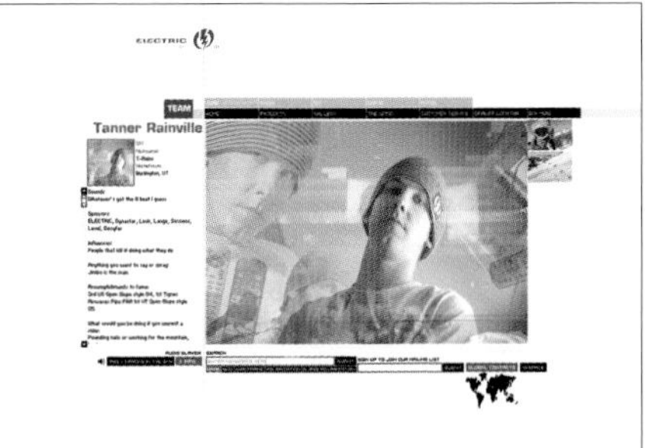

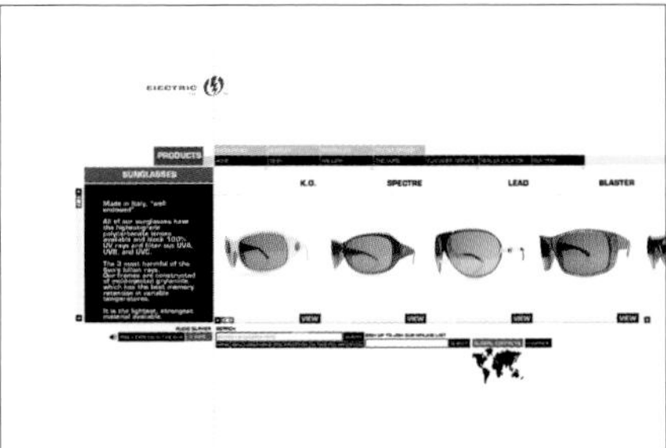

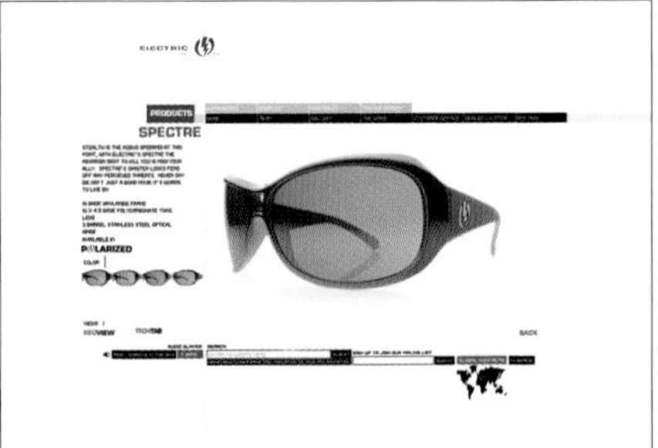

www.holidaydominator.com

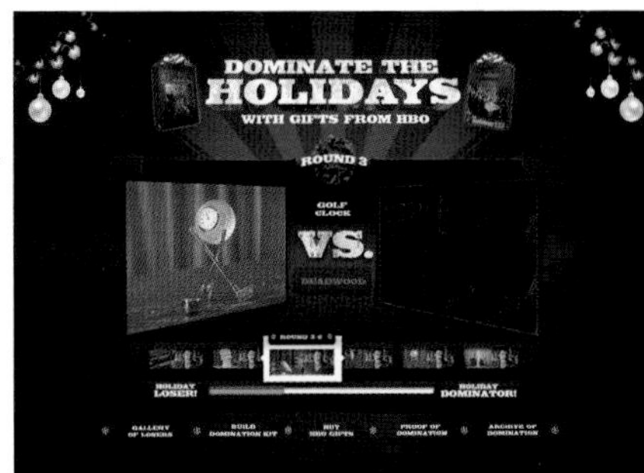

Clients

Nike, HBO, California Tourism, Pebble Beach Resorts, Sony BMG, Interscope Records, Virgin, Capitol Records.

Awards

FWA, Macromedia (Site of the Day), e-Creative (Site of the Day).

BLOC

UK

www.blocmedia.com

since 2000

Mission

Bloc is a multi-award winning digital creative agency with 6 years experience in producingeffective and groundbreaking creative digital marketing for blue chip entertainment brands. Bloc is focussed on youth marketing and works with some of the biggest youth focussed brands in the world today.

www.stackopolis.com

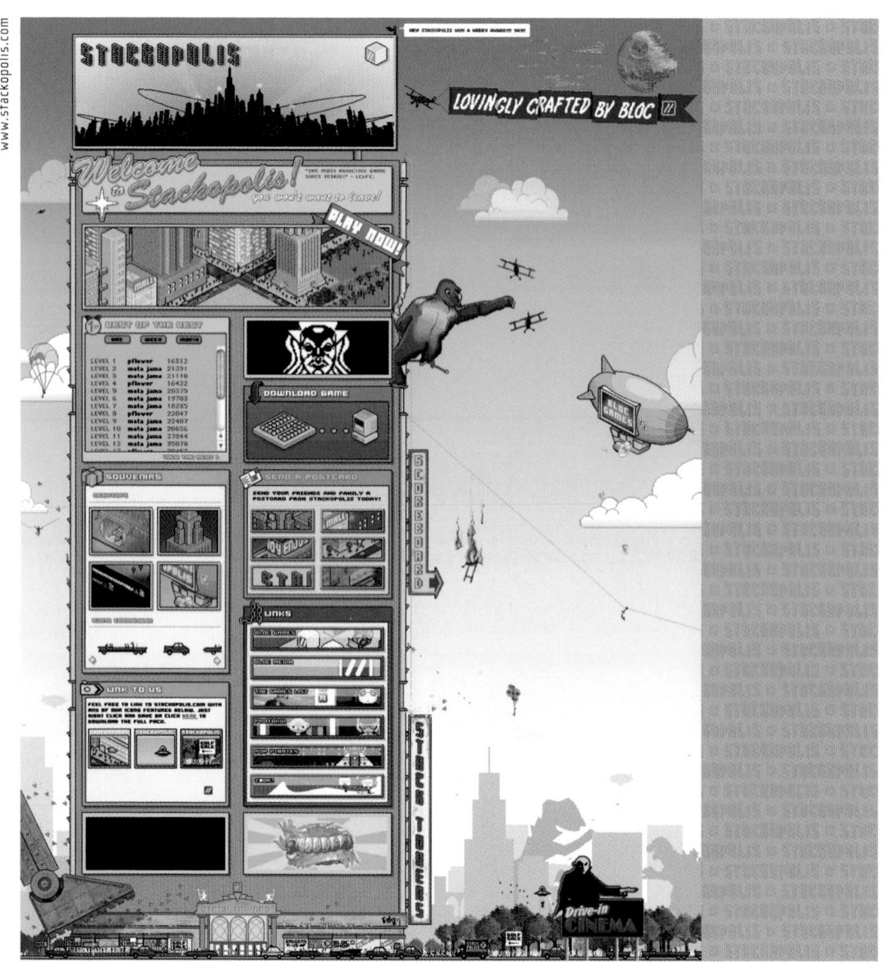

Location

Bloc
61 Charlotte Road
London, EC2A 3QT
United Kingdom
<hello@blocmedia.com>

Team

1 CEO/Chief Creative Officer, 2 Creative Directors, 1 Account Director, 1 Technical Director, 1 Operations Director, 1 Studio Director, 1 Art Director, 3 Senior Creatives, 5 Creatives, 6 Developers.

Bloc Media est une agence de création numérique plusieurs fois primée et avec 6 années d'expérience dans la production de marketing numérique créatif et d'avant-garde pour des marques de loisirs de premier ordre. Bloc Media est centrée sur le marketing jeunesse et travaille avec certaines des plus grandes marques mondiales ciblant les jeunes. /// **Bloc ist eine mehrfach ausgezeichnete Agentur für digitales Design mit sechsjähriger Erfahrung in der Konzeption und Realisation effektiver, Bahn brechender digitaler Marketing-kampagnen für Topmarken der Unterhaltungsindustrie. Bloc ist auf Jugendmarketing spezialisiert und arbeitet für einige der weltweit aktuell führenden Jugendmarken.**

http://zwok-game.com

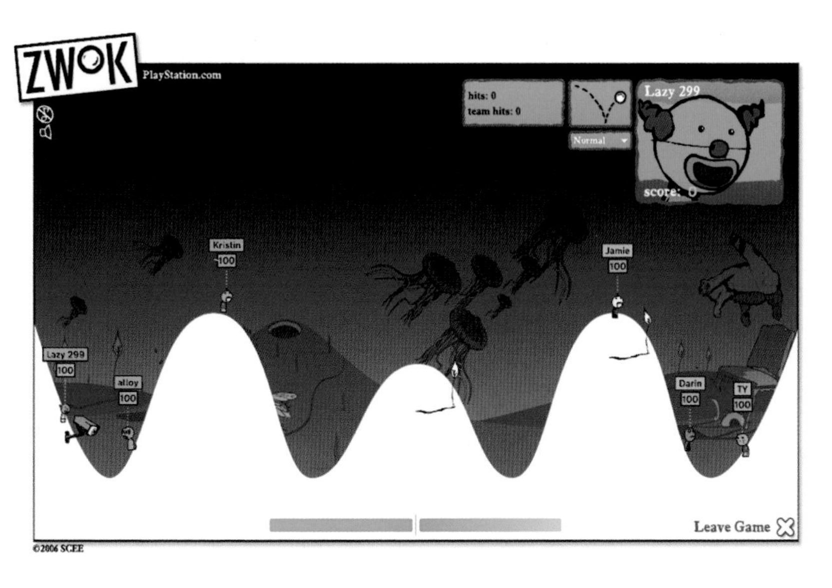

Clients

Electronic Arts Europe, Electronic Arts UK, Sony Computer Entertainment Europe, Playstation.com, Diesel, EMI, Turner Networks, Pogo.

Awards

IMAA (Gold), BIMA (Gold), Campaign Digital Awards, Webby Awards (Gold/Honouree), The ONE Show, Cannes Lions (Bronze), FWA (Site of the Day), Cresta Awards, Eurobest Awards, Future Marketing Awards, Future Marketing Awards, FITC, NMA Effectiveness Awards, Design Week, Digital Music Awards.

BUBBLE

UK

www.thebubblesite.co.uk

since 1998

Mission

Our clients' confidence in our work allows us to produce bespoke projects that push all aspects, not only in graphic treatments but also across full production. We think freely, create solid relationships and build our interactive, moving-image, sound and print portfolio with pieces that inspire, captivate and satisfy our creative appetite.

www.arca.uk.com

arca

Home | Most Recent | Slaidburn Community Centre | Ideas | 1014

About

Works

White wall

Contact

19 Sep 06

Description

Slaidburn required a new building for their various community activities, to be sited next to a meadow on the River Hodder. Arca considered the pattern of buildings that already existed in the village, marked by their informal relationship to each other, particularly as they moved away from the main roads.

Information

Title : Slaidburn Community Centre
Location : Slaidburn, Lancashire
Programme : 2002 – 0
Type : Limited Competition
Client : Slaidburn
Contract Value : £400000

Download PDF

Latest News

10 Oct 06

Burnley Update : 2006-10-10

On 29 September, Arca submitted a Parameters Outline Planning Application for the Weavers' Triangle sites in Burnley, on behalf of Hurstwood Group. The design features a wide mix of uses, including offices, homes, shops, and a live music venue. A decision is expected in early 2007.

Image

Burnley Update

Weavers Triangle
July Jobs
Tate Gallery win
Michael Combden
Arca Appointed

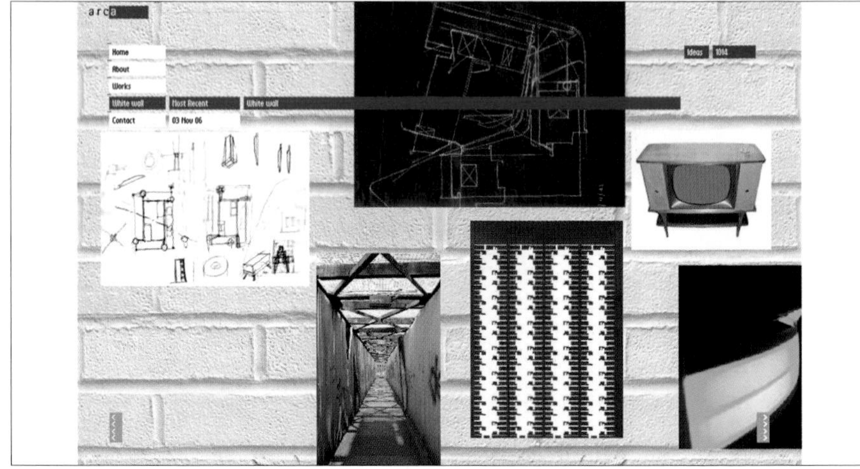

Location

Bubble
51 Turner St
Manchester, M4 1DN
United Kingdom
<paul@thebubblesite.co.uk>

Team

1 MD, 1 Interactive Director, 1 Production Director, 1 Creative Director, 2 Designers, 1 Programmer.

Nos clients font entièrement confiance en notre travail, ce qui nous permet de produire des projets sur mesure dans tous leurs aspects, non seulement pour ce qui est des traitements graphiques, mais également en ce qui concerne l'ensemble de la production. Nous pensons librement, établissons des relations solides et construisons notre portefeuille interactif d'images animées et de sons au moyen de morceaux qui inspirent, captivent et satisfont notre appétit de création. /// **Das Vertrauen unserer Kunden ermöglicht uns, maßgeschneiderte Kreativkonzepte zu realisieren, die sowohl in Bezug auf das grafische Design als auch den gesamten Produktionsprozess Bahn brechend sind. Wir legen Wert auf freies, unvoreingenommenes Denken und auf den Aufbau solider Beziehungen. Auf dieser Grundlage kreieren wir für unsere Kunden voller Inspiration und Kreativität kraftvolle Kampagnen in den Bereichen interaktive Medien, bewegtes Bild, Ton und Print.**

www.nikal.uk.com

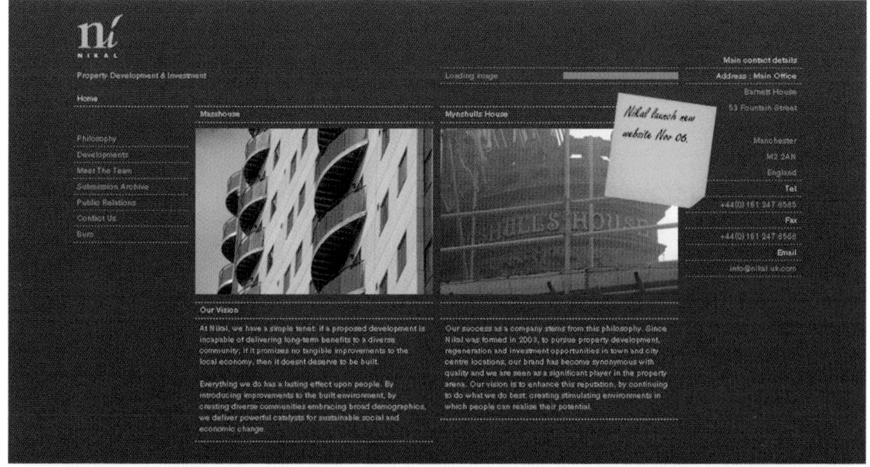

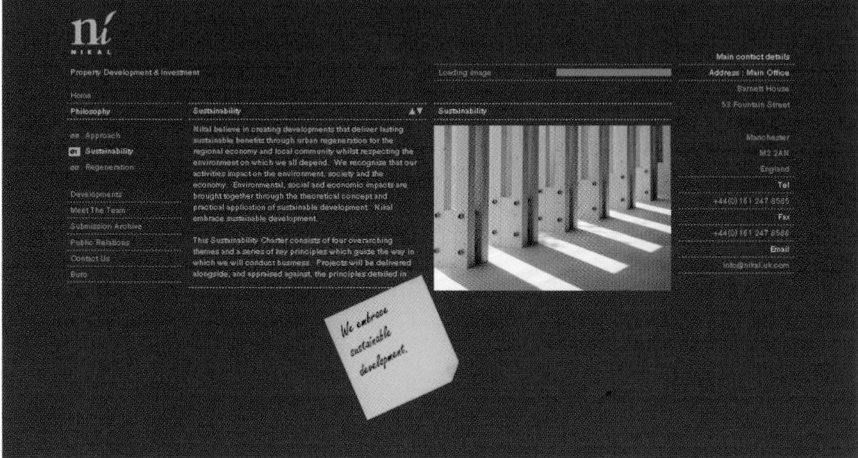

Clients

Orange, SCEE (Sony Computer Entertainment Europe), Size / JD Sports, UDEN Media, Argent PLC, BBC, The Championship Committee, Marketing Manchester.

Awards

Roses Design Award (Gold).

COTTONBLEND

USA

www.cottonblend.com

since 2005

Mission

To think big from concept to completion – creating cutting-edge websites for every client. /// Penser en grand, du concept au produit fini, et créer des sites Internet d'avant-garde pour chaque client. /// Wir denken vorausschauend - vom Konzept bis zur Realisierung – um für jeden unserer Kunden innovative Webseiten zu kreieren.

www.herbiehancock.com

Location

Cottonblend
8833 West Sunset Blvd.
West Hollywood, CA 90069
USA
<hello@cottonblend.com>

Team

1 Senior Creative Director, 1 Senior Art Director, 1 Associate Art Director, 2 Designers, 1 Senior Software Engineer, 1 Front-End Developer, 1 Senior Account Manager, 1 Content Manager.

www.troubadour.com

Troubadour

9081 SANTA MONICA BLVD
WEST HOLLYWOOD, CA 90069

JOIN OUR EMAIL LIST! CLICK HERE!

EVENTS TICKET INFO HISTORY GALLERY FAQ MAP CONTACT+BOOKING

01 ABOUT

Since opening in **1957**, the legendary Troubadour club in West Hollywood has helped launch some of contemporary music's most talented performers. Greats such as **Elton John**, **James Taylor** and **Tom Waits** performed there early in their careers, and it continues to be a destination for cutting-edge acts from around the world.

The Troubadour also remains a popular venue among serious music fans who enjoy listening to live music in an intimate and historically rich setting.

01.1 SPOTLIGHT + CALENDAR

MONDAY DECEMBER 4

THROUGH THE EYES OF THE DEAD

From A Second Story Window · THE ACACIA STRAIN · LIGHT THIS CITY

«			NOVEMBER 2006			»
SUN	MON	TUE	WED	THU	FRI	SAT
			1	2	3	4
5	6	7	8	9	10	11
12	13	14	15	16	17	18
19	20	21	22	23	24	25
26	27	28	29	30		

01.2 FEATURED EVENTS

The Lovemakers & Gram Rabbit
Tuesday, November 28

A Static Lullaby
Wednesday, November 29

Sea Wolf
Saturday, December 2

© 2006 Troubadour. All Rights Reserved. Privacy Policy RSS

www.viejasentertainment.com

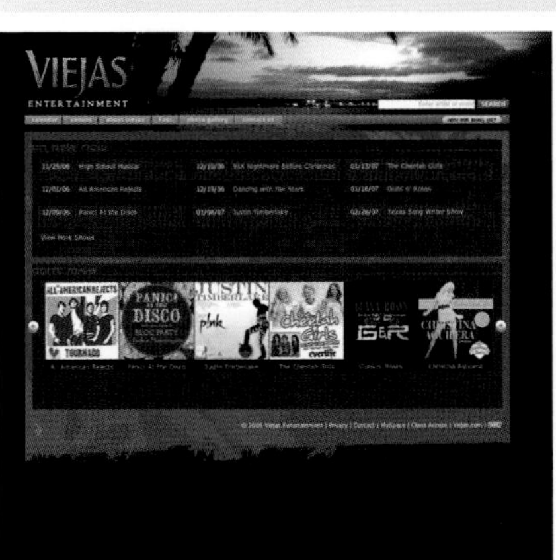

Clients

American Express, BMX Plus! Magazine, Gifts.com, Herbie Hancock, LiveDaily, The Orpheum Theatre, The Pasadena Civic, Simon & Schuster, Ticketmaster, TicketWeb, The Troubadour, UCLA, Viejas Entertainment.

Awards

Webby Awards (Nominee), SXSW (Finalist).

CRASH!MEDIA

CANADA

www.crashmedia.com

since 1997

Mission

At CRASH! we strive to create engaging, compelling and entertaining interactive experiences. We believe that interactive is not just bound to the screen and keyboard, but to environments, people and motion – to sound and video. We use technology to create entertaining tools for the masses. We love what we do.

www.thirststudio.com

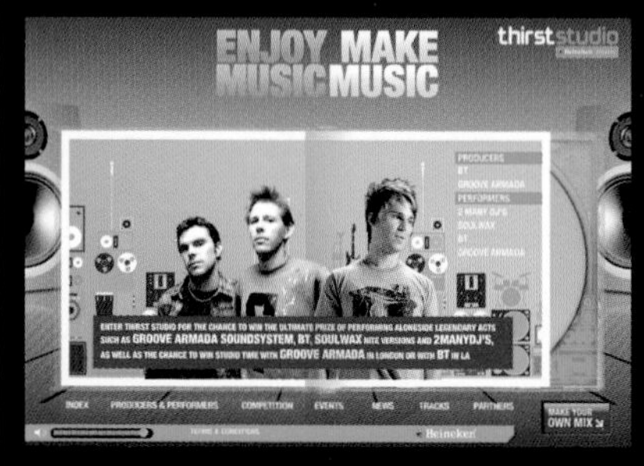

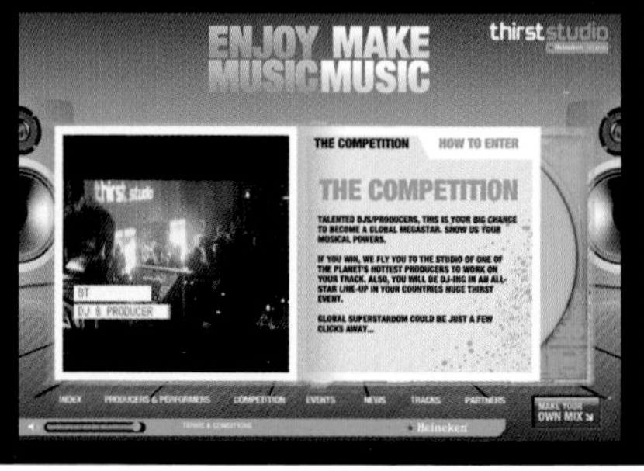

Location

CRASH!MEDIA
58 Stewart St.#201
Toronto, Ontario M5V 1H6
Canada
<info@crashmedia.com>

Team

1 Creative Director, 1 Art Director, 2 Designers, 2 Programmers.

Chez CRASH!, nous nous efforçons de créer des expériences intéressantes et amusantes. Nous pensons que l'interactivité ne concerne pas uniquement un écran et un clavier, mais des environnements, des personnes et des mouvements, du son et de la vidéo. Nous utilisons la technologie pour créer des outils divertissants pour els visiteurs. Nous aimons ce que nous faisons. /// Fesselnde, faszinierende und unterhaltsame interaktive Erlebniswelten zu kreieren – das ist die Mission von CRASH! Wir bei CRASH! finden, dass Interaktivität etwas mit Umgebungen, mit Menschen und mit Bewegung zu tun hat – mit Ton und Video. Mit modernster Technologie kreieren wir deshalb unterhaltsame Tools für die Massen. Wir lieben das, was wir machen.

www.webcamtastic.com

ESPN

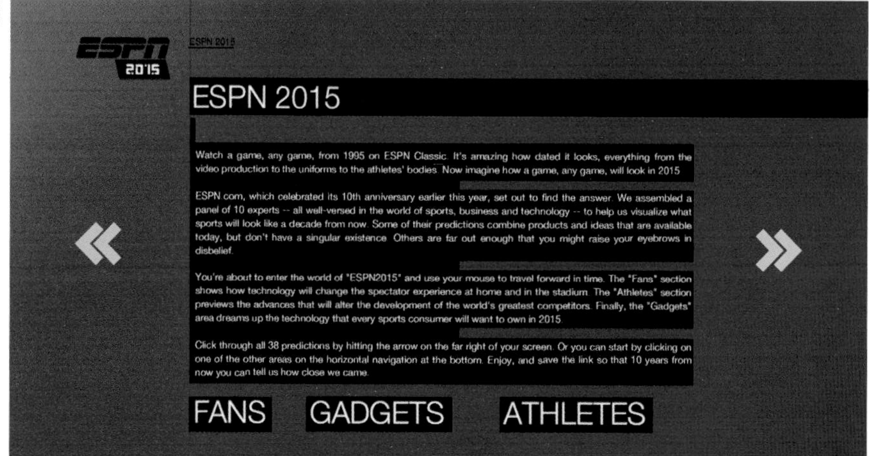

Clients

Sony, Intel, Volvo, ESPN, Napster, Mercedes, Reebok, Cadillac, Bacardi, Heineken, Honda, Toyota, Dodge, RollingStone, Calvin Klein, CBC, University of Toronto, Harlequin.

Awards

Webby Awards, Flashforward (Best Audio), FlashInTheCan (Sound), Communication Arts Interactive Annual (Entertainment), SXSW Interactive, Macromedia (Site of the Day), FWA, IronFlash.

DE-CONSTRUCT

UK

www.de-construct.com

since 2001

Mission

A digital communications agency with a passion for design, creativity and good ideas. From brands we all know to niche boutiques, we apply our thinking and attention to detail to create engaging and stimulating experiences. The craft of design lies at the heart of our offering, transferring our love of typography and layout into the digital landscape.

www.lumixdifference.com

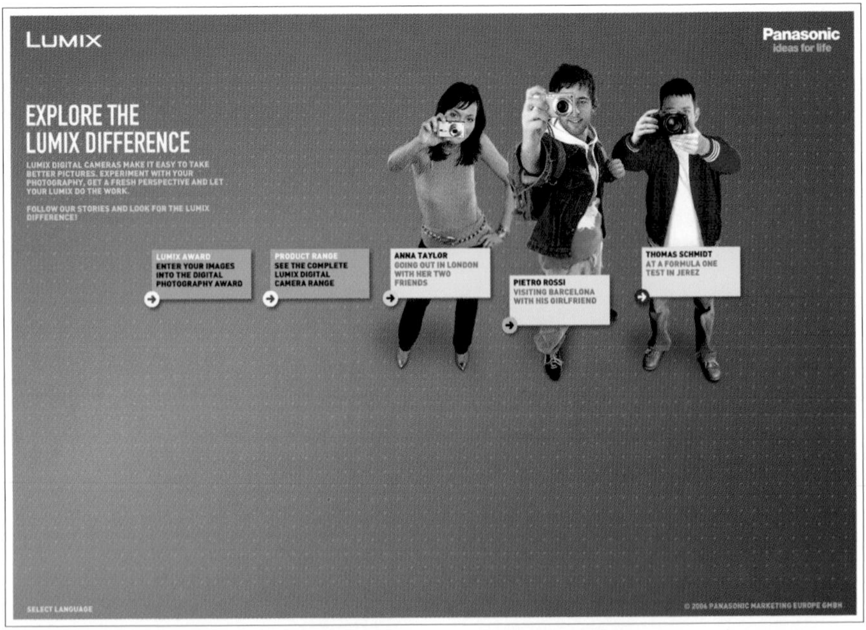

LUMIX
Panasonic
ideas for life
EXPLORE THE LUMIX DIFFERENCE
LUMIX DIGITAL CAMERAS MAKE IT EASY TO TAKE BETTER PICTURES. EXPERIMENT WITH YOUR PHOTOGRAPHY, GET A FRESH PERSPECTIVE AND LET YOUR LUMIX DO THE WORK.
FOLLOW OUR STORIES AND LOOK FOR THE LUMIX DIFFERENCE!
LUMIX AWARD
ENTER YOUR IMAGES INTO THE DIGITAL PHOTOGRAPHY AWARD
PRODUCT RANGE
SEE THE COMPLETE LUMIX DIGITAL CAMERA RANGE
ANNA TAYLOR
GOING OUT IN LONDON WITH HER TWO FRIENDS
PIETRO ROSSI
VISITING BARCELONA WITH HIS GIRLFRIEND
THOMAS SCHMIDT
AT A FORMULA ONE TEST IN JEREZ
SELECT LANGUAGE
© 2006 PANASONIC MARKETING EUROPE GMBH

LUMIX
Panasonic
ANNA TAYLOR
CAMERA: DMC-FX01

LUMIX
Panasonic
ANNA TAYLOR
CAMERA: DMC-FX01
DMC-FX01
STYLISH AND COMPACT
GET CREATIVE

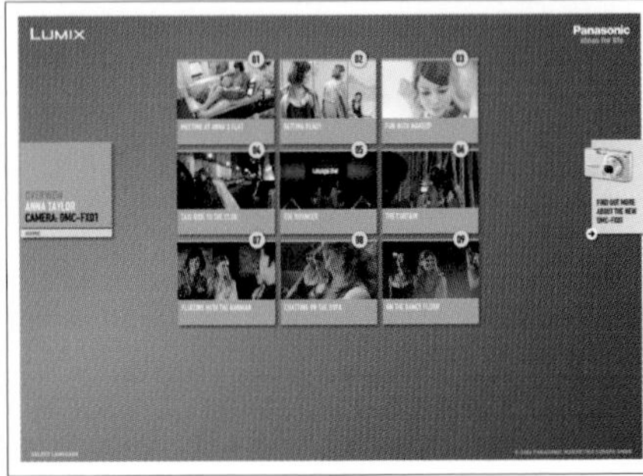

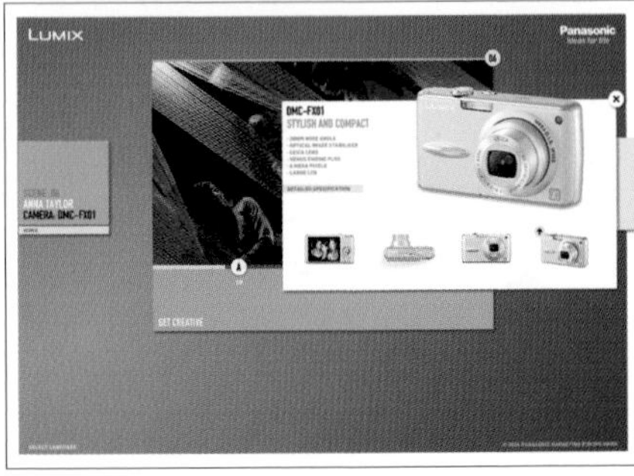

Location

de-construct
10-18 Vestry Street
London, N1 7RE
United Kingdom
<info@de-construct.com>

Team

4 Account/Management Directors, 2 Creative Directors, 1 Design Director, 6 Designers, 4 Flash Developers, 1 Technical Director, 4 Web Developers, 1 Project Director, 4 Project Managers.

Agence de communications numériques avec une passion pour le design, la créativité et les bonnes idées. Nous savons comment trouver un créneau pour les boutiques des marques, nous mettons en application nos idées et notre souci des détails pour créer des expériences intéressantes et stimulantes. L'art du design se trouve au cœur de nos propositions, et nous transposons notre passion de la typographie et de la présentation dans l'environnement numérique. /// **Eine Agentur für digitale Kommunikation mit einer Leidenschaft für Design, Kreativität und gute Ideen. Ob bekannte Marken oder Nischenunternehmen – für unsere Kunden kreieren wir mit brillanten Ideen und Liebe zum Detail spannende und stimulierende Erlebniswelten. Das Design steht im Mittelpunkt unserer Arbeit: Typografie und Layout sind die wichtigsten Elemente unserer digitalen Kampagnen.**

www.adidas.com/stella

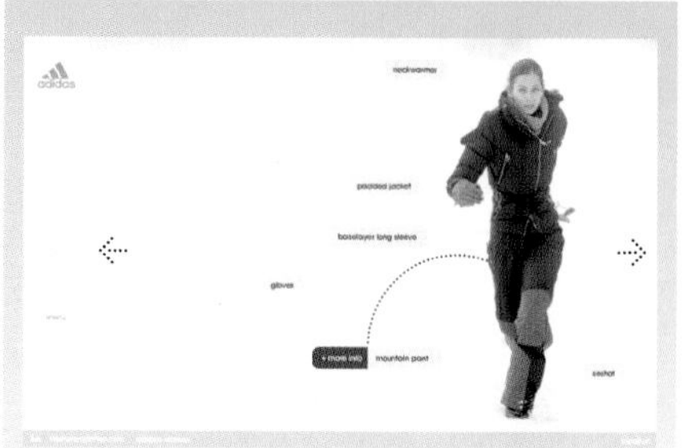

www.vitra.com/headline

Clients

adidas, Panasonic, Vitra, Barbican, Hayward Gallery, Eurostar, Established & Sons, Viaduct.

Awards

D&AD, Clio, OneShow, DesignWeek, LIAA, Webby Awards.

DIET STRYCHNINE CORP.

USA

www.dietstrychnine.com

since 1999

Mission

Initially motivated by our pursuit to reject the inescapable formula of contemporary web design, now our sights are set on being the best interactive designers alive. Stay true, create something with a soul and we will stand at the top of the hill looking down on the competition.

www.georginagoodman.com

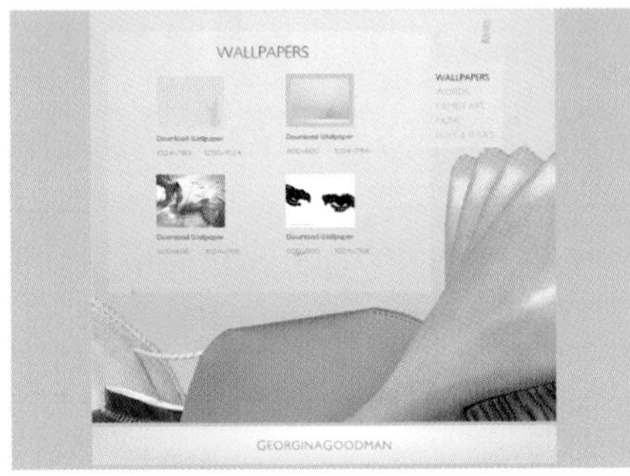

Location

Diet Strychnine Corp.
2701 N. Janssen Ave.
Chicago, IL 60614, USA
Satellite office locations: LA, NYC, London
<noonan@dietstrychnine.com>

Team

1 Head of Operations, 2 Creative Directors, 3 Designers, 2 Flash Gurus, 3 Programmers, 1 Copywriter, 1 Photographer, 1 Bichon Frise.

Désireux au départ de rejeter les inévitables formules du design web contemporain, notre objectif consiste à présent à être les meilleurs designers Web du marché. En restant vrais, en créant quelque chose avec une âme, nous pourrons demeurer au top et regarder nos concurrents de haut. /// **Am Anfang stand die Motivation, uns von den vorherrschenden Prinzipien zeitgenössischen Webdesigns zu verabschieden. Jetzt besteht unser Ziel darin, unsere Kreationen zu den weltbesten Beispielen für interaktives Design zu machen. Unsere Philosophie: Wir bleiben authentisch und füllen unsere Kreationen mit Seele. Darin liegt unsere größte Stärke.**

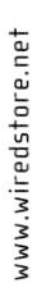

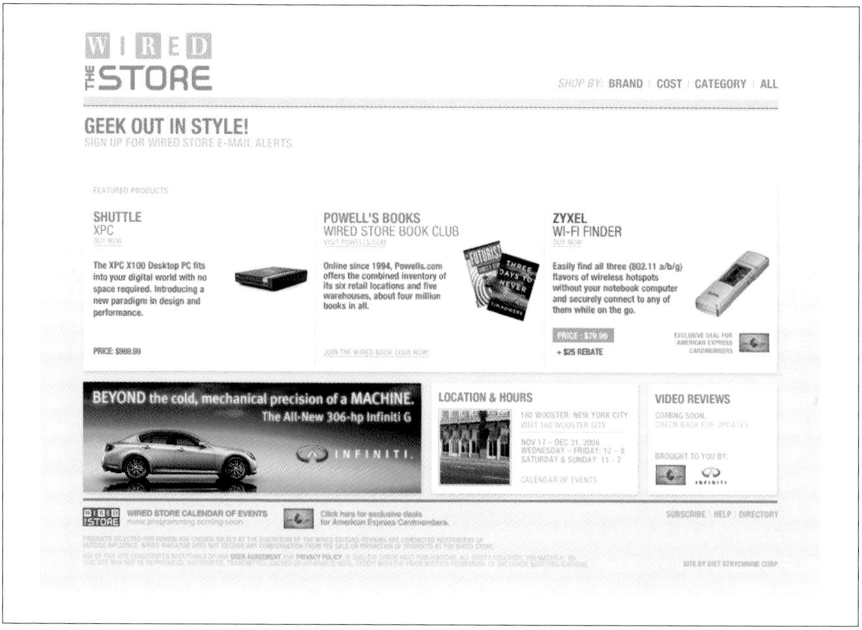

www.zitaelze.com

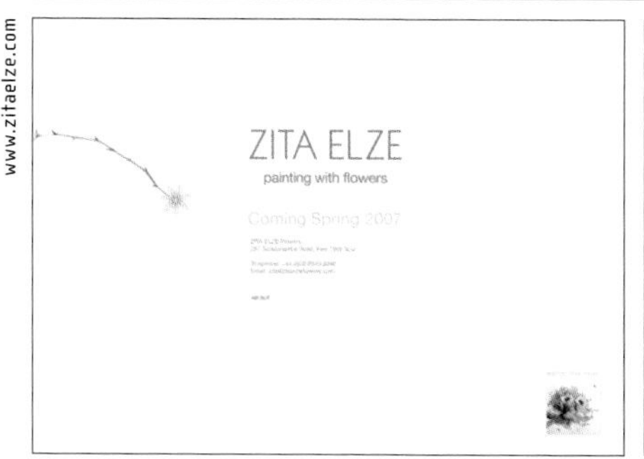

Clients

WIRED Magazine, Georgina Goodman, Zita Elze Flowers, Andrew Blake, Pompei AD, U'Luvka Vodka, Condé Nast, Yahoo!, Warner Bros. Records, Foote, Cone & Belding, Rag & Bone.

Awards

Communication Arts Interactive, AIGA, MTV Europe Music Awards (nomination).

DRIFTLAB

USA

www.driftlab.com

since 2003

Mission

The driftlab philosophy is simple: Create high-impact web experiences, which engage and captivate the user. This means a relentless pursuit of innovation in design and development, which will result in an inspiring experience while maintaining a high level of usability.

www.chevrolet.com/silverado/launch

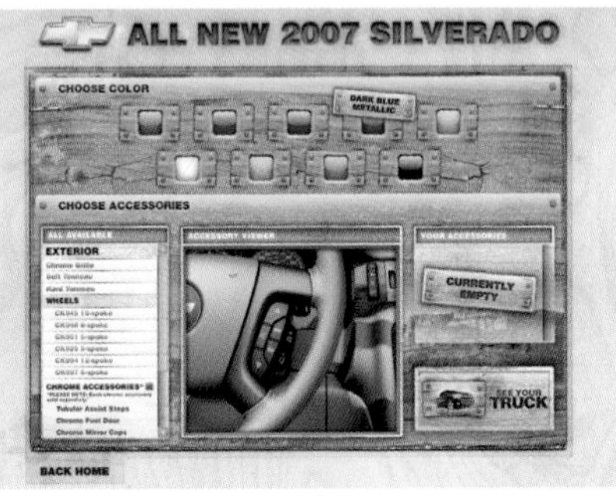

Location

driftlab
2222 Flowering Drive
Grayson, GA 30017
USA
<scott@driftlab.com>

Team

1 Creative Director, 2 Designers, 1 Programmer.

La philosophie de Driftlab est simple : créer des expériences Internet impressionnantes qui intéressent et captivent l'utilisateur. Pour cela, nous cherchons sans cesse à innover en matière de design et de développement, pour créer une expérience enrichissante et un niveau élevé de convivialité. /// **Die Philosophie von driftlab ist einfach: Eindrucksvolle Web-Erlebniswelten kreieren, die den User fesseln und faszinieren. Unsere Designer und Entwickler sind unaufhörlich auf der Jagd nach den innovativsten Ideen. Das Resultat: inspirierende Erlebniswelten mit gleichzeitig hoher Userfreundlichkeit.**

Night Watch

Clients: Sony, Campbell-Ewald, Fox, Bacardi®.

Awards: FWA, Bombshock, Fcukstar.

EURO RSCG 4D

WORLDWIDE

www.eurorscg4d.com

since 2001

Mission

What: We help you to create and keep promises to build your brand and business momentum. **How:** We select and combine the right digital techniques to leverage your marketing budget. We are young, collaborative and relentless. Our network of agencies is only 5 years old, yet is already N° 1 in terms of revenue. We believe our most valuable asset is our international perspective on the latest trends and emerging techniques. Get to the future first with Euro RSCG 4D.

Pepperidge Farms Goldfish

Location

Euro RSCG 4D
Argentina, Australia, Austria, Belgium, Brazil, Chile, China, Czech Republic, France, Germany, India, Italy, Mexico, Netherlands, Poland, Portugal, Russia, Spain, Taiwan, Thailand, Turkey, United Kingdom, United States.

Team

Euro RSCG 4D has over 1,170 employees, including: 75 media, 300 production, 325 client service, 95 engineers, 250 creatives, 50 analyst/measurement, 75 administrative.

Ce que nous faisons : nous vous aidons à créer et construire votre marque et votre momentum commercial. **Comment nous procédons :** nous sélectionnons et associons les techniques numériques appropriées afin d'exploiter au mieux votre budget marketing. Nous sommes jeunes, enthousiastes et nous aimons travailler en équipe. Notre réseau d'agences, qui n'a que 5 ans, est déjà numéro un en termes de recettes. Nous pensons que notre ressource la plus précieuse est notre perspective internationale des toutes dernières tendances et des techniques émergentes. Avec Euro RSCG 4D, soyez les premiers à entrer dans l'avenir. /// **Was:** Wir helfen Ihnen dabei, Versprechen zu gestalten und zu halten, damit Sie Ihre Marke und Ihr Geschäft erfolgreich aufbauen und weiter entwickeln können. **Wie:** Wir wählen für Sie im Rahmen Ihres Marketingbudgets geeignete Digitaltechniken aus und bündeln diese zu einer maßgeschneiderten Kombination. Wir sind ein junges und sehr engagiertes Team. Unser Agenturnetzwerk ist erst 5 Jahre alt, doch in punkto Einnahmen bereits jetzt die Nummer 1. Unsere wertvollste Stärke ist unser internationaler Blick auf die neuesten Trends und Techniken. Sprinten Sie als Erster in die Welt der Zukunft – mit EURO RSCG 4D.

Volvo C70

Nokia

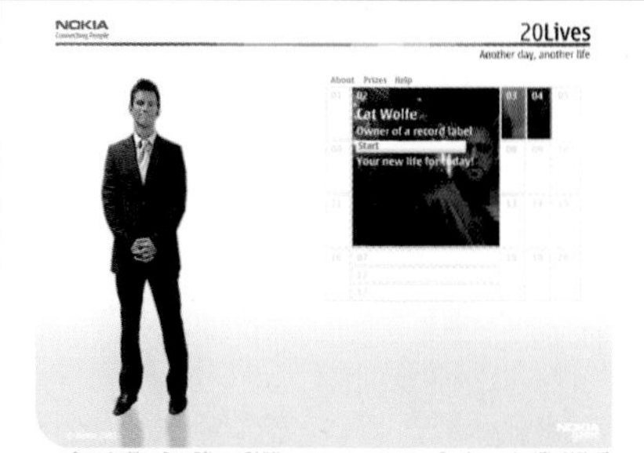

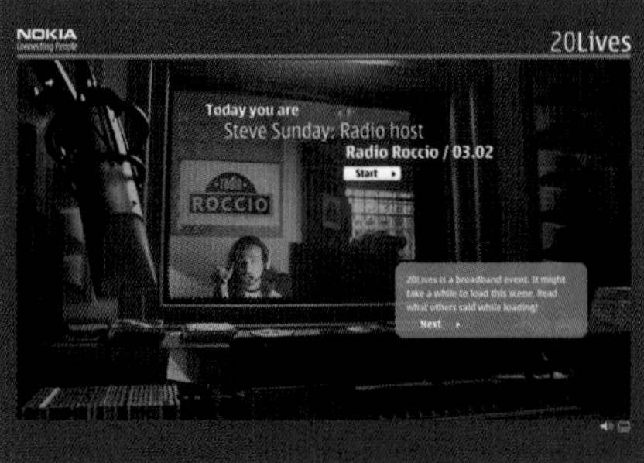

Intel - Crimescene

Clients

Bank One, Barclays, British Gas, Canal+, Carrefour – Promodes, Citigroup, Citroen, Danone, General Motors, Glaxosmithkline, Hewlett Packard, IBM, Intel, Jaguar, L'Oreal, Land Rover, Mobility Products Limited, Novartis, Peugeot, Pfizer, Reckitt Benckiser, Sanofi-Aventis, Schering Plough, Sprint, Symantec, Volvo, etc.

Awards

AIMIA (Winner), John Caples Awards, Premio Iman (Silver), ADC Netherlands (Silver), Club de Criação São Paulo (Bronze), FIAP (Silver/Bronze), IAC, The One Show Interactive, Cannes Lions (Gold/Silver/Bronze), New York Festivals, Web Awards, Cresta (Winner), El Ojo de Iberoamerica/El Ojo Interactivo (Gold/Bronze).

FICC

JAPAN

www.ficc.jp

since 2004

Mission

To keep things simple. To craft beyond visible details. To develop, experiment and communicate. /// Rester simple. Faire un travail de création au-delà des détails visibles. Développer, expérimenter et communiquer. /// Weniger ist oft mehr. Kreationen, die über das Sichtbare hinausgehen. Entwickeln, experimentieren und kommunizieren.

www.anteprima.com

Location

FICC inc.
501 Akasaka Plaza 7-4-18
Akasaka, Minato-ku, 107-0052 Tokyo
Japan
<info@ficc.jp>

Team

1 Creative Director, 2 Art Directors, 4 Designers, 3 Project Managers, 1 Illustrator, 1 Photographer, 3 Flash Developers/Programmers.

www.gorakadan.com

www.sevensalotti.jp

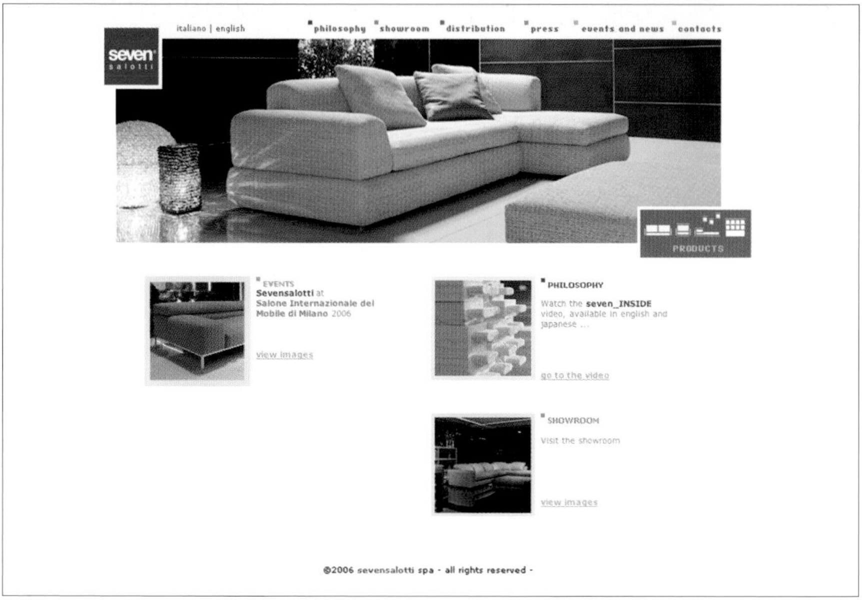

Clients

Anteprima Ltd., Louis Vuitton Japan Group, Gorakadan, Nihon Loreal Inc., Dentsu E-Marketing One, Arflex, Seven Salotti, Emeco, WSI

Awards

FWA, Macromedia (Site of the Week).

FREEDOM INTERACTIVE DESIGN USA

www.freedominteractivedesign.com since 2002

Mission

By fostering a creative environment based on teamwork and a shared passion to do groundbreaking work, we attract and keep smart, talented and happy people. Together, our mission is to deliver superior marketing and communications projects in the areas of design and technology.

www.calamityphysics.com

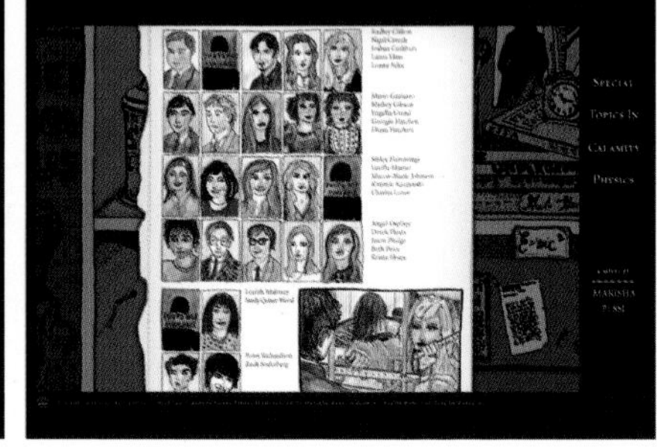

Location

Freedom Interactive Design
462 Broadway, Suite 510
New York, NY 10013
USA
<info@freedominteractivedesign.com>

Team

1 Creative Director/Executive Producer, 1 Director, Business Development, 1 Senior Art Director, 2 Vice President, Senior Flash Developers, 2 Flash Developers, 1 Production Artist, 01 Project Coordinator.

En favorisant un environnement créatif fondé sur un travail en équipe et la passion commune d'un travail d'avant-garde, nous attirons et conservons des professionnels intelligents, talentueux et satisfaits. Notre mission commune : fournir des projets de marketing et de communications d'excellente qualité dans les domaines du design et de la technologie. /// **Für uns ist eine kreative Umgebung wichtig, die auf Teamwork und einer gemeinsamen Leidenschaft für innovatives Arbeiten basiert. Deshalb können wir auf smarte, talentierte und zufriedene Mitarbeiter zählen, die gern zu uns kommen und auch gern bei uns bleiben. Unsere gemeinsame Mission sind hervorragende Marketing- und Kommunikationslösungen, die sich durch außergewöhnliches Design und ausgefeilte Technologie auszeichnen.**

www.berrybones.com

www.wouldyoulikeawebsite.com

Clients

Comedy Central, Estee Lauder, Fox Searchlight, Godiva, Goodby Silverstein & Partners, Imperial Palace Hotel & Casino, Kellogg's, Leo Burnett, L'Oreal

Awards

FWA (Site of the Day), Flashforward (Sound Design Finalist), FlashInTheCan (Best e-Commerce).

GLOW INTERACTIVE

USA

www.glowinteractive.com

since 2000

Mission

A digital solutions provider comprised of experts who share a passion to dream, develop and deliver rich internet content. Whether it's surfing a website, purchasing a product, playing a game, or simply clicking on a banner, our work is recognized for generating positive reactions that stimulate sales, increase awareness and build brand loyalty.

www.bravotv.com/Project_Runway/mashups/index

Location

Glow Interactive
333 Hudson St. Suite #302
New York, NY 10013
USA
<info@glowinteractive.com>

Team

2 Creative Directors, 2 Art Directors, 3 Designers, 3 Programmers.

Fournisseur de solutions numériques employant des experts partageant la passion de rêver, développer et proposer des contenus Internet très intéressants. Que l'utilisateur surfe sur un site Internet, achète un produit, joue à un jeu ou clique sur une banderole, notre travail est reconnu pour générer des réactions positives qui stimulent les ventes, sensibilisent et assurent la loyauté envers les marques. /// **Digitale Lösungen von einem Team aus Experten mit der gemeinsamen Leidenschaft, anspruchsvollen Rich Content für Webseiten zu kreieren. Ob Webseitengestaltung, Online-Shopping, Games oder Bannerwerbung – unsere Arbeit ist bekannt dafür, positive Aufmerksamkeit bei den Konsumenten zu erreichen, ihre Bindung zu Marken zu festigen und so den Umsatz unserer Kunden zu steigern.**

www.usanetwork.com/series/psych/games/memorygame/index.php

Clients

A&E, AMC, Atari, Bravo, Biography Channel, Cartoon Network, Golf Magazine, SciFi Channel, The History Channel, USA Network, VH1.

Awards

Omma Awards (Finalist Rich Media Banner), Promax/BDA (World: Gold – North America: Gold/Silver), Webby Awards, Mixx Awards, Macromedia (Site of the Day), International Webpage Awards (Creative Excellence), FWA, AdTech (Winner: Best Broadcast Streaming), k10k, Moluv's, CoolHomepages.

H2D2

GERMANY

www.h2d2.de

since 2000

Mission

H2D2 acts strategically and designs with heart. As an office for communication design we give companies, brands and products a visual identity. The starting point of our work is always a strong idea for content. This provides the beat, decides the medium just as it does the graphical style.

www.frontlineshop.com

Location

H2D2
Kaiserstraβe 79
60329 Frankfurt
Germany
<markus@h2d2.de>

Team

1 Creative Director, 2 Designer, 1 Online Marketing & Copywriting, extern Programmers.

H2D2 travaille de façon stratégique et conçoit avec le cœur. En tant qu'agence de design de communication, nous offrons une identité visuelle aux entreprises, marques et produits. Le point de départ de notre travail est toujours une grande idée de contenu, qui donne le rythme et décide du média et du style graphique. /// **H2D2 handelt strategisch und gestaltet mit Herz. Als Büro für Kommunikationsdesign geben wir Unternehmen, Marken und Produkten eine visuelle Identität. Ausgangspunkt unserer Arbeit ist immer eine starke inhaltliche Idee. Sie gibt den Takt vor, entscheidet über die Wahl des Mediums genau so wie über den grafischen Stil.**

www.wwf.de

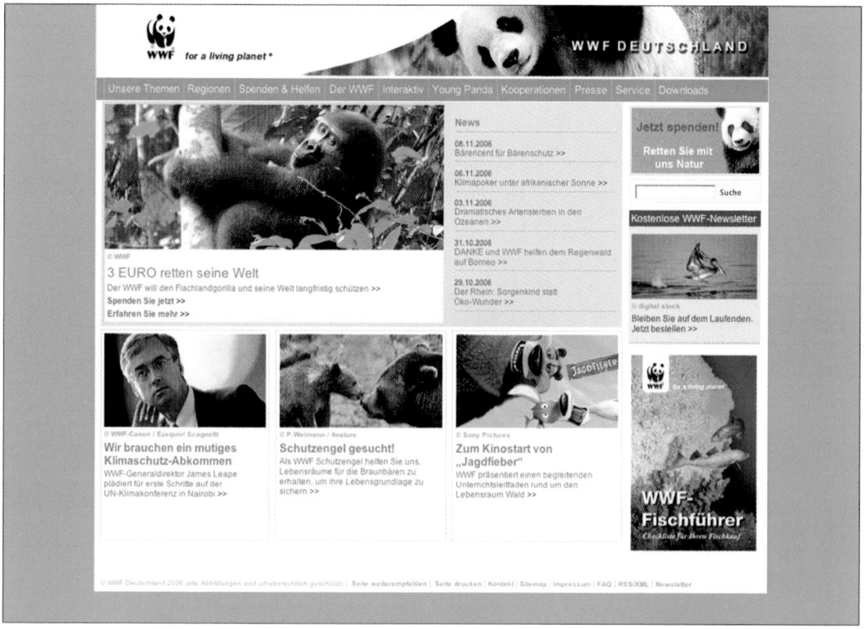

Clients

adidas, DaimlerChrysler AG, DEVK Versicherungen, Dresdner Bank AG, Evangelisches Stadtjugendpfarramt Frankfurt, Frontline GmbH, Guise Store Chicago, Neue Digitale, Polydor/Zeitgeist, Procter & Gamble Service GmbH, WWF Deutschland.

Awards

Input-Output (No. 5), Annual Multimedia, Multimedia Rheinland-Pfalz (1st Prize).

IN2MEDIA

DENMARK

www.in2media.dk

since 1994

Mission

In2media is a full-service new media design agency which bridges the gap between business insights, creativity, innovation, and technology to create effective communication solutions across digital platforms such as web, IPtv, mobile phone, iPod and Media Center.

www.lafamilia.dk

Location

In2media
Skt. Peders Stræde 30C
DK-1453 Copenhagen K
Denmark
<contact@in2media.dk>

Team

1 CEO, 1 Strategic Director, 1 Creative Director, 2 Art Directors, 3 Designers, 3 Rich Media Developers, 3 Programmers, 2 Project Managers.

In2media est une nouvelle agence de design à service complet qui comble l'écart entre les informations commerciales, la créativité, l'innovation et la technologie pour créer des solutions efficaces de communication entre les plates-formes numériques telles qu'Internet, IPtv, les téléphones portables, iPod et les centres multimédias. /// **In2media ist eine Full-Service-Agentur für neues Mediendesign, die eine Brücke zwischen Markenverständnis, Kreativität, Innovation und Technologie spannt, um effektive Kommunikationslösungen für digitale Plattformen wie Internet, IPTV, Mobiltelefone, iPod und Media Center zur Verfügung zu stellen.**

www.annhagen.com

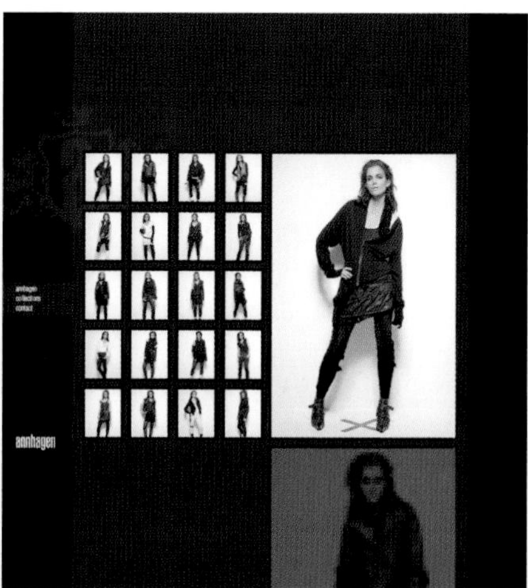

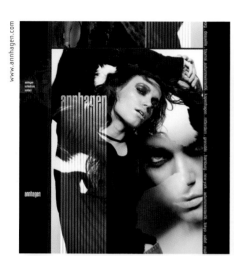

www.cafenoir.dk

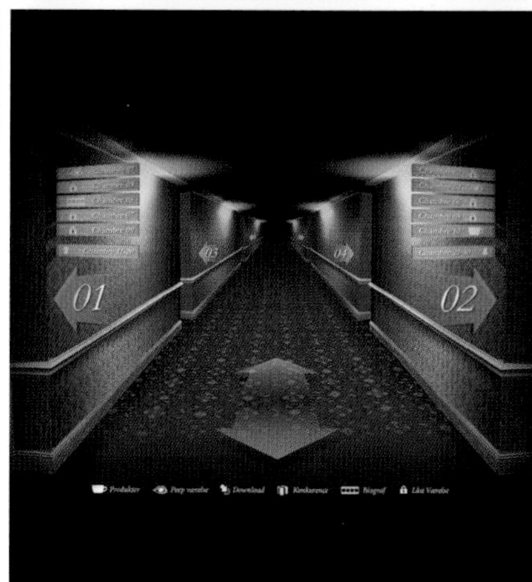

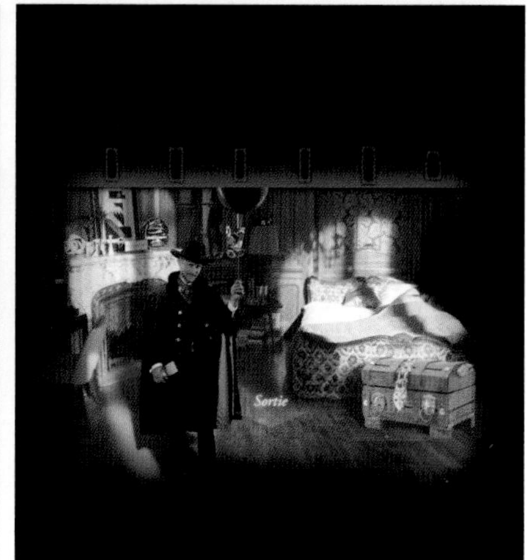

Clients
MTV, Nokia, Philips, Elite Models, Sara Lee, Georg Jensen, Lundbeck, Nilfisk, Red Green, Pfizer.

Awards
FWA, Adobe (Site of the Day), DOPE, Fcukstar, Flash Kit (Site of the Day).

JUXT INTERACTIVE

USA

www.juxtinteractive.com

since 1998

Mission

JUXT Interactive is committed to creating innovative user experiences that position brands and organizations. JUXT produces websites, micro sites, original content, and rich media advertising that focuses on achieving specific business objectives, leveraging our expertise in branding, storytelling, Flash design and development. Moreover, we strive to ensure an efficient use of technology.

www.nesteaice.com

Location

JUXT Interactive
858 Production Place
Newport Beach, CA 92663
USA
<josh@juxtinteractive.com>

Team

1 Executive Producer, 1 Creative Director, 1 Account Director, 4 Art Directors, 5 Designers, 2 Programmers, 3 Web Developers, 5 Project Managers, 1 Copywriter, 2 Marketing.

JUXT Interactive s'efforce de créer des expériences nouvelles pour les utilisateurs qui positionnent les marques et les entreprises. JUXT produit des sites Internet, des micro-sites, des contenus originaux et une excellente publicité multimédia centrée sur des objectifs commerciaux spécifiques, l'exploitation de notre expertise de marque, la création d'histoires, le design Flash et le développement. En outre, nous nous efforçons d'utiliser de façon efficace la technologie. /// **JUXT Interactive konzentriert sich darauf, innovative Online-Erlebniswelten zu kreieren, die Marken und Unternehmen optimal positionieren. Mit Fokus auf den spezifischen Geschäftszielen unserer Kunden produzieren wir Webseiten, Mikroseiten, Original-Content und Rich-Media-Werbung und nutzen dabei unser umfangreiches Know-hows in punkto Branding, Storytelling, Flash-Design und Entwicklung. Dabei legen wir großen Wert auf einen effizienten Einsatz von Technologie.**

www.justforthefofit.com

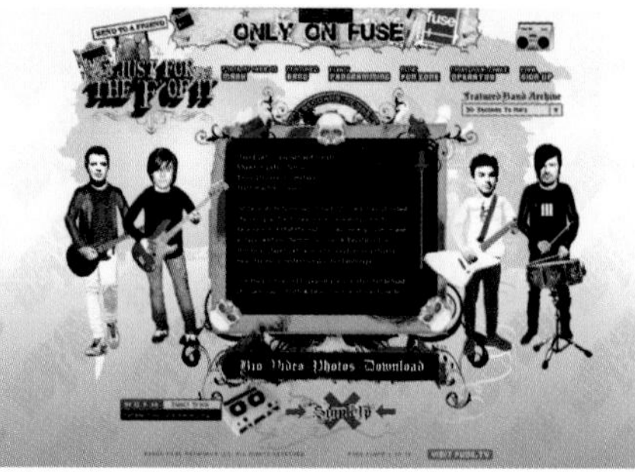

www.springbydannon.com

Clients

Coca-Cola, Boost Mobile, DirecTV, Fuse TV, Target.

Awards

National Gold Addy, London International Advertising Award, Step In Design Grand Prize, Clio, Communication Arts, One Show Interactive, Ad:Tech, SXSW.

KNI

USA

www.kurtnoble.com

since 2000

Mission

Our goal is to make awesome websites, give great service to our clients, and be good people. /// Notre objectif consiste à créer des sites Internet exceptionnels, à fournir un excellent service à nos clients et à être les meilleurs. /// Wir geben unser Bestes, um erstklassige Webseiten für unsere Kunden zu realisieren und ihnen zudem einen Top-Service zu bieten.

www.thrillvillegame.com

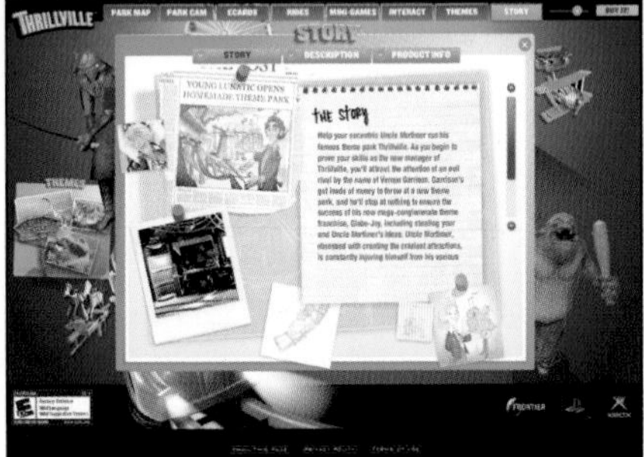

Location

KNI
720 York St. #103, San Francisco, CA 94110, USA
2021 21st Ave. South Suite c-100, Nashville, TN 37212, USA
<Kurt@kurtnoble.com>

Team

1 Creative Principal, 1 Creative Director, 2 Technical Director, 1 Math & Animation Wizard.

www.bacardilive.com

www.tacobell.com

Clients

LucasArts, Goodby, Silverstein and Partners, Foote, Cone and Belding, Push Inc., J. Walter Thompson, Dane Cook, Specialized Bicycle Components, Maverick Records, Virgin Records, Geffen Records, MCA Records, Dreamworks Records, Hollywood Records, Mailboat Records, James Taylor, US Marine Corps, Napster...

Awards

Comm Arts (Award of Excellence: Interactive Advertising), One Show (Silver), ADC (Merit), FWA (Site of the Day/Site of the Year), Bombshock, Yahoo Cool Sites, StyleBoost, Macromedia (Sites of the Day).

LARGE

UK

www.largedesign.com

since 1998

Mission

Large delivers World Class Websites for innovative and powerful brands. /// Large crée des sites Internet exceptionnels pour les nouvelles marques puissantes. /// **Large liefert Webseiten der Spitzenklasse für innovative und starke Marken.**

www.AgentProvocateur.com

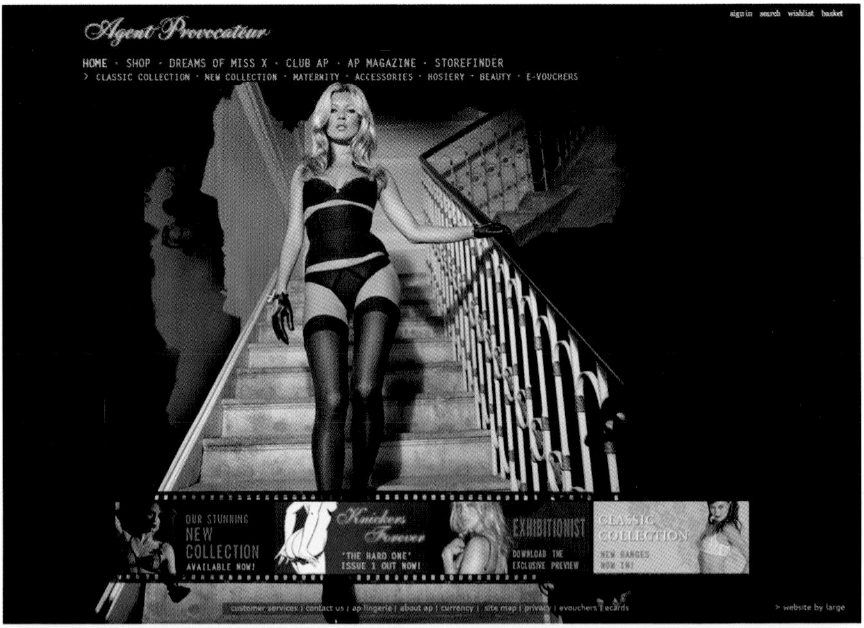

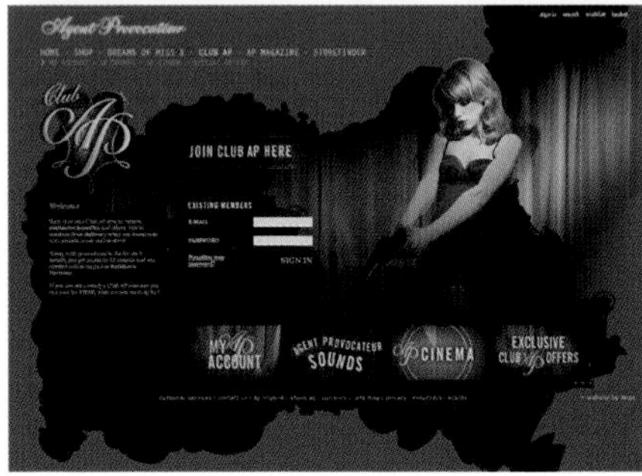

Location

Large
36-42 New Inn Yard
London EC2A, 3EY
United Kingdom
Lars Hemming Jorgensen <l.jorgensen@largedesign.com>

Team

14 Creatives, 11 Programmers, 6 Project Managers.

www.Oasis-Stores.com

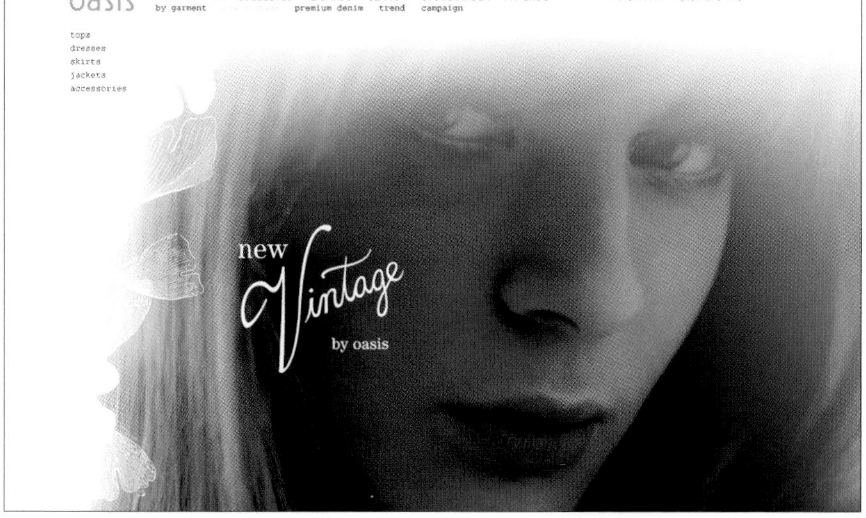

www.LuluGuinness.com

Clients

Agent Provocateur, BBC, De Beers, Empire Cinemas, LEGO, Lulu Guinness, Oasis Stores, Pout, Sunglass Hut and YO! Sushi.

Awards

1# American Graphic Design Awards, Vogue's World's Sexiest Site, D&AD Annual.

LESS RAIN

UK/GERMANY/JAPAN

www.lessrain.com

since 1998

Mission

To create small interactive and emotional worlds. /// Création de petits mondes interactifs et émotionnels. /// Interaktive und emotionale kleine Welten zu erschaffen.

www.interact10ways.com/usa/less_rain.asp

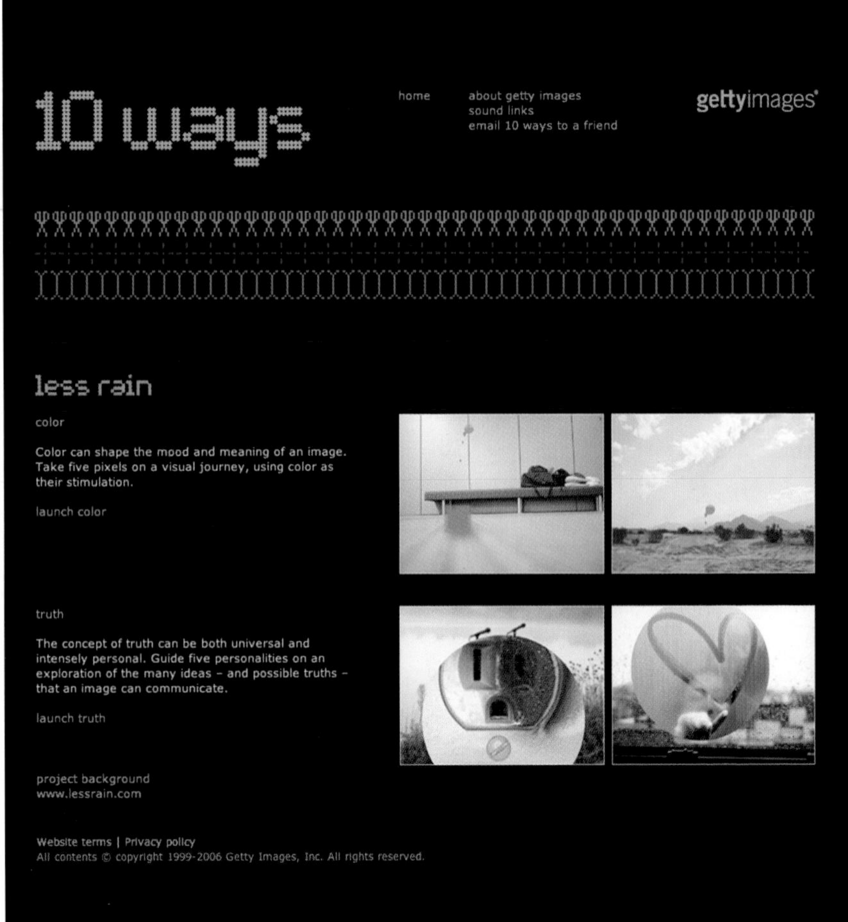

Location

Less Rain
London, United Kingdom: <www.lessrain.co.uk>
Berlin, Germany: <www.lessrain.de>
Tokyo, Japan: <www.lessrain.co.jp>
<reception@lessrain.com>

Team

2 Creative Directors, 2 Art Directors, 4 Designers, 5 Programmers.

www.sonjamueller.org

www.vw-eos.jp

Clients Red Bull, Red Bull Racing, BBC, Nike, VW.

LIBERONLINE

ITALY

www.liberonline.com

since 2000

Mission

LIBEROnline is the harmony between communication, design and interaction in our creative projects. At LIBEROnline, we get asked to interpret the style or the goal of the customer effectively transforming it into a spectacular and communicative interface.

www.stefanel.it

Location

LIBEROnline
Via Duca d'Aosta 51
30170 Venezia-Mestre
Italy
<libero@liberonline.com>

Team

1 Creative Director/Designer, 2 Programmers.

Dans ses projets de création, LIBEROnline représente l'harmonie entre la communication, le design et l'interaction. Chez LIBEROnline, nous devons interpréter le style ou l'objectif du client et le transformer en une interface spectaculaire et communicative. /// **LIBEROnline steht für kreative Projekte mit einer harmonischen Ausgewogenheit zwischen Kommunikation, Design und Interaktion. LIBEROnline versteht sich darauf, den Stil und die Ziele seiner Kunden neu zu interpretieren und wirkungsvoll in Aufsehen erregende und kommunikative User-Interfaces zu transformieren.**

www.augustovalentinidesign.it

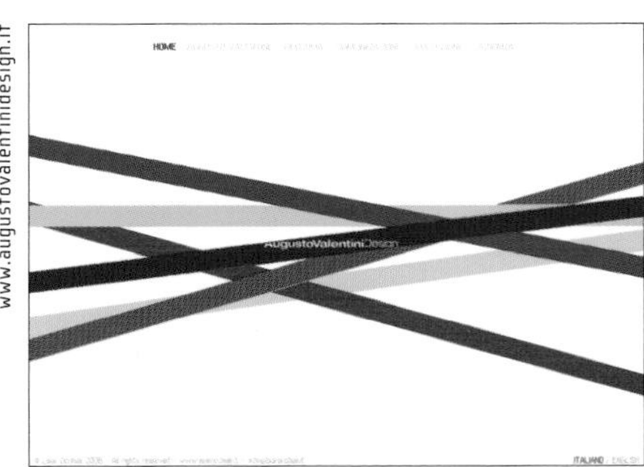

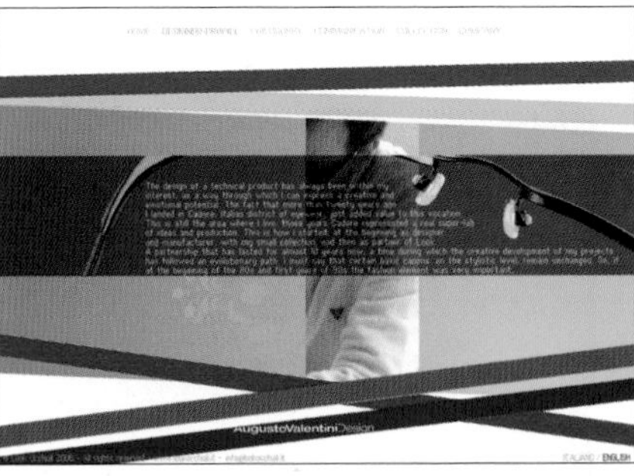

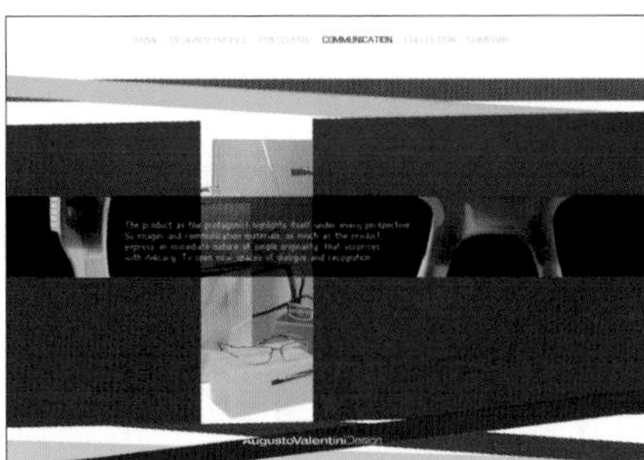

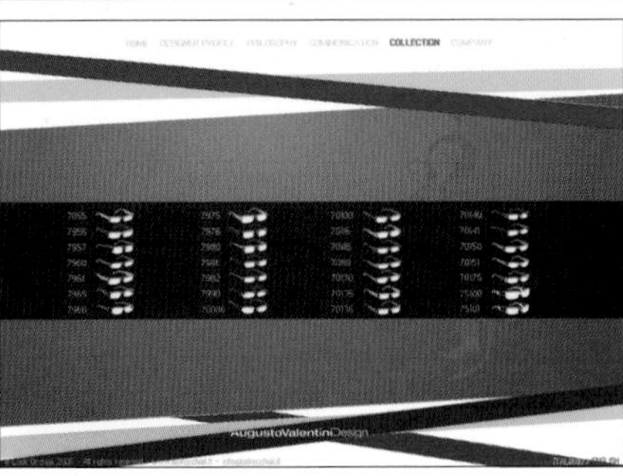

www.c151.com

Clients

Stefanel, Alessi, Alpes Inox, Diadora, E-play, Theodore Trancu & Associates.

Awards

Webby Awards, FlashInTheCan, Flashforward, American Design Awards, Horizon Interactive Awards, Italian Web Awards.

LOWE TESCH

SWEDEN

www.lowetesch.com

since 2002

Mission

LOWE Tesch is an award-winning full-service agency delivering world class interactive work, creating effective, entertaining, objective and result-focused digital platforms. /// LOWE Tesch est une agence primée à service complet qui effectue un excellent travail Web et crée des plates-formes numériques efficaces, amusantes, objectives et axées sur les résultats. /// **LOWE Tesch, eine preisgekrönte Full-Service-Agentur, liefert weltweit führende, ergebnisorientierte, kreative und unterhaltsame interaktive Lösungen für digitale Plattformen.**

www.saab.com/microsites/pilotswanted/GLOBAL/en/index2.shtml

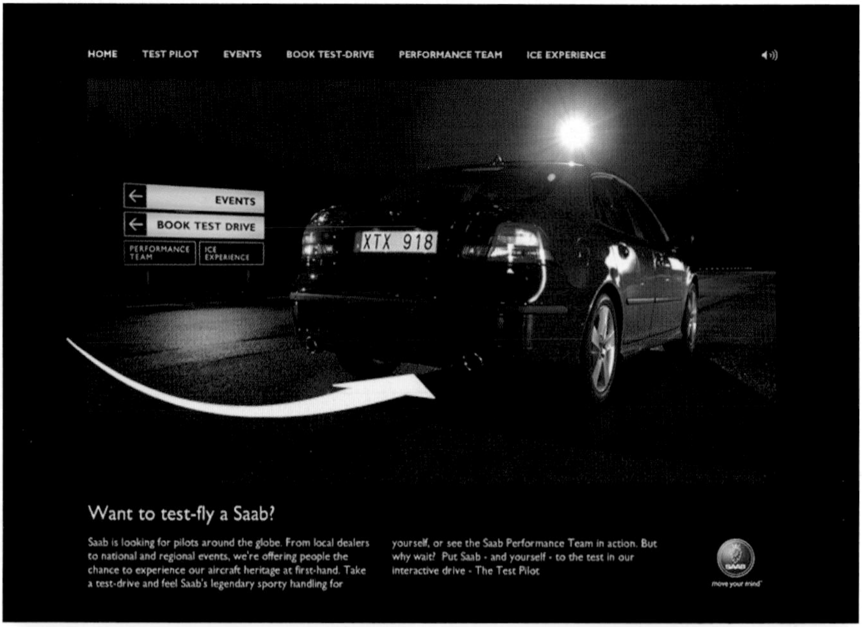

Location

LOWE Tesch
Box 6518, SE – 113 83 Stockholm
Sweden
<info@lowetesch.co>

Team

1 Creative Director, 3 Art Directors, 2 Flash Designers, 1 Web Designer.

www.ledefi-stellaartois.com

www.letranger-stellaartois.com

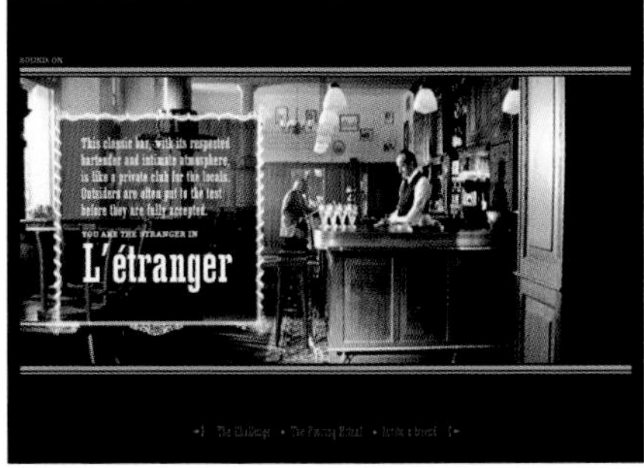

Clients

Saab Automobile (worldwide), Stella Artois (worldwide), TV 3, Tiger of Sweden, Coop.

Awards

New York Festivals (2 Silver), One Show (Bronze), Creative Review (Best Digital Campaign), Cannes Lions (2 Gold/Bronze), London International Advertising Festival (Gold), Epica (Silver/Bronze), Eurobest (Bronze), Golden Egg Sweden (Gold).

MEDIABOOM

USA

www.mediaboom.com

since 2002

Mission

mediaBOOM is an award winning interactive media company. We create extraordinary online brand experiences, designed not just to attract customers, but also to engage them. We combine cutting-edge technology and powerful visuals to produce highly interactive, atmospheric websites, games and broadcast animation. Our mission is to exceed our client's expectations.

www.mediaboom.com

Location

mediaBOOM
96 Broad Street
Guilford, Connecticut 06437
USA
<info@mediaBOOM.com>

Team

1 Creative Director, 1 Art Director, 2 Designers, 3 Programmers, 1 Sound Designer, 1 Photographer, 1 Content Writer.

mediaBOOM est une société Web primée. Nous créons des expériences de marques extraordinaires sur le Net, conçues pour attirer les clients, mais surtout pour les impliquer. Nous associons une technologie de pointe à de puissantes bandes images pour produire des sites Internet très interactifs et avec beaucoup d'ambiance, des jeux et des animations radio. Notre mission : aller au-delà des attentes de nos clients. ///

mediaBOOM ist eine mehrfach ausgezeichnete Agentur für interaktive Medien. Wir entwickeln und realisieren außergewöhnliche Markenwelten für das Internet, die nicht nur die Aufmerksamkeit der Verbraucher wecken, sondern sie auch langfristig an die Marken binden. Dabei kombinieren wir modernste Technologie mit kraftvollen Visuals, um Webseiten, Games und 3D-Animationen mit viel Atmosphäre und einem hohen Interaktivitätsgrad zu produzieren. Dabei setzen wir uns immer wieder das Ziel, die Erwartungen unserer Kunden weit zu übertreffen.

www.salsaritas.com

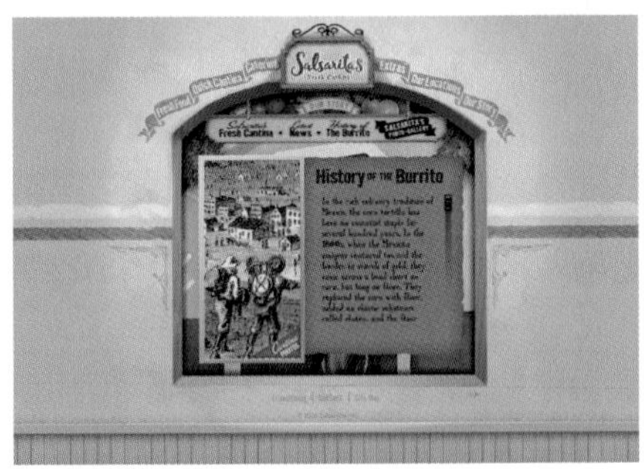

www.northeastdomestics.com

Clients

Salsarita's Fresh Cantina, Golfoholics, Northeast Domestics, ESPN, Marvel Comics, American Institute for Foreign Study, Cardiovascular Research Foundation, Conglomeride Entertainment, Local Thunder, Prospect Denim

Awards

Webby Awards (Winner/People's Voice Winner), Winter Semi-Annual American Design Awards (Winner), Web Design International Festival (Butterfly Award), PixelAwards, American Design Awards (Site of the Month/Platinum Award), ITA (Site of the Week), FWA (Site of the Day), DOPE, PixelMakers (Site of the Week).

MEDIALAND

TAIWAN

www.medialand.com.tw

since 2002

Mission

Unlimited Creation + Professional Planning + High Motivation + Effective Marketing = Medialand. /// Création sans limites + Planification professionnelle + Motivation + Marketing efficace = Medialand. /// Grenzenlose Kreativität + Professionelle Planung + Hohe Motivation + Effektives Marketing = Medialand.

www.toyota.com.tw/event/2006_motorshow/main.asp

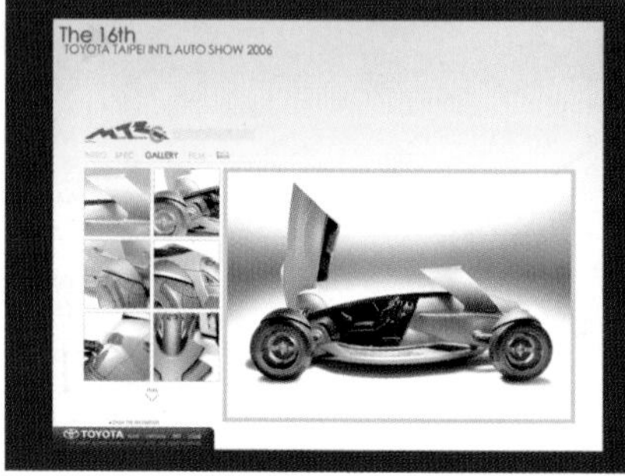

Location

Medialand Digi-Tech. Inc.
3F-6, No.3, Songjiang Rd.
Zhongshan District, Taipei City 104
Taiwan
<tim@mail.medialand.com.tw>

Team

1 Creative Director, 1 Art Director, 9 Designers, 3 Programmers, 2 Flash Programmers, 2 Web Planners, 5 Project Managers.

http://formosa.ntm.gov.tw/formosa

www.yamaha-motortown.com.tw

Clients

Yamaha, Toyota, Lexus, Epson, Shiseido, Subaru, Ford, Bausch & Lomb, Msn, Sony, Eva Air, Citibank, etc.

Awards

Click! Awards (Taiwan), e-Creative (Site of the day), Fcukstar (Site of the day), theDreamer (Site of the day), DOPE.

MILK AND COOKIES

BELGIUM

www.milkandcookies.be

since 2003

Mission

Milk and cookies is a small, almost super-tiny, company. We spend our days (and nights) making websites. We like: trees, flowers, happy thoughts, tender sensual feelings, satellite tv-shows that make you laugh, carrots and broccoli, animals that can talk, being big in little Asia, la fille d'O, our mums and dads.

www.kurtstallaert.com

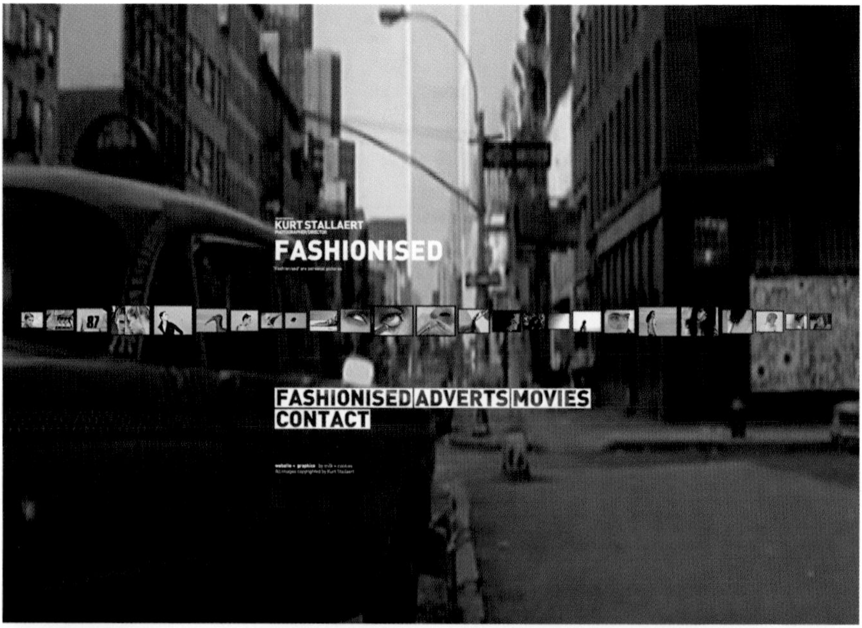

KURT STALLAERT
PHOTOGRAPHER/DIRECTOR
FASHIONISED
FASHIONISED ADVERTS MOVIES
CONTACT

Location

Milk and Cookies
Rue Royale 35 / Koningsstraat 35
1000 Brussels
Belgium
<crumbs@milkandcookies.be>

Team

1 Creative Director, 1 Business Manager (CEO), 2 Art Directors.

Milk and Cookies est une toute petite entreprise. Nous occupons nos journées (et nos nuits) à créer des sites Internet. Nous aimons : les arbres, les fleurs, les pensées positives, les sentiments tendres, les émissions de télévision par satellite qui font rire, les carottes et le brocoli, les animaux qui peuvent parler, être grands dans la petite Asie, la fille d'O, nos parents. /// **Milk and Cookies ist eine kleine, ja geradezu winzige Firma. Wir verbringen unsere Tage (und Nächte) damit, Webseiten zu gestalten. Wir mögen: Bäume, Blumen, schöne Gedanken, Zärtlichkeit und Sinnlichkeit, TV-Shows, die uns zum Lachen bringen, Karotten und Broccoli, Tiere, die sprechen können, being big in little Asia, la fille d'O, unsere Mamas und Papas.**

www.exdrummer.com

www.soulwax.com

Clients

Soulwax, MTV, Sony, Coca-Cola, Canon, Delvaux, Dirty Dancing, La Fille d'O, Devilles Harem Girls, Culture Club, Absolut Vodka, Kurt Stallaert (Photographer), and many many more.

NEUE DIGITALE

GERMANY

www.neue-digitale.de

since 1997

Mission

Never Stop — Standstill is our enemy! Only constant and systematic advancement coupled with a healthy amount of ambitious restlessness permit genuine progress. We always strive to provide excellent solutions that convince and fascinate, and which bring about measurable success, across all areas of our work.

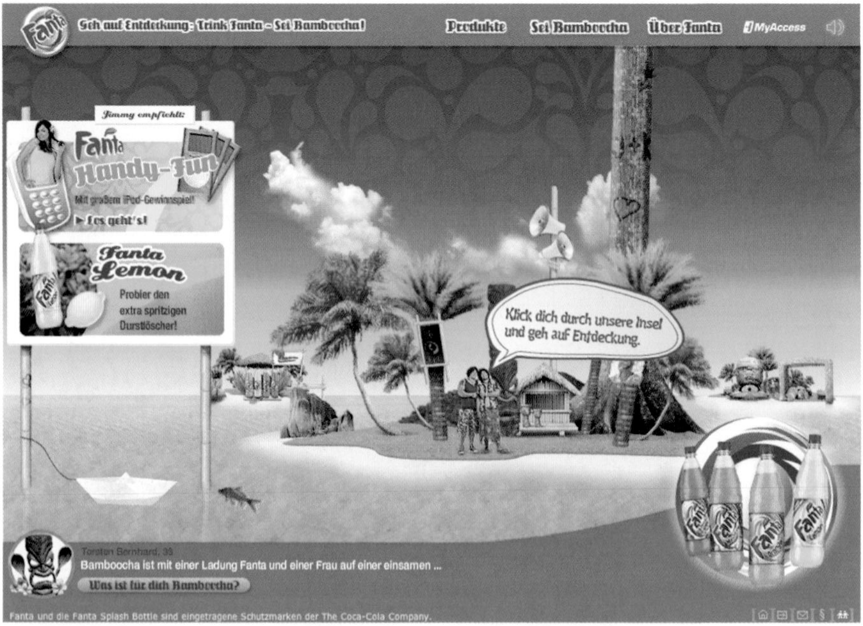

Location

NEUE DIGITALE GmbH
Falkstr. 5
60487 Frankfurt am Main
Germany
<info@neue-digitale.de>

Team

CEO (Andreas Gahlert), CCO (Olaf Czeschner), and 62 employees.

Nous sommes toujours en mouvement. L'immobilisme est notre ennemi. Seul le progrès constant et systématique associé à une bonne dose d'agitation ambitieuse nous permet d'avancer. Nous nous efforçons sans cesse de fournir d'excellentes solutions convaincantes et intéressantes qui entraînent une réussite mesurable dans tous les domaines de notre travail. /// **Never Stop – Niemals stehen bleiben, denn Stillstand ist unser größter Feind! Nur eine kontinuierliche und systematische Weiterentwicklung gepaart mit einer gesunden Portion von rastlosem Ehrgeiz ermöglicht echten Fortschritt. In allen Bereichen unserer Arbeit streben wir stets danach, exzellente Lösungen zu liefern, die nicht nur faszinieren und überzeugen, sondern auch messbaren Erfolg bringen.**

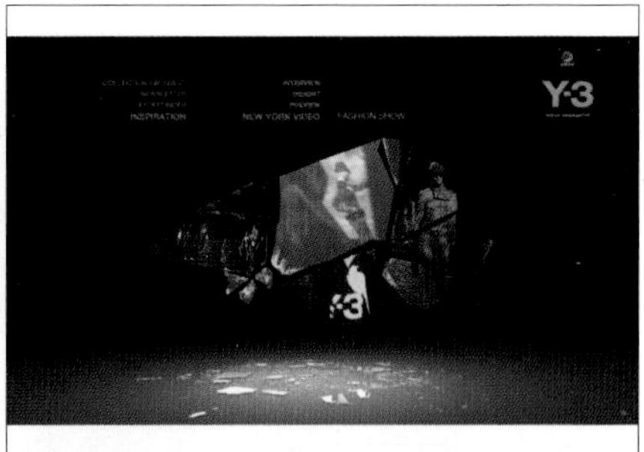

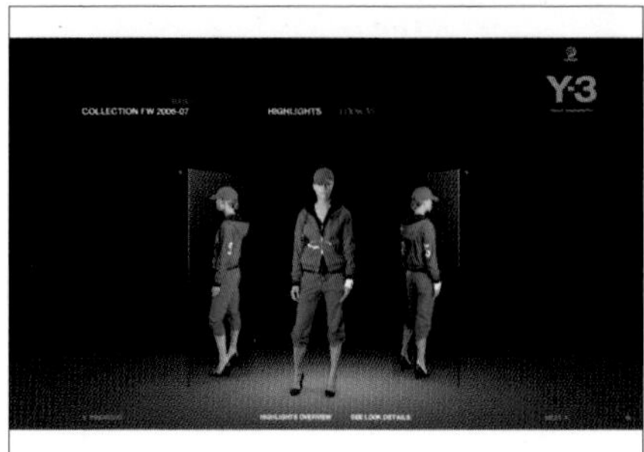

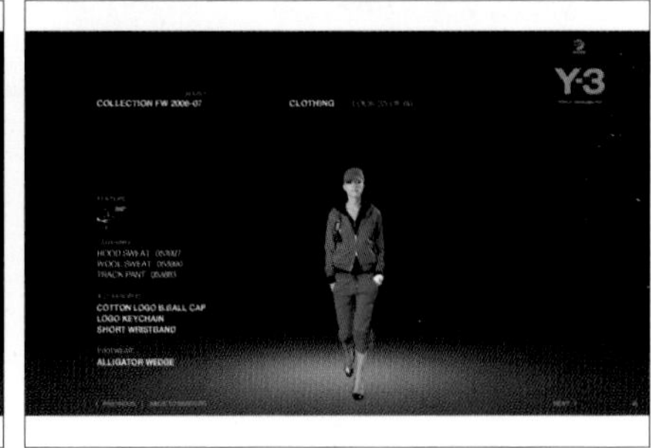

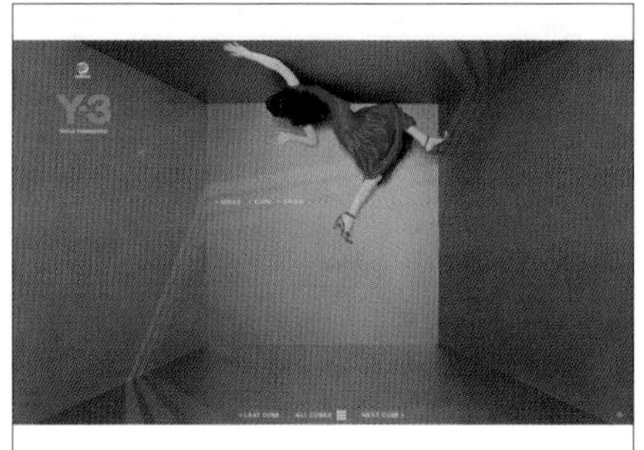

Clients

adidas, Germanwings, Olympus Europa, Coca Cola, Wilkhahn, Schirn Kunsthalle Frankfurt, Twentieth Century Fox, DaimlerChrysler.

Awards

New York Festivals (Grand Award/2 Gold /Silver/4 Bronze), iF communication design (2 Gold/Special Media), Cannes Lions (Gold), Clio (Silver/Bronze), D&AD (Bronze), One Show (2 Silver/Bronze), Golden Award of Montreux (Gold), ANDY Awards (Silver), ADC Deutschland (Gold/2 Bronze), Eurobest Award, etc.

NORTH KINGDOM

SWEDEN

www.northkingdom.com

since 2003

Mission

North Kingdom is a provider of innovative, interactive design solutions. We facilitate every aspect of project delivery, from conceptualising, through to design, production and post-production. Each piece of work we take on becomes the basis of our relationship with our clients, with every aspect crafted to our very highest standard.

Toyota Aygo

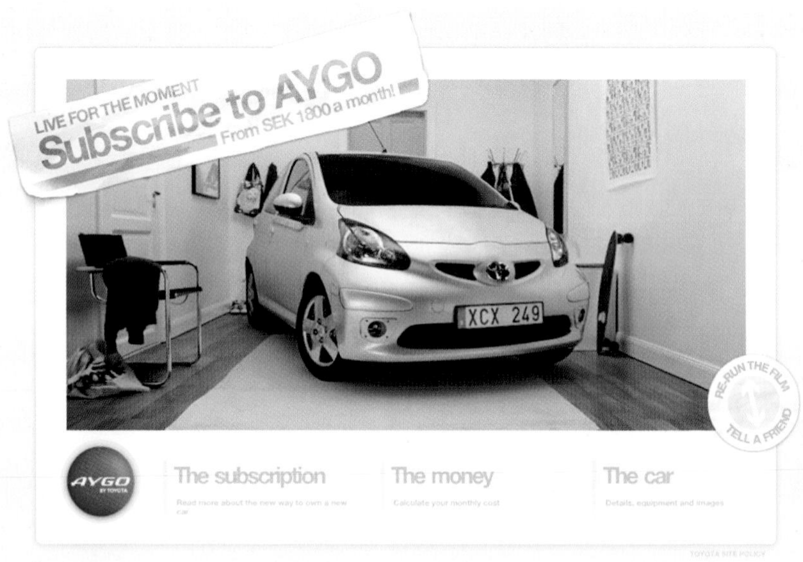

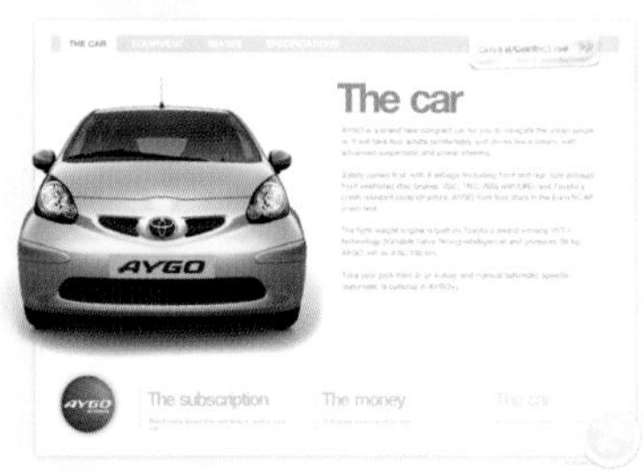

Location

North Kingdom
Storgatan 32, 93131 Skellefteå, Sweden
Skeppsbron 36, 11130 Stockholm, Sweden
<info@northkingdom.com>

Team

Undisclosed.

North Kingdom est un fournisseur de nouvelles solutions de design Web. Nous nous chargeons de tous les aspects d'un projet, de la conceptualisation au design, en passant par la production et la postproduction. Chaque travail que nous entreprenons devient la base de notre relation avec nos clients, et nous en travaillons chaque aspect avec le plus grand soin. /// **North Kingdom bietet innovative interaktive Designlösungen. Unser Portfolio umfasst die komplette Projektabwicklung, vom Konzept über das Design und die Produktion bis hin zur Postproduktion. Jedes Projekt, das wir übernehmen, wird zur Basis unserer Beziehung mit unseren Kunden, wobei wir uns immer das Ziel setzen, auch den allerhöchsten Ansprüchen zu genügen.**

www.vodafonejourney.com

www.absolutkravitz.com

Clients

Vodafone Group, BRIO, ABSOLUT, Toyota Sweden, Goodby, Silverstein & Partners.

Awards

Cannes Lions (4 Gold/Silver/Bronze).

OGILVYINTERACTIVE

WORLDWIDE

www.ogilvy.com

since 1983

Mission

Born in 1983, OgilvyInteractive was the first dedicated interactive group formed by a global agency network. Digital Strategy. Digital Marketing. Digital Media. Technology. Websites. Intranets. Extranets. Mobile. Rich Media. E-commerce. Content Management. Today, OgilvyInteractive innovates in 42 offices across 39 countries, in languages ranging from Hindi to French to Mandarin.

IBM

IBM

United States [change] | Terms of use

Search

Home | Products | Services & industry solutions | Support & downloads | My IBM

what makes you* special?

WATCH

Watch how IBM can help guide you from inspiration to execution.

Special stories

All around you, companies are cultivating an ecosystem of innovation. Learn how they've infused it into their thinking, products, processes and people.

→ How IBM has helped companies do special things.

Get started

Everybody talks innovation, but here's how IBM can help you do it. Where do you start? You start with IBM, and these six potential "doorways" to innovation in your company.

- Revitalize your business
- Exploit your capabilities
- Secure your enterprise
- Strengthen customer connections
- Transform your workforce
- Manage your operations

Industry expertise

We've helped companies in almost every industry succeed in the on demand world. How? By knowing their businesses as well as they do. Find out more.

→ Find your industry.

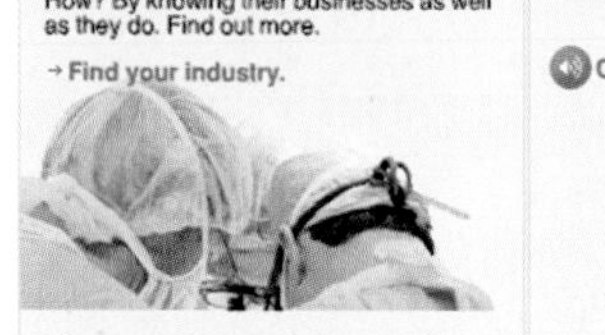

Voices of innovation

The innovation revolution will be Podcasted.

Click to listen.

Stay informed

See how IBM is helping to lead the innovation charge.

→ The Global CEO Study.

→ IBM's Global Innovation Outlook.

→ View the advertising campaign.

Location

OgilvyInteractive

42 offices in 39 countries.

Please refer to <www.ogilvy.com>.

Team

Undisclosed.

Fondé en 1983, OgilvyInteractive a été le premier groupe Web dédié formé par un réseau mondial d'agences. Stratégie numérique. Marketing numérique. Média numérique. Technologie. Sites Web. Intranets. Extranets. Portables. Média enrichi. Commerce électronique. Gestion des contenus. À l'heure actuelle, OgilvyInteractive ne cesse d'innover dans ses 42 bureaux situés dans 39 pays du monde, et utilise des langues telles que l'hindi, le français ou le mandarin. /// **OgilvyInteractive entstand 1983 durch die Bildung eines weltweiten Agenturnetzwerks als erste Gruppe, die sich speziell mit interaktivem Design beschäftigte. Digitale Strategien. Digitales Marketing. Digitale Medien. Technologien. Webseiten. Intranets. Extranets. Mobile Netze. Rich-Media-Inhalte. E-Commerce. Content Management. Heute hat OgilvyInteractive 42 Niederlassungen in 39 Ländern und kreiert dort innovative Kampagnen in zahlreichen Sprachen, von Hindi über Französisch bis Mandarin.**

American Express

Levi's

Clients

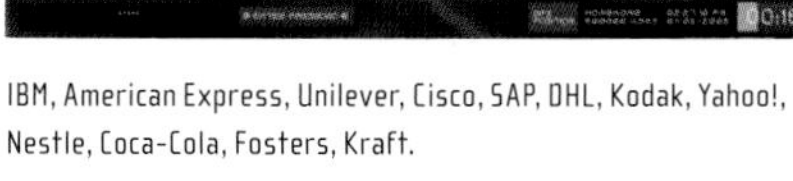
IBM, American Express, Unilever, Cisco, SAP, DHL, Kodak, Yahoo!, Nestle, Coca-Cola, Fosters, Kraft.

Awards

Cannes Grand Prix +other Lions, Clios Grand Prix + and other Clios, LIAA Grand Prix, One Show Pencils, Diamond Echo from DMA, Asia Awards.

ONSCREEN CREATIVE

UK

www.onscreencreative.com

since 2003

Mission

We do things on screens! We make sites, create animations and design online ads. On any screen of any size in any place... We like to be convergent, classic and fun in our approach to everything we're doing.

www.onscreencreative.com

www.zero7.co.uk

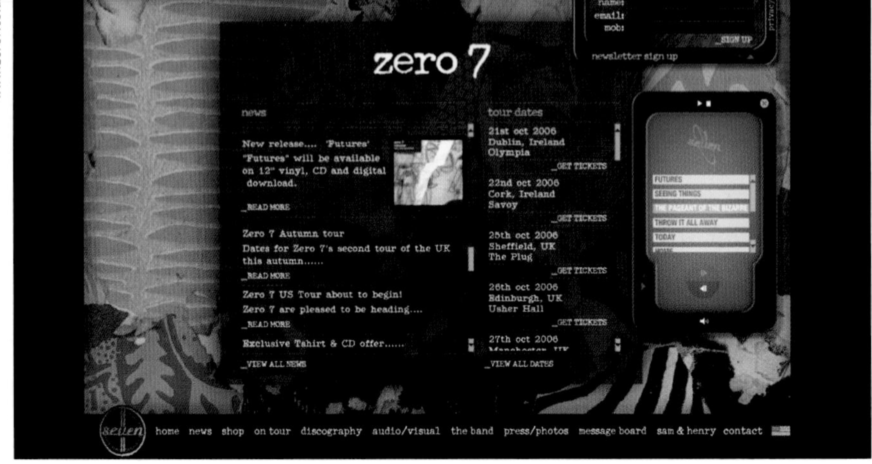

Location

Onscreen Creative
Camden & Clerkenwell
London
United Kingdom
<tim@onscreencreative.com>

Team

1 Creative Director, 2 Designers, 2 Programmers.
Technical agency: <www.marotori.com>.

C'est nous qui faisons apparaître des choses sur les écrans. Nous créons des sites, des animations et des publicités sur Internet, sur tous les écrans, quelle que soit leur taille, et où qu'ils se trouvent. Nous aimons avoir des avis convergents et une manière classique et amusante de travailler. /// **Wir machen Sachen auf Bildschirmen! Wir machen Webseiten, gestalten Animationen und designen Online-Werbung. Das machen wir für Bildschirme aller Größen, egal wo sie stehen. Wir sind zielorientiert, haben gern Spaß und außerdem den Ehrgeiz, echte Klassiker zu liefern.**

www.tigerbeer.co.uk

Clients

Tiger Beer, United International Pictures, Zero 7, Dan Pearson.

ON CLICK

SPAIN

www.onclick.es

since 2001

Mission

We make personal and efficient solutions in new media communication. We are improving continuously. We take each project as a new and personal aim. Thus we are able to improve day-by-day offering the best results for any New Media Creative Project.

www.converse.es/setumismo

Location

On Click
Zabalbide 6
48600 Sopelana-Bizkaia
Spain
<info@onclick.es>

Team

1 Project Manager/Creative Director, 1 Interactive/Graphic Designer, 1 Designer/Programmer.

Nous créons des solutions personnelles et efficaces dans la nouvelle communication média et nous cherchons sans cesse à nous améliorer. Nous considérons chaque projet comme un objectif nouveau et personnel, ce qui nous permet de nous améliorer et d'obtenir les meilleurs résultats possibles pour chaque projet de création. /// **Wir bieten individuell zugeschnittene und effiziente Kommunikationslösungen für neue Medien. Wir sind immer dabei, noch besser zu werden. Wir übernehmen jedes neue Projekt mit frischem Ehrgeiz und Elan. Deshalb können wir uns jeden Tag aufs Neue steigern und unseren Kunden bei jedem New-Media-Projekt kreative Spitzenergebnisse liefern.**

www.vectordefenders.com

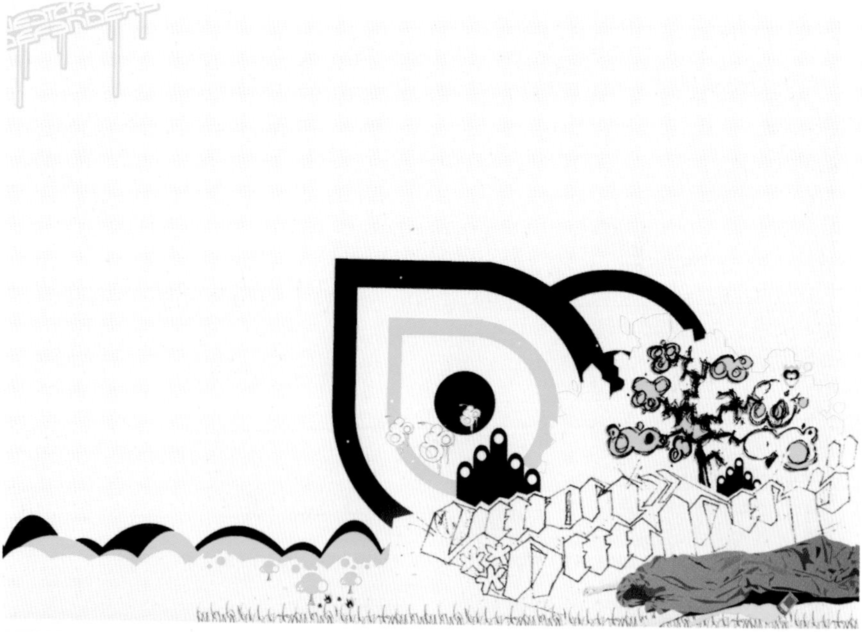

www.cabezadeperro.es

Clients

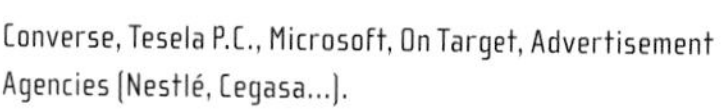

Converse, Tesela P.C., Microsoft, On Target, Advertisement Agencies (Nestlé, Cegasa...).

Awards

FWA, CiberArt Bilbao, El Correo Digital (People's Choice).

ONYRO

GREECE

www.onyro.com

since 2004

Mission

We have an obsession for design and technology and whilst believing in quality over quantity we aim to continuously pioneer the change within our marketplace so that we can offer our clients beautifully unique ground breaking online experiences which provide real business results and exceed the clients expectations time after time.

www.adel.gr

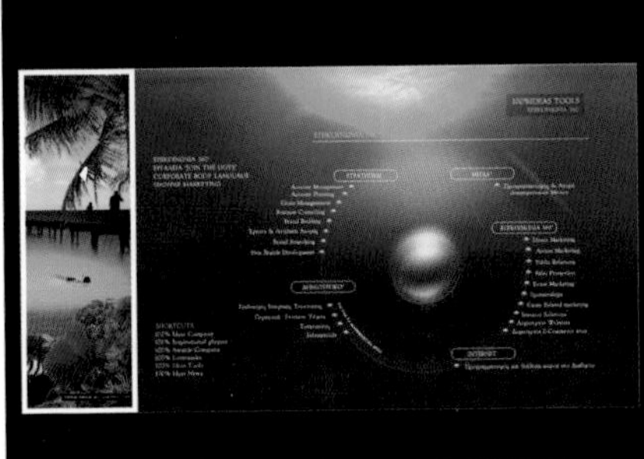

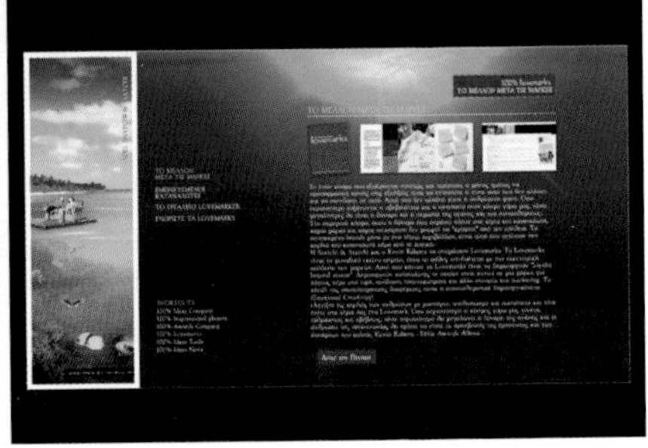

Location

Onyro
Paraschou 11
15233 Chalandri, Athens
Greece
<info@onyro.com>

Team

1 Creative Director, 1 Technical Director, 2 Designers, 2 Flash Programmers.

Nous adorons le design et la technologie et privilégions la qualité à la quantité. Nous nous efforçons d'être à l'avant-garde des évolutions de notre marché afin de proposer à nos clients des expériences Internet révolutionnaires et exceptionnelles permettant d'obtenir des résultats commerciaux réels et d'aller au-delà des attentes des clients, jour après jour. /// **Wir haben eine Passion für Design und moderne Technologien. Wir setzen auf Qualität statt Quantität. Wir streben unaufhörlich danach, Pionierleistungen auf unserem Markt zu vollbringen. Wir möchten unseren Kunden wirklich einzigartige und Weg weisende Online-Erlebniswelten bieten, die ihnen einen echten Wettbewerbsvorteil verschaffen und ihre Erwartungen jedes Mal aufs Neue übertreffen.**

www.mcdonalds.gr

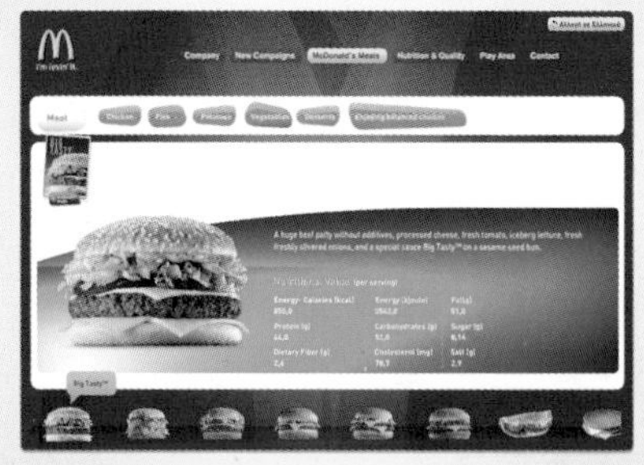

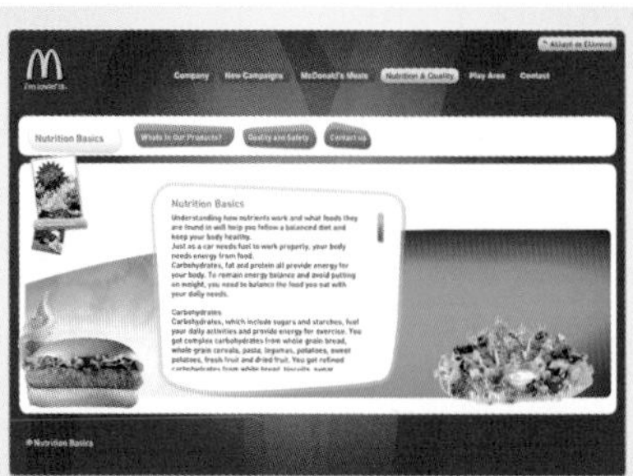

Toyota Tundra

Clients

Toyota USA, Cingular, Snickers, Emi, Positiva, JPMorgan, Cannon, Royal Velvet, BBC, WRC, McDonalds Greece, Sato Greece, Toyota Greece, CuttySark, Nissan Greece, Superfast Ferries, OTE.

OPCOM

POLAND

www.opcom.pl

since 2001

Mission

Opcom is like a woman. Elegant and sophisticated. About thirty. Extremely ambitious. When needed, she lays aside the marketing jargon and trusts her intuition. Always in tune with current trends. Incredibly envious. She would never don an outfit worn by the competition. Striving for new experiences that will catch your eye.

www.alwaysfresh.pl

Location

Opcom
Cracow, Poland
Jeleniogorska 17
Chris Adamus <k@opcom.pl>

Team

1 CEO, 1 Creative Director, 6 Client Services, 1 Administration, 8 Production Department.

Opcom est semblable à une femme. Élégante et sophistiquée. La trentaine. Extrêmement ambitieuse. Lorsque cela est nécessaire, elle fait abstraction du jargon marketing pour suivre son intuition. Elle est toujours en accord avec les tendances du moment. Incroyablement envieuse. Elle ne mettra jamais de tenue portée par la concurrence. Elle recherche de nouvelles expériences qui vous taperont à l'œil. ///
Opcom ist wie eine Frau. Elegant und raffiniert. Um die dreißig. Extrem ehrgeizig. Wenn es nötig ist, legt sie den Marketing-Jargon beiseite und vertraut ihrer Intuition. Sie weiß immer über die neuesten Trends Bescheid. Sie ist unglaublich neidisch. Niemals würde sie sich mit einem Outfit schmücken, das die Konkurrenz bereits getragen hat. Sie ist stets auf der Suche nach neuen Blickfängen, die Ihre Aufmerksamkeit erregen werden.

www.noblesurfer.com

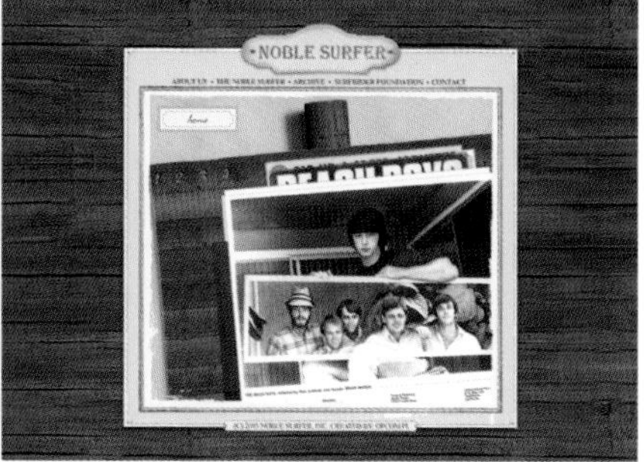

Clients

Procter & Gamble, Puma, Always, Tampax, BreBank and others.

Awards

FWA, Kreatura 2005, Webstarfestival 2005.

PARK

RUSSIA

www.designpark.ru

since 2003

Mission

Rock, ideas, experiments, understanding, peace, adequacy, manipulations, fun, open mind, goodness, friendship, absorption, control, inspiration, action, concept, interactive, future, random, work, art, music, fashion, abstractionism, speed, movies, city, feelings, eating, excitement, sex, order, sleep, love, simplicity, motion, party, people, miracle, space, boys, complexity, positive, w.e.s.d., nature, girls, possibilities, communication, interest, design.

www.instinct.ru

Location

PARK
9/3 Maly Ivanovsky pereulok
Moscow, Russia, 109028
<info@designpark.ru>

Team

2 Art Directors, 7 Designers, 2 Programmers, 4 Managers.

Rock, idées, expériences, compréhension, paix, capacité, manipulations, amusement, ouverture d'esprit, bonté, amitié, absorption d'Opcom, contrôle, inspiration, action, concept, interaction, avenir, caractère aléatoire, travail, art, musique, mode, abstraction, vitesse, films, ville, sentiments, nourriture, enthousiasme, sexe, ordre, sommeil, amour, simplicité, mouvement, fête, personnes, miracle, espace, garçons, complexité, positivisme, week-end, nature, filles, possibilités, communication, intérêt, design. /// **Rock, Ideen, Experimente, Verständnis, Frieden, angemessen, Manipulationen, Spaß, offen für alles, gut, Freundschaft, aufsaugen, Kontrolle, Inspiration, Aktion, Konzept, interaktiv, Zukunft, Zufall, Arbeit, Kunst, Musik, Mode, Abstraktion, Geschwindigkeit, Filme, Stadt, Gefühle, Essen, Erregung, Sex, Ordnung, Schlaf, Liebe, Schlichtheit, Bewegung, Party, Leute, Wunder, Weltall, Boys, Komplexität, w.e.s.d., Natur, Girls, Möglichkeiten, Kommunikation, Interesse, Design.**

www.fashionpoint.ru

Clients

Bacardi-Martini, Motorola, Ogilvy, BBDO, Beeline.

Awards

Moscow Advertising Festival, Golden Award for Russian Music Awards (Website), Golden Drum (Golden Drum/Bronze Drum).

PERFECT FOOLS

SWEDEN

www.perfectfools.com

since 2002

Mission

We give your online branding full power, We stop at (almost) nothing to deliver online campaigns and corporate websites that captivate your target audience, challenge expectations and get results.

Samsung SGH D600

Location

Perfect Fools
Drottninggatan 57
111 21 Stockholm
Sweden
<info@perfectfools.com>

Team

1 Creative Director, 4 Art Directors, 1 3d Designer, 2 Project Leaders, 1 Sound Designer, 5 Flash Developers, 1 Script Writer.

Nous conférons tous les pouvoirs à notre stratégie de marque. Rien (ou presque) ne nous arrête pour fournir des campagnes Internet et des sites d'entreprises qui captivent le public visé, répondent à ses attentes et permettent d'obtenir des résultats. /// **Wir geben Vollgas, damit Ihre Marke im Internet die Pole Position erreicht. Wir machen vor (fast) nichts Halt, um Onlinekampagnen und Unternehmenswebseiten an den Start zu bringen, die nicht nur Ihre Zielgruppen, sondern auch Sie begeistern und Ihren Umsatz steigern werden.**

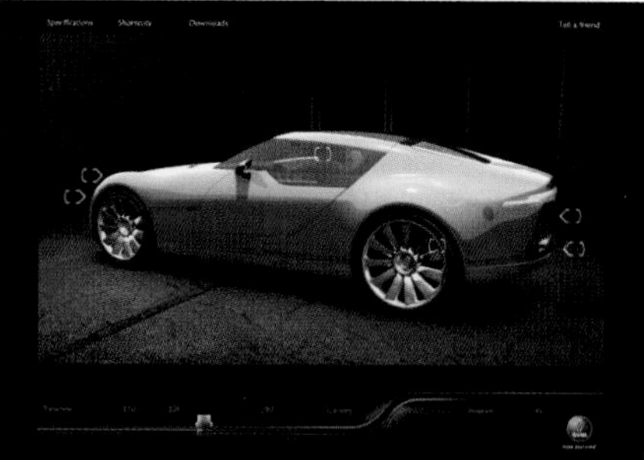

Samsung D820

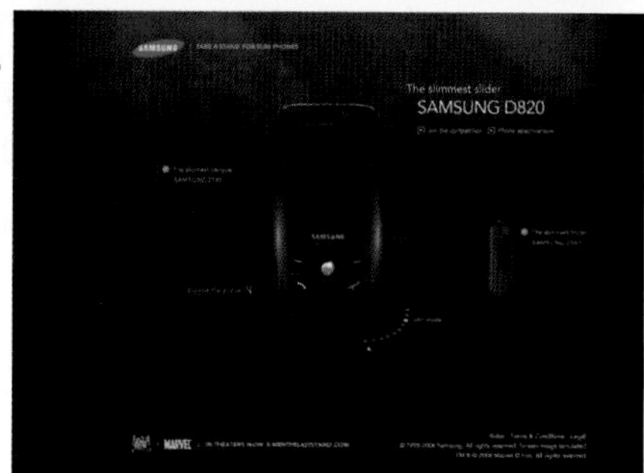

Clients

adidas, British Airways, Coca-Cola, Electrolux, Ericsson, Incepta Group, Kraft Foods, Nokia, Ogilvy, PEAB, Pfizer, Publicis, Saab, Samsung, Schwarzkopf & Henkel, Seat, SEB, Sprite, Swedish Armed Forces, Swedish Radio, Svenska Spel, Volvo.

Awards

Flash Film Festival, Cannes Cyber Lions (Shortlist), London International Advertising Awards, FITC, FWA, Eurobest, etc.

PILL & PILLOW

HONG KONG

www.pillandpillow.com

since 2004

Mission

We don't just design websites. We design experiences. /// Nous ne concevons pas uniquement des sites Internet, nous créons des expériences. /// Wir gestalten nicht einfach nur Webseiten. Wir gestalten Erlebniswelten.

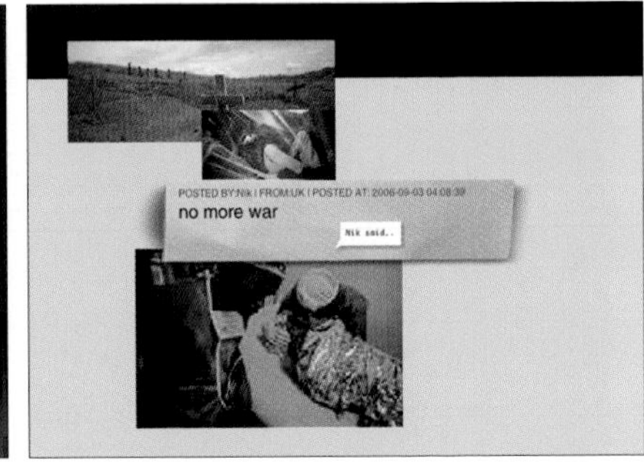

Location

pill & pillow
9/F, 15 Caroline Hill Road
Causeway Bay
Hong Kong
<curious@pillandpillow.com>

Team

1 Creative Director, 1 Art Director, 2 Designers, 1 Programmer.

www.ovalpartnership.com

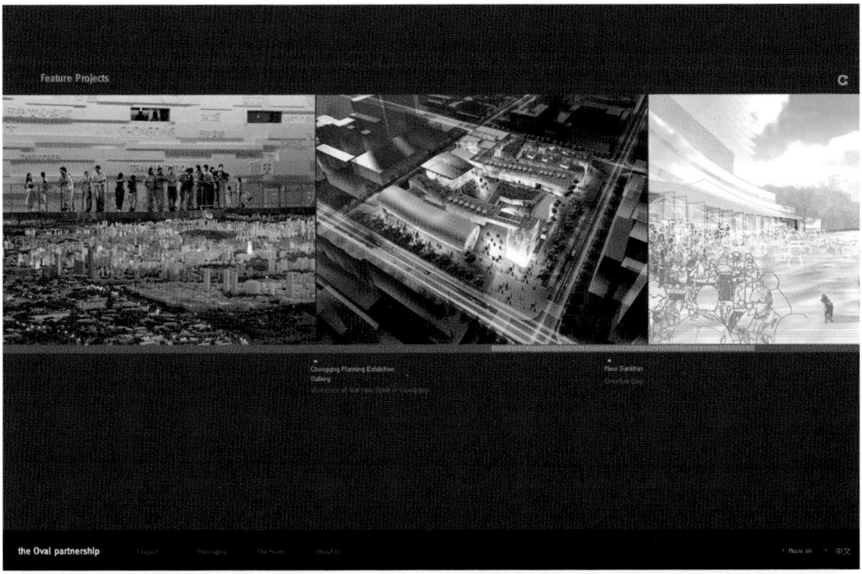

www.happypylones.com

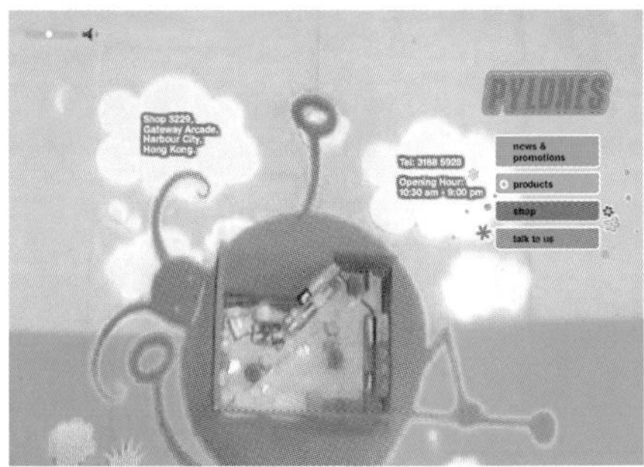

Clients

Médecins Sans Frontières, Pylones, The Oval Partnership.

Awards

London International Awards Finalist, FWA, HKDA (Hong Kong Designer Association), IFVA (Silver).

PLANK

CANADA

www.plankdesign.com

since 1998

Mission

Plank set out to make the Web a better-looking place, but soon realized that wasn't enough. Sites need to be about results, usefulness, user-friendliness, AND good aesthetics. So Plank's mission is to deliver sites that meet all of those requirements, ones that can make a difference. Plank – websites that matter.

www.fantasiafest.com/2006/en

Location

Plank
101-372 rue Ste-Catherine o.
Montréal, Québec, H3B 1A2
Canada
<info@plankdesign.com>

Team

1 Creative Director/President, 1 Art Director/Senior Designer, 1 Production Director, 1 Interactive Director, 1 Marketing Director, 2 Programmers, 1 Designer/Integrator, 1 Programmer/Integrator.

La société Plank a été créée pour rendre Internet plus séduisant, mais nous nous sommes rapidement rendu compte que ce n'était pas suffisant. Les sites doivent être liés aux résultats, être utiles, conviviaux et très bien présentés. La mission de Plank consiste à créer des sites possédant toutes ces qualités, des sites qui font la différence. Plank, des sites qui incitent. /// **Plank fing an mit dem Ziel, dem Web zu einem besseren Look zu verhelfen, doch bald wurde klar, dass das allein nicht reicht. Webseiten müssen Ergebnisse liefern, nützlich und userfreundlich sein UND obendrein gut aussehen. Deshalb besteht die Mission von Plank nun darin, Webseiten zu kreieren, die all diese Anforderungen erfüllen und zudem einzigartig sind. Plank – Webseiten mit dem gewissen Etwas.**

www.ultrabland.com

info
work
bios
news

work

Cinemax Image 2006

Cinemax IDs 2006

HBO The Wire 4

USA Character

USA Psych

USA The Starter Wife

Sci Fi Twilight Zone

Clients Michael Moore, Governor-General of Canada, ultrabland, 1-800-GOT-JUNK?, Buzz Image, Airborne Entertainment, Fantasia Film Festival.

Awards Macromedia (Site of the Day), Forbes Magazine (Best Mobile Industry Site), SXSW (Best Film Website), Webby Awards.

POSTGAL WORKSHOP

HONG KONG

www.postgal.com

since 2003

Mission

To deliver creative work which simultaneously enables clients to deliver their message effectively. /// Travail créatif permettant aux clients de transmettre efficacement leur message. /// Kreative Lösungen liefern, mit denen unsere Kunden ihre Werbebotschaften effizient vermitteln können.

www.postgal.com

Location

Postgal Workshop
Unit 3, 11/F, Siu Wai Ind Bldg, 29-33 Wing Hong St
Cheung Sha Wan
Hong Kong
<info@postgal.com>

Team

1 Creative Director, 2 Designers, 1 Programmers, 2 Animators.

www.ifva.com

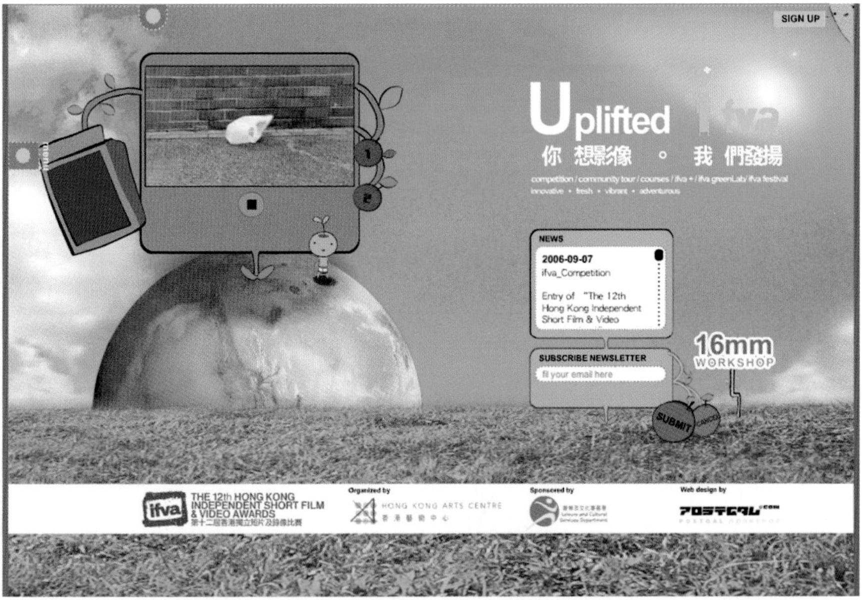

Clients

Nike, Levi's, Lee Kum Kee, etc.

Awards

Flashforward, Macromedia Pocket PC Flash Contest, E-Creative.

PREZENCE

SOUTH AFRICA/UK

www.prezence.co.za + www.prezence.co.uk since 2000/2002

Mission

Prezence's mission is to change the face of new media, by delivering cutting-edge online digital solutions that are 100% accessible to the target market. Implementing innovative and exciting ideas that enable users to interact with brands on completely new levels.

www.sterkinekor.com

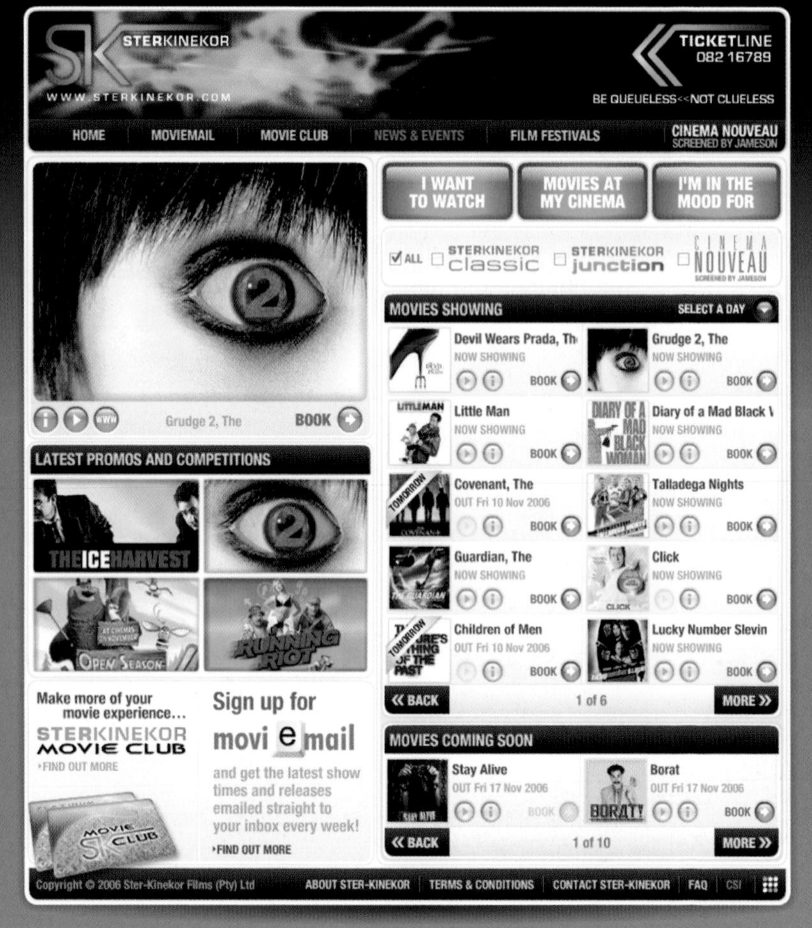

Location

Prezence South Africa <info@prezence.co.za>
2A Nautica, The Water Club, Granger Bay, Cape Town
Diamond House, Hammets Crossing, Fourways, Johannesburg
Prezence United Kingdom <info@prezence.co.uk>
Denby Buildings, Regent Grove, Leamington Spa, UK

Team

4 Creative Directors, 4 Programmers, 12 Designers/Flash Developers, 4 Flash Action Scripters, 6 Content Editors, 4 Studio/Business Development.

La mission de Prezence : changer la face des nouveaux médias en fournissant des solutions numériques Internet de pointe entièrement accessibles aux marchés ciblés, et mettre en place des idées intéressantes permettant aux utilisateurs d'entrer en interaction avec les marques à de nouveaux niveaux. /// **Prezence hat die Mission, den neuen Medien ein neues Gesicht zu geben und modernste digitale Onlinelösungen zu bieten, die zu 100% auf die Zielgruppe zugeschnitten sind. Wir realisieren innovative und spannende Ideen und ermöglichen Nutzern, auf völlig neuen Ebenen mit Marken zu kommunizieren.**

www.klipdrift.co.za

Clients

Ster Kinekor, Telkom, Warner Gallo, EMI, SonyBMG, British American Tobacco, South African Breweries, Hip2b2, Vodacom Direct, Vodafone Live, South African Music Awards, Barclays, Virgin Active, Distell Group, FCB, Oasis, Sony Pictures, RCA, Columbia, UIP, Universal Music, EA (Electronic Arts), etc.

PROD4EVER

USA

www.prod4ever.com

since 2001

Mission

We wanna make the web not boring + push our design skills. /// Nous voulons donner du punch à Internet et tirer profit de nos compétences en design. /// Wir treiben unsere Designfähigkeiten auf die Spitze, damit das Internet auch in Zukunft aufregend bleibt.

www.headautomatica.com

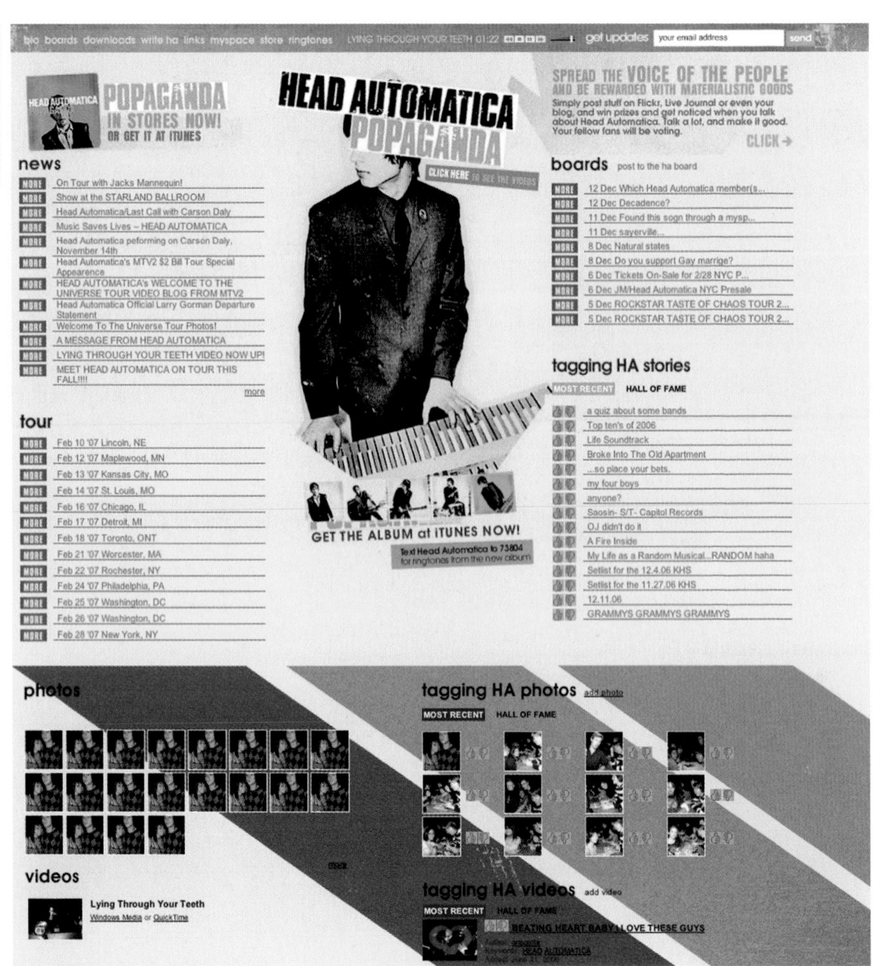

Location

PROD4ever
306 Dartmouth Street, Suite 205
Boston, MA 02116
USA
<info@prod4ever.com>

Team

4 Designers, 1 Project Manager.

www.mychemicalromance.com

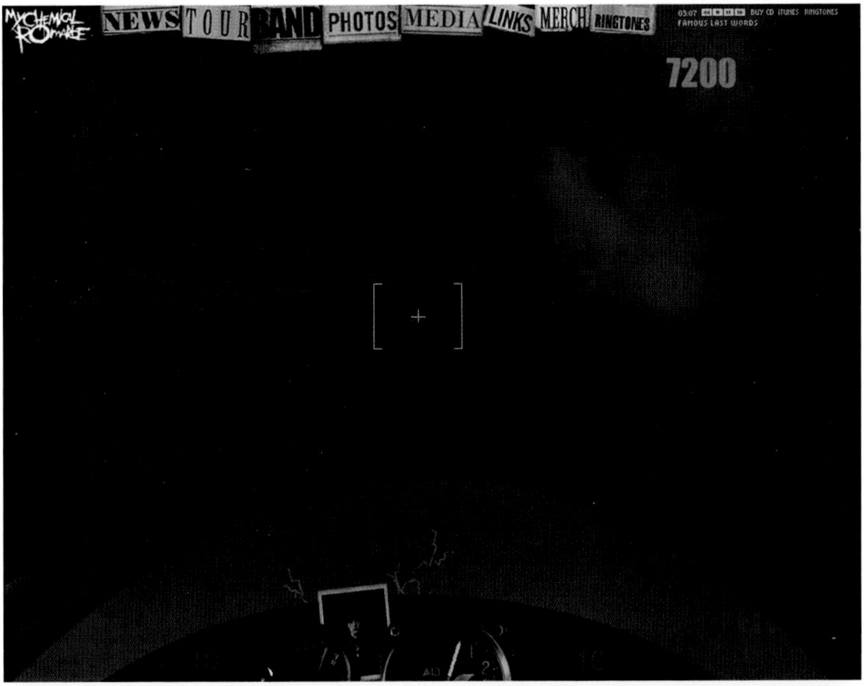

www.spoontheband.com

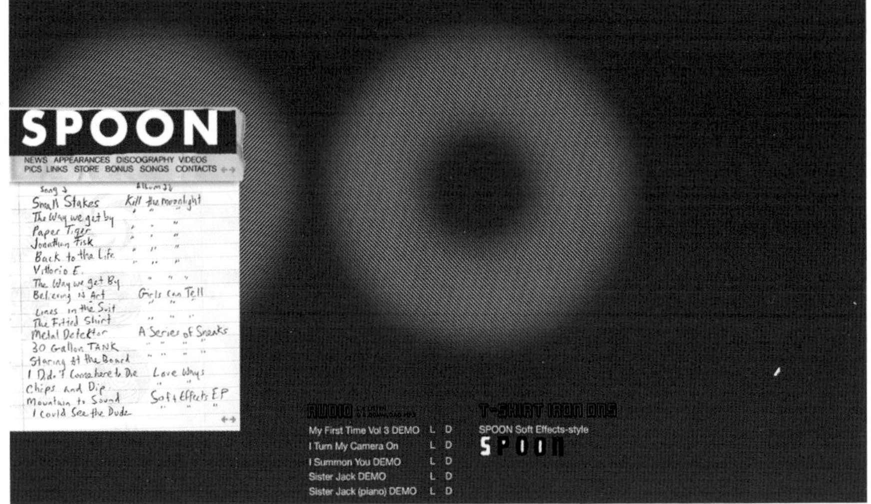

Clients

Warner Brothers Records, Capital Records, Universal Records, Astralwerks, AOL, Madonna, Spoon, Mary Timony.

PUBLICIS NET

FRANCE

www.publicisnet.fr

since 1997

Mission

The best agency in town. /// La meilleure agence du marché. /// Die beste Agentur der Stadt.

www.coca-colablak.fr

Location

Publicis Net
36 rue Vivienne
75002 Paris
France
<psimonet@publicisnet.fr>

Team

1 Creative Director, 4 Senior Art Directors, 6 Junior Art Director, 4 Web Designers, 10 Programmers.

www.experiencewonderyou.com

C Koi Ce Hold Up

Clients

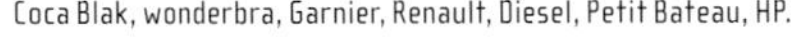

Coca Blak, wonderbra, Garnier, Renault, Diesel, Petit Bateau, HP.

Awards

Cannes Cyber Lion, W³, Webaward (USA), Golden Award of Montreux, Clic d'OR, Phoenix VDA, Club des DA, Tom Com.

RADIANT CORE

CANADA

www.radiantcore.com

since 2003

Mission

We build websites that build our clients' businesses. Our projects are beautifully handcrafted and provide ease of mind through the Foundation Website Management Platform. Plus, we're really swell!

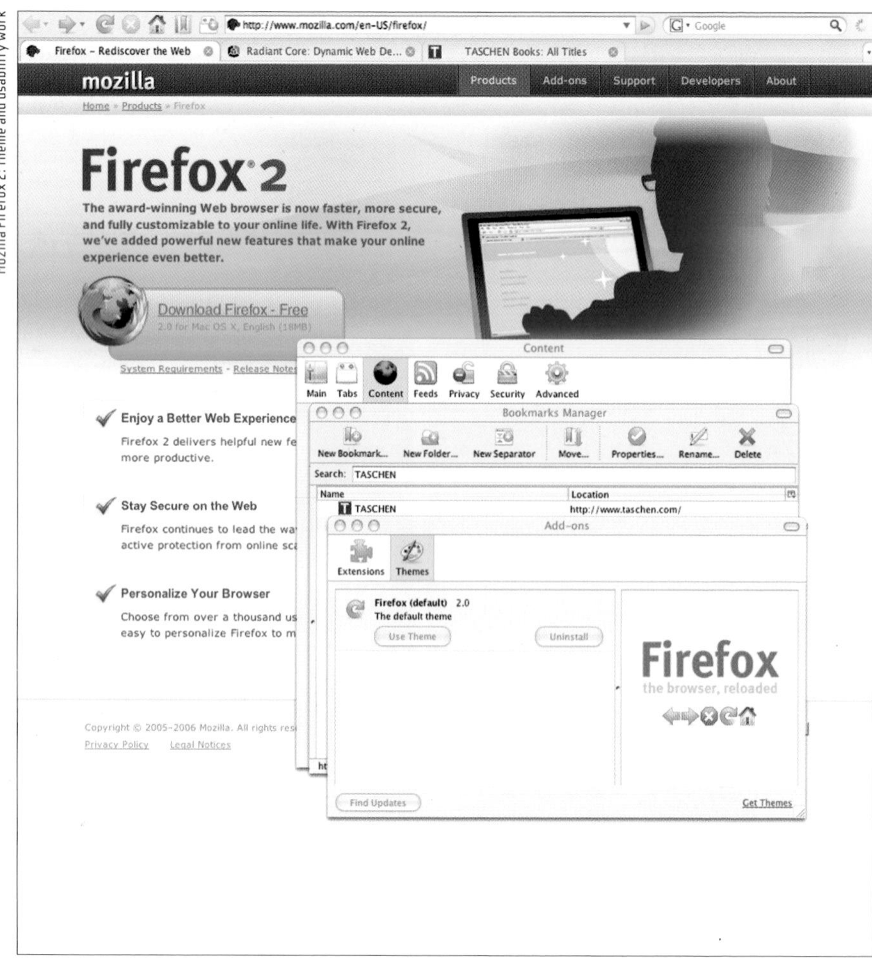

Mozilla Firefox 2: theme and usability work

Location

Radiant Core, Inc.
171 East Liberty St., Suite 253
Toronto, ON, M6K 3P6
Canada
<sales@radiantcore.com>

Team

1 President, 1 Vice-President/Technology, 1 Creative Director, 3 Developers, 1 Project/QA Manager.

Nous créons des sites Internet qui construisent l'activité de nos clients. Nos projets sont travaillés avec soin et permettent d'avoir l'esprit tranquille par le biais de la fondation Plate-forme de gestion des sites Internet. Et nous sommes vraiment supers ! /// **Wir bauen Webseiten, mit denen unseren Kunden ihren Umsatz steigern können. Unsere Projekte werden in echter Handarbeit individuell auf jeden unserer Kunden zugeschnitten. Außerdem bieten wir unseren Kunden mit unserer Foundation Website Management Platform einen besonderen Service. Wir sind wirklich gut - probieren Sie uns aus!**

www.agoracom.com

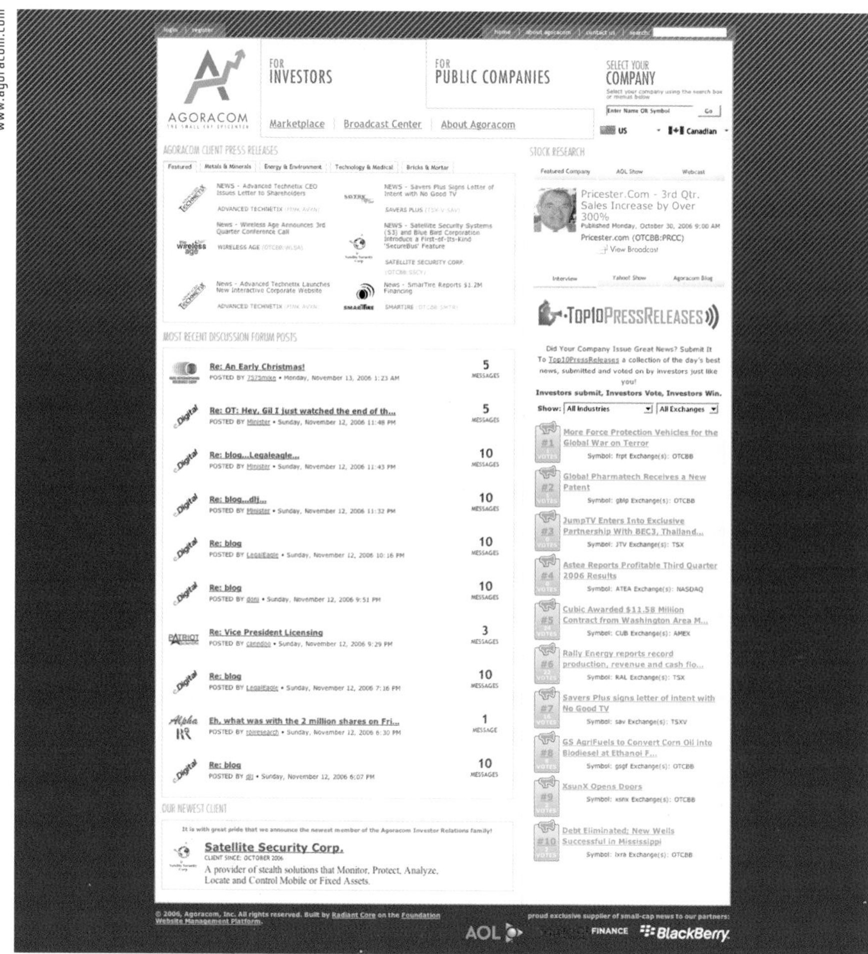

Clients

Mozilla Corporation, Kraft, Clorox, Bacardi, Symantec, Scott Paper, Brookfield Homes, Foxy Originals, Agoracom, TargetVacations.ca.

Awards

Ontario Home Builders Association (Best Internet Website), CNET Editor's Choice Award, PC Magazine Editor's Choice Award.

RAISE MEDIA

ROMANIA

www.raise-media.com

since 2004

Mission

We are a grown up agency providing our clients with unique products that are different from your every day websites. A team of professionals working with care, determination and consideration, focuson putting their full talent, energy and expertise into each project.

www.onestopconcept.com

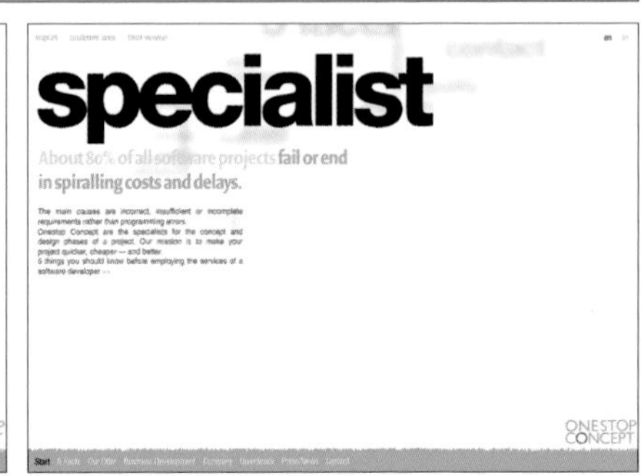

Location

Raise Media
300042 Timisoara
Romania
Bd Take Ionescu 44 ap 14
<contact@raise-media.com>

Team

1 Project Manager, 1 Designer, 1 Developer and collaborators.

Notre agence adulte fournit à nos clients des sites exceptionnels et différents des sites habituels, grâce à notre équipe de professionnels qui travaillent avec le plus grand soin et mettent à contribution tout leur talent, leur énergie et leur expertise dans chaque projet. /// **Wir sind eine erfahrene Agentur und bieten unseren Kunden einzigartige Webseiten, die sich vom Mainstream abheben. Für jedes neue Projekt wirft unser kreatives und kompetentes Team sein ganzes Können in die Waagschale und behält dabei immer genau die Ziele unserer Kunden im Auge.**

www.hotelsavoy-tm.com

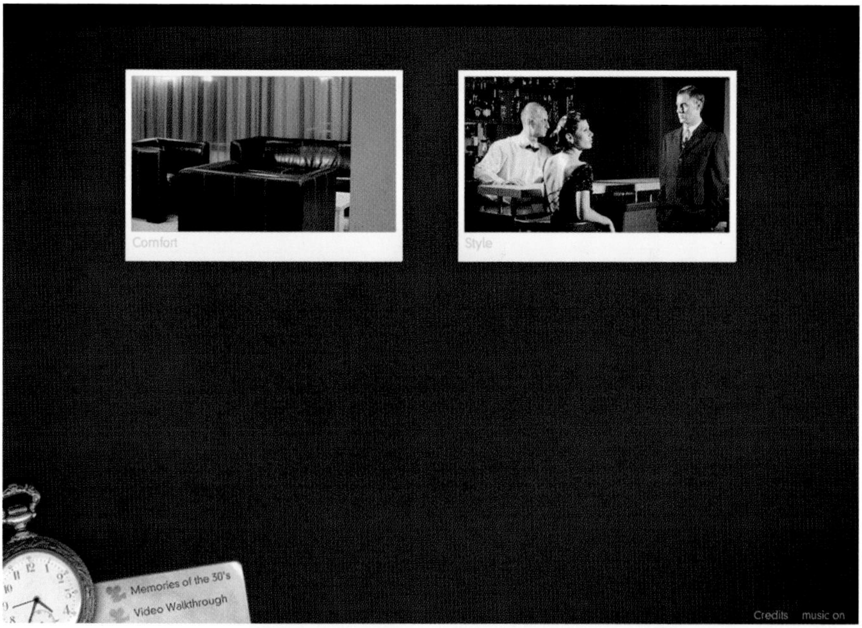

Clients

Lafarge Cements, OneStop Concept, Andreescu and Gaivoronski Associated Architects, Savoy Hotel, Rankine Jewellery, City Business Centre Timisoara, Trio Katharsis.

Awards

FWA, Internet TINY Awards, British Council (Interactive Work), Fcukstar, and more.

RESN

NEW ZEALAND

www.resn.co.nz

since 2004

Mission

RESN aims to inspire people, clients, our friends and ourselves. To create well-crafted websites, engaging online experiences, fun games, memorable visuals, and to shock, surprise, please and humour people.

www.resn.co.nz

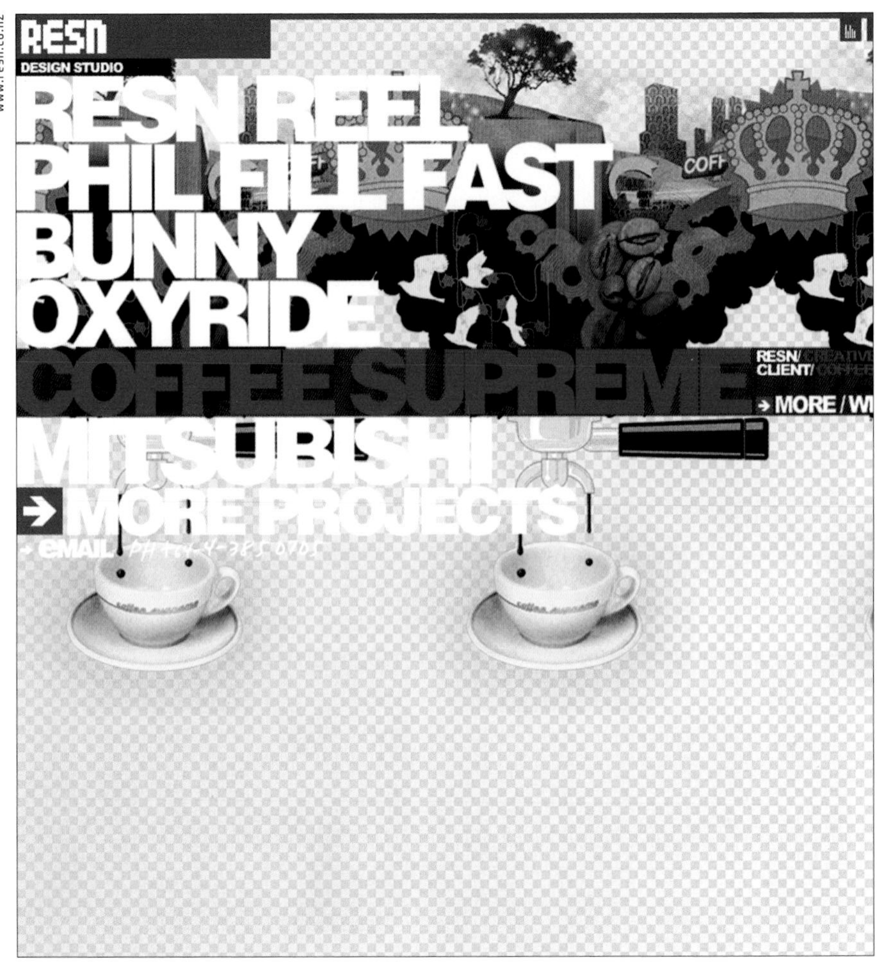

Location

RESN
Te Aro, Wellington
New Zealand
<hello@resn.co.nz>

Team

2 Creative Directors/Producers, 2 Designers, 1 Illustrator/ Animator, 2 Developers.

RESN souhaite inspirer les personnes, les clients, nos amis et nous-mêmes, pour créer des sites soignés, des expériences Internet intéressantes, des jeux amusants, des bandes images mémorables, et pour choquer, surprendre, plaire et amuser. /// **Wir bei RESN möchten Menschen, Kunden, Freunde und auch uns selbst inspirieren. Wir möchten erstklassige Webseiten machen, aufregende Online-Erlebnisse vermitteln, unterhaltsame Spiele bieten und Visuals liefern, die in Erinnerung bleiben; wir möchten die Menschen überraschen, sie manchmal schockieren, sie gern auch zum Lachen bringen und sie dabei immer unterhalten.**

www.theblackseeds.com

http://play.resn.co.nz

www.3ccd.co.nz

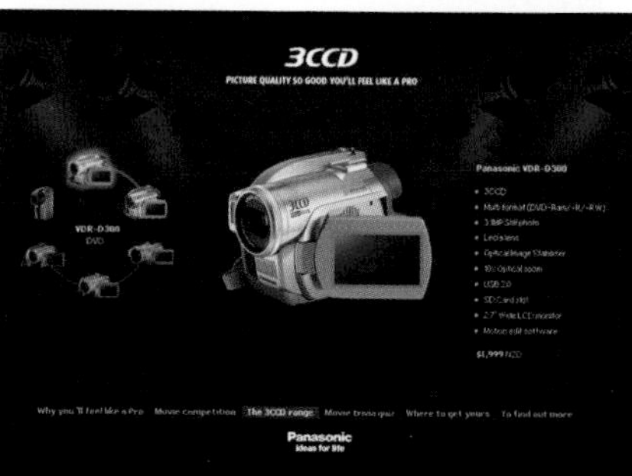

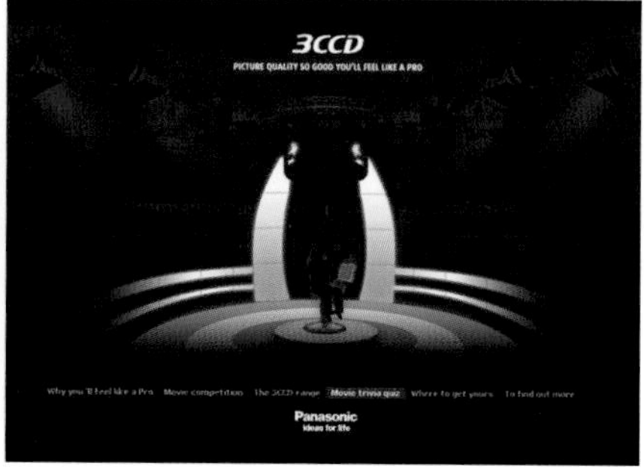

Clients
Panasonic, Mitsubishi, Clemenger BBDO, Naked, Coffee Supreme, Victoria University School of Design, Musicians, Ourselves

Awards
Semi Permanent Auckland and Sydney 2005, Webby Awards, DOPE.

RICE 5

HONG KONG

www.rice5.com

since 2003

Mission

Be fun! /// Soyons drôles ! /// Am wichtigsten ist Spaß!

www.rice5.com

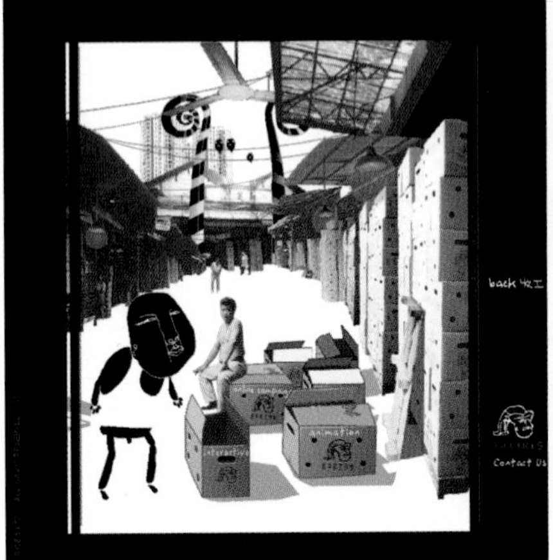

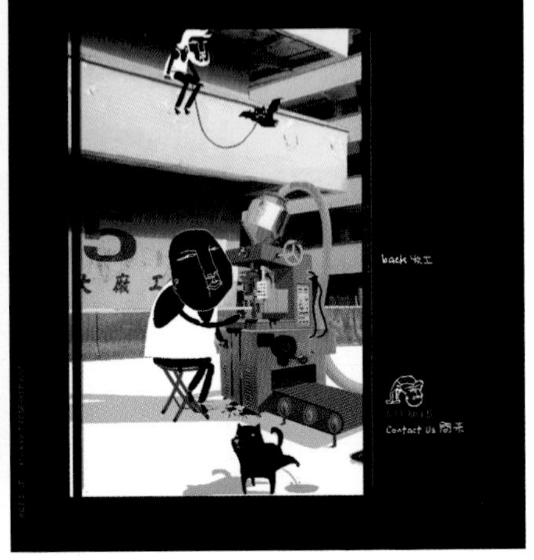

Location

Rice 5
Unit 906, Eastern Harbour Centre, 28 Hoi Chak Street
QuarryBay
Hong Kong
<andrewlee@rice5.com>

Team

1 Creative Director, 2 Art Directors, 3 Designers, 4 Technical Developers, 5 Project Managers.

www.calbeefun.com

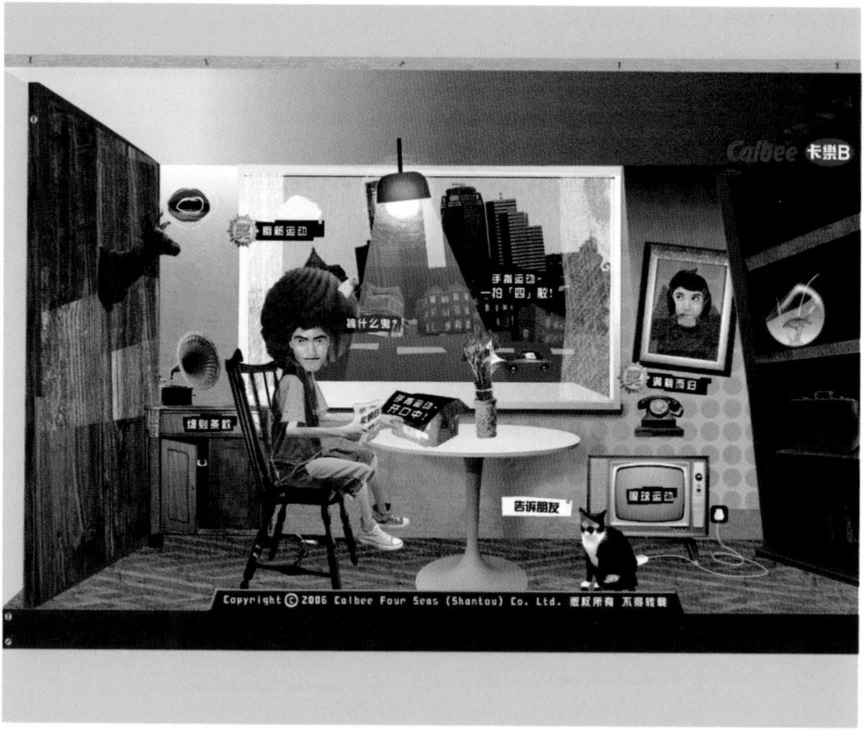

Calbee 卡樂B
告诉朋友
Copyright © 2006 Calbee Four Seas (Shantou) Co. Ltd. 版权所有 不得转载

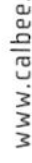

www.calbee.hk

Go!Go!Gold!大抽獎
Calbee 卡樂B
Send俾朋友睇
得獎結果
我想抽!

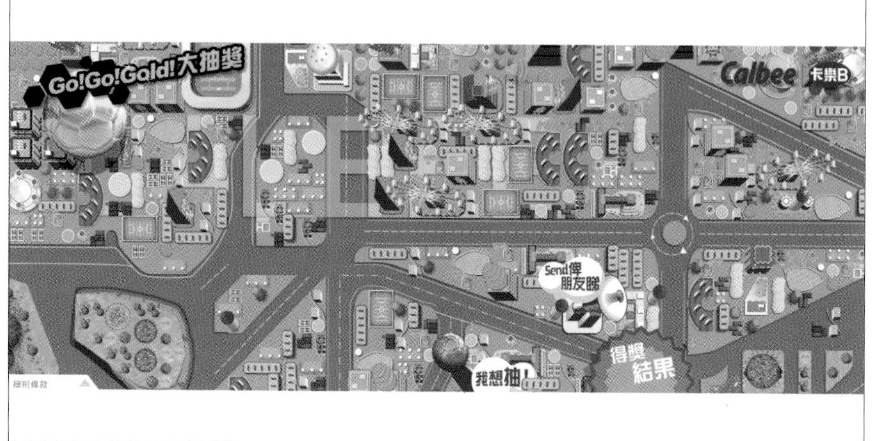

Clients

adidas HK, adidas regional.

Awards

FWA, Interactive & Direct Awards (iDA) The HK4As, HKDA Award.

SAATCHI & SAATCHI INTERACTIVE WORLDWIDE

www.saatchi.com

since 1998

Mission

We know people have become their own creators, editors and broadcasters of content. They want to be part of the creative process, connect with others and control the tidalwave of information. We believe in the power of Sisomo: sight, sound and motion. We create using interactive and emerging technologies as threads to weave together an integrated solution

www.customseries.com.br

Location

Saatchi & Saatchi Worldwide – Interactive

USA (NYC, LA, TeamOne), Belgium, Italy, Germany, Israel, Brazil, Mexico, Australia, New Zealand, Singapore, China, France, UK, South Africa, Holland.

Tom Eslinger <tom.eslinger@saatchila.com>

Team

1 WW Creative Dir., 19 Creative Dir., 14 Strategy Dir., 20+ Online Media Planners (LA/TeamOne), 17 Creative Leads, 16 Copywriters, 28 Creative Technologists, 30 Flash Progr., 62 Graphics Designers, 28 Producers, 9 3d Artists, 6 Mobile Specialists, 36 Account Exec., 16 Gen. Managers, global partnership with the Hyperfactory.

Nous connaissons des personnes qui sont devenues les propres créateurs, responsables de l'édition et diffuseurs de leurs sites. Elles veulent participer au processus de création, être en relation avec d'autres personnes et contrôler l'immense vague d'informations. Nous croyons au pouvoir de Vusomo : vue, son et mouvement. Nous créons au moyen de technologies interactives émergentes pour tisser une solution intégrée. /// Es gibt inzwischen sehr viele Leute, die das Internet auf kreative Weise nutzen, um eigene Texte und auch Audio- oder Video-Content hinein zu stellen. Sie wollen am kreativen Prozess teilhaben, zu anderen Leuten Verbindung aufnehmen und die Informationsüberflutung auf ihre Weise steuern. Wir glauben an die Kraft von sisomo: sight (Bild), sound (Ton) und motion (Bewegung). Für unsere Kreationen nutzen wir modernste interaktive Technologien, die zu einer integrierten Lösung bündeln.

www.toyota.com/yaris

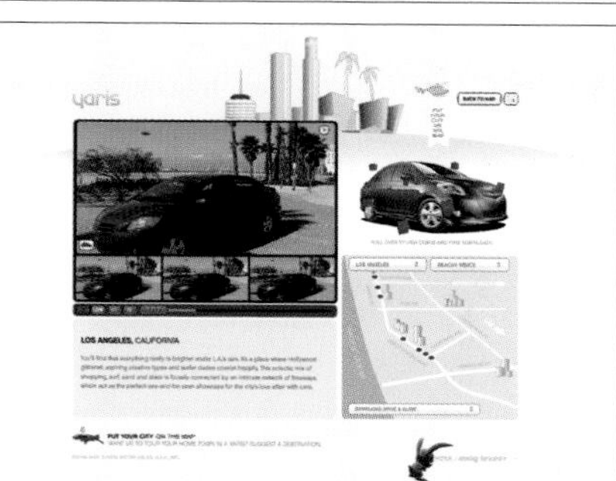

Clients

Toyota, Procter & Gamble, Lexus, Nike, T-Mobile, Guinness, Hewlett Packard, ESPN, Sony Pictures, Emirates, Visa, Sony Ericsson, Telecom Italia, Singapore Navy, NZ Army, Telecom NZ, Westpac, 42 Below Vodka, Royal Navy, Dr. Martens, Tiger Beer, Fox Sports, United Nations, Double A Paper, Skol Beer, Toshiba.

Awards

Cannes International Advertising Festival, D&AD, One Show Interactive, CLIOs, Effies, YoungGuns, Eurobest, NY Festivals, London International Advertising Awards, Future Marketing Awards, IAAA, Webbies, Communication Arts.

SENNEP

UK

www.sennep.com

since 2003

Mission

To infuse design and technology with a human element and create experiences which capture and expand upon our clients' visions. /// Conférer au design et à la technologie un élément humain et créer des expériences qui captent la vision de nos clients et vont au-delà. /// Wir machen Design und Technologie mit einem Hauch von Menschlichkeit lebendig, um Erlebniswelten zu kreieren, die die Vorstellungskraft unserer Kunden sprengen.

www.bowwowlondon.com

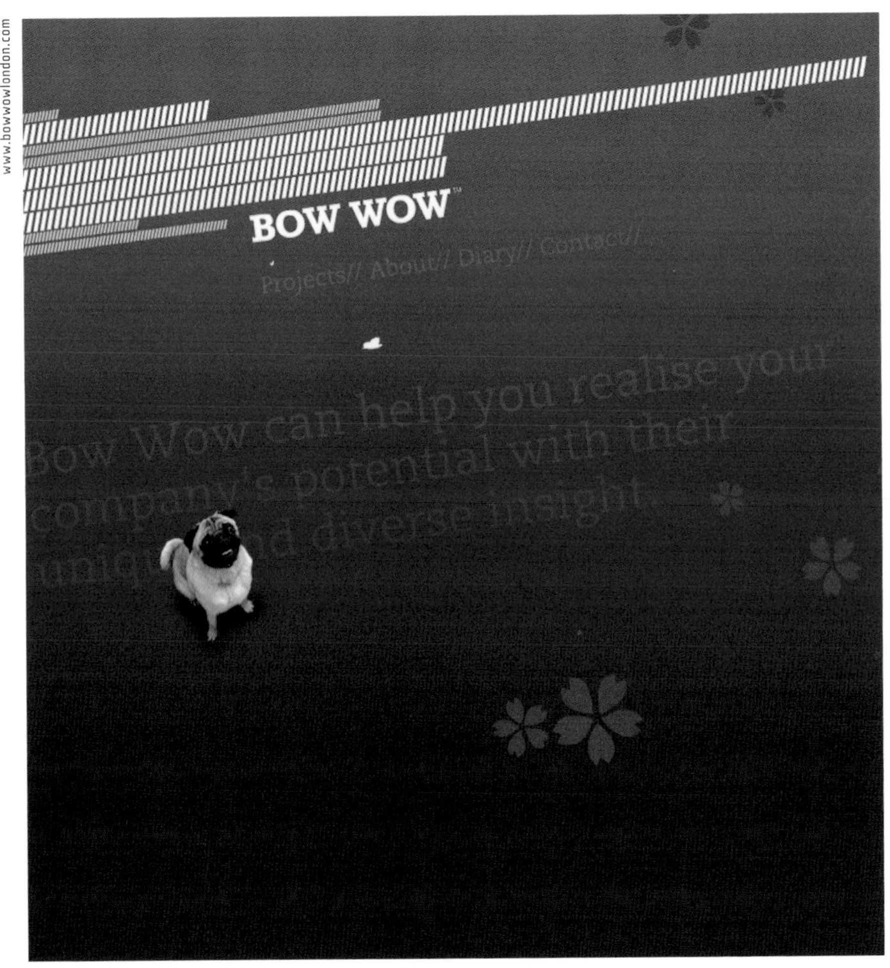

Location

Sennep
6 Disney Street
London, SE1 1JF
United Kingdom
<info@sennep.com>

Team

3 Creative Partners, 1 Programmer, 1 Project Manager.

www.jacksons-of-piccadilly.com

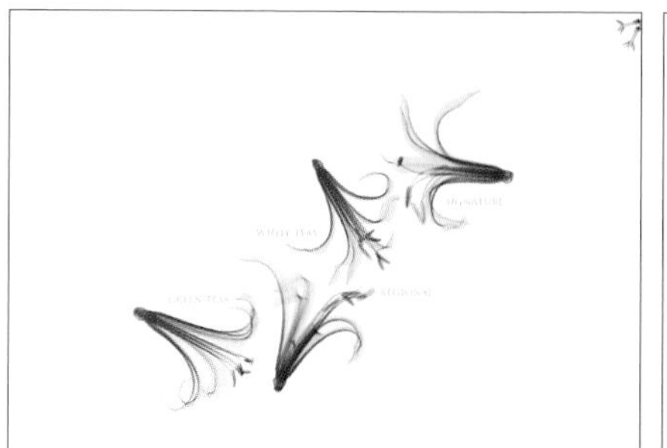

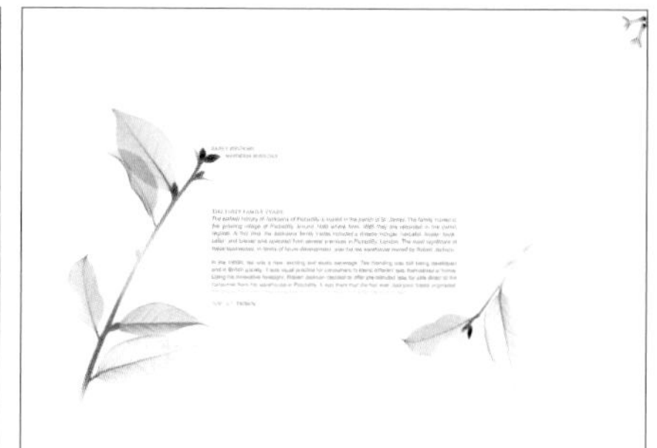

www.suso100.com

Clients

Sky, Horlicks, onedotzero, rpm, Norwegian Embassy, Motorola, Fallen Vodka, SUSO Drinks, Jacksons of Piccadilly.

Awards

D&AD, Design Week (Commended), Marketing Week Awards (Winner), New York Festivals (World Medal), Webby Awards, FWA.

SEPTIME CREATION

FRANCE

www.septime-creation.com

since 2001

Mission

Septime is made up of people keen on web design evolution and graphic arts in general. We aimto create professional multimedia products by combining originality and efficiency. Our goal is to create new experiences for the user, new trips, and explorations of the creative potential that the creation and development tools offer us.

www.billabongjrpro.com

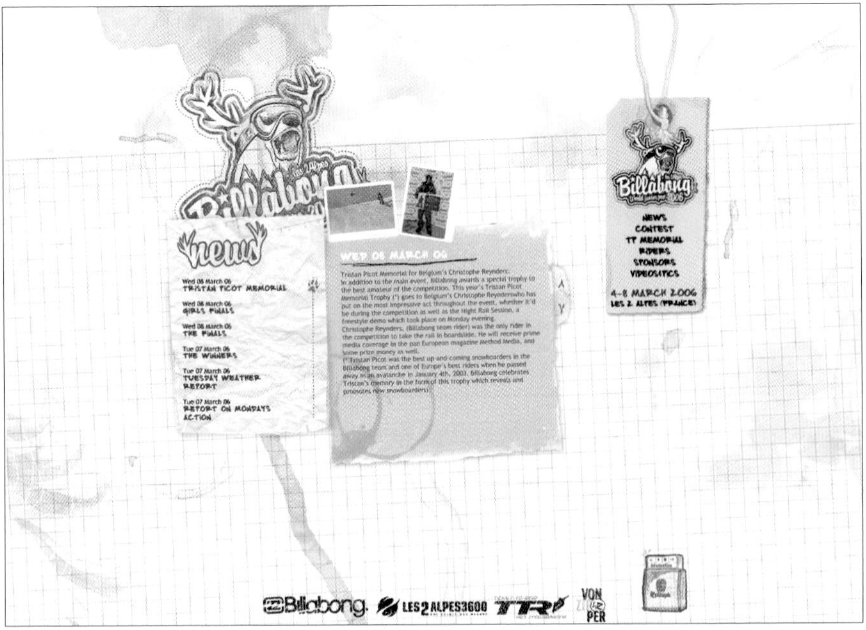

Location

Septime Creation
6, boulevard Gambetta
12000 Rodez
France
<info@septime.net>

Team

1 Creative Director, 1 Art Director & Flash Programmer, 1 2d/3d Designer, 2 Programmers, 1 Assistant Manager.

Septime se compose de personnes intéressées par l'évolution du design Web et des arts graphiques en général. Nous cherchons à créer des produits multimédias professionnels en associant l'originalité et l'efficacité. Notre objectif : créer de nouvelles expériences pour l'utilisateur, de nouveaux voyages et explorer le potentiel créatif des outils de création et de développement. /// **Septime besteht aus** einem Team von Leuten, die sich der Mission verschrieben haben, die Evolution von Webdesign und Grafikdesign voranzutreiben. Wir kreieren professionelle Multimediaprodukte, die Einzigartigkeit und Effizienz in sich vereinen. Wir wollen unser kreatives Potenzial mithilfe der neuesten Technologien voll ausschöpfen, um die User in neue virtuelle Welten zu entführen und ihnen einprägsame Erlebnisse zu vermitteln.

www.freeasadog.com

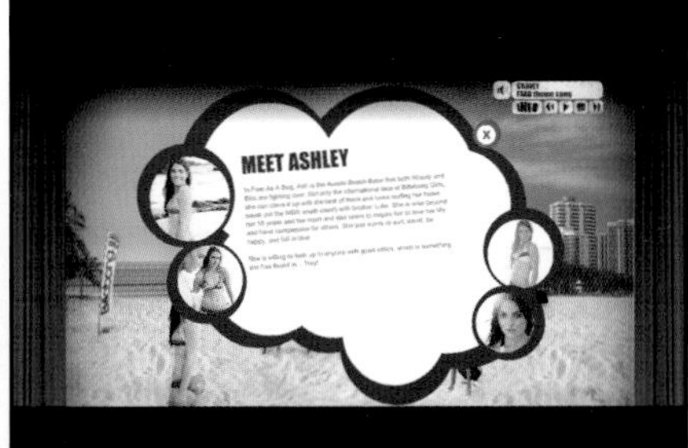

http://thesettlers.uk.ubi.com/settlers2

Clients

Ubisoft Europe, Billabong Europe, Capy Joulia Architects, Fondation du Patrimoine.

Awards

FWA, DOPE, ITA, French and fresh, NewWebPick.

SHOP AROUND

THE NETHERLANDS

www.shop-around.nl

since 1997

Mission

Shop Around is a production company whose activities span the fields of internet, motion design (TV) and print. Our work is characterized by it's contemporary style. /// Shop Around est une société de production dont les activités englobent Internet, le design de mouvement (TV) et l'impression. Notre travail se caractérise par un style contemporain. /// Shop Around ist eine Produktionsgesellschaft, deren Aktivitäten die Bereiche Internet, Motion Design (TV) und Print abdecken. Unsere Arbeit ist vor allem eins: sehr modern.

www.willemwever.nl

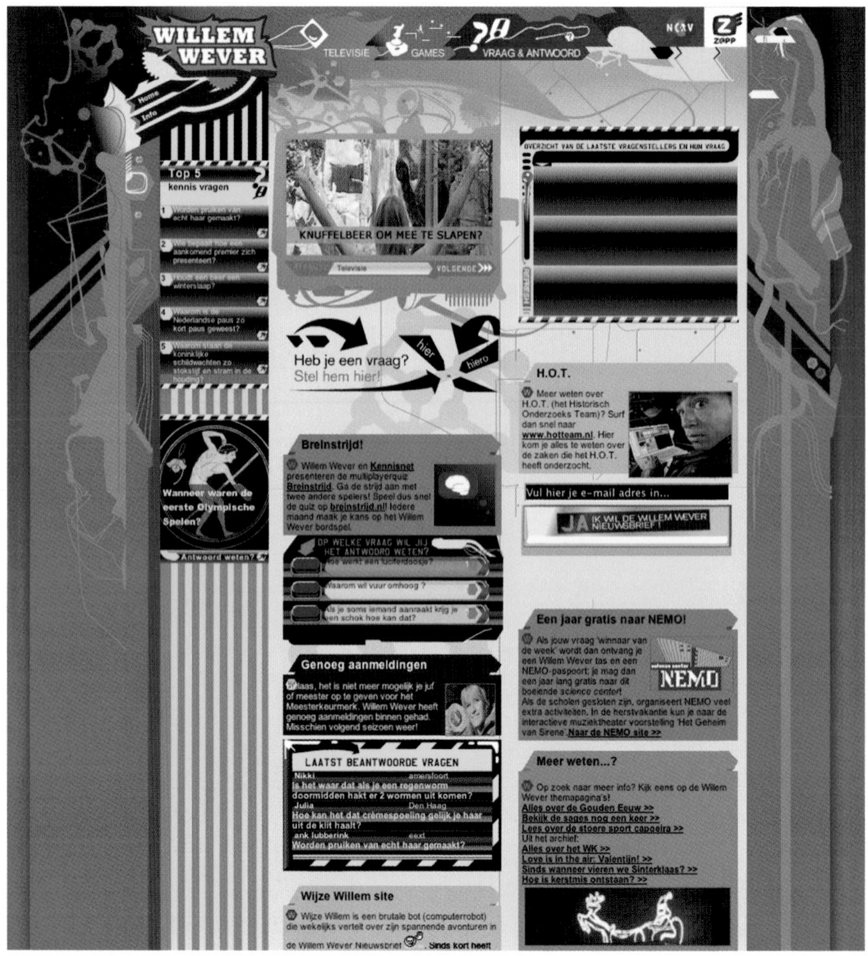

Location

Shop Around
Voorhaven 19
3025 HC Rotterdam
The Netherlands
<info@shop-around.nl>

Team

1 General Director, 1 Creative Director, 3 Designers, 1 Animator, 1 Programmer, 2 Project Managers, 2 Sales Managers.

www.rails.nl

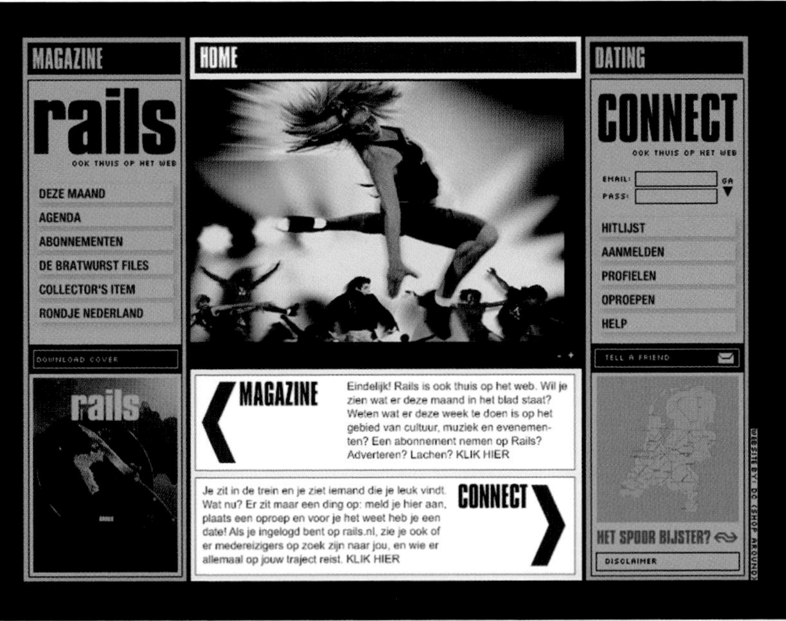
MAGAZINE
HOME
DATING
rails
OOK THUIS OP HET WEB
DEZE MAAND
AGENDA
ABONNEMENTEN
DE BRATWURST FILES
COLLECTOR'S ITEM
RONDJE NEDERLAND
DOWNLOAD COVER
CONNECT
OOK THUIS OP HET WEB
EMAIL:
PASS:
GA
HITLIJST
AANMELDEN
PROFIELEN
OPROEPEN
HELP
TELL A FRIEND
MAGAZINE
Eindelijk! Rails is ook thuis op het web. Wil je zien wat er deze maand in het blad staat? Weten wat er deze week te doen is op het gebied van cultuur, muziek en evenementen? Een abonnement nemen op Rails? Adverteren? Lachen? KLIK HIER
CONNECT
Je zit in de trein en je ziet iemand die je leuk vindt. Wat nu? Er zit maar een ding op: meld je hier aan, plaats een oproep en voor je het weet heb je een date! Als je ingelogd bent op rails.nl, zie je ook of er medereizigers op zoek zijn naar jou, en wie er allemaal op jouw traject reist. KLIK HIER
HET SPOOR BIJSTER?
DISCLAIMER

www.hansvanbentem.nl

HANS VAN BENTEM

news
works
resume
links
contact

Clients

Advertising Agencies: FHV/BBDO, TBWA, DDB, Ogilvy, etc.
MTV networks, Rails , FFWD Heineken Dance Parade.

SITESEEING

GERMANY

www.siteseeing.de

since 2002

Mission

SiteSeeing is an interactive media agency. Our work is characterized by coherent structures, innovative user guidance and a distinct design. Our approach ensures that every new project is an experience for the viewer.

www.victorbyhasselblad.com

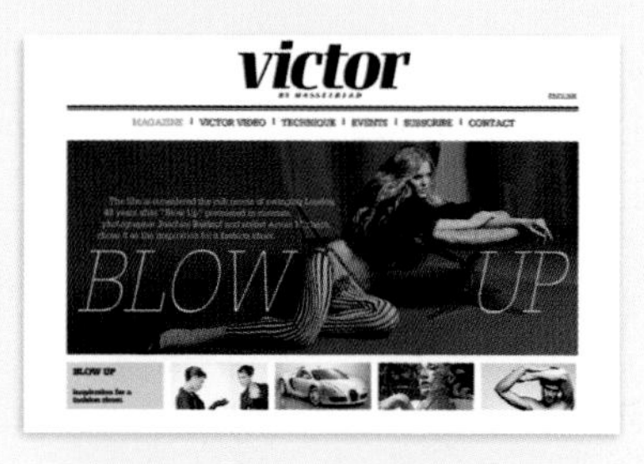

Location

SiteSeeing Interaktive Medien
Bernhard-Nocht-Str. 89-91
20359 Hamburg
Germany
<info@siteseeing.de>

Team

1 Managing Director, 1 Technical Director, 2 Designers, 2 Programmers.

SiteSeeing est une agence média interactive qui se caractérise par des structures cohérentes, des conseils aux utilisateurs et un design instinctif. Nous faisons en sorte que chaque projet soit une expérience pour le visiteur. /// SiteSeeing ist eine Agentur für interaktive Medien. Merkmale unserer Arbeit sind verständliche Strukturen, innovative Benutzerführung und eine klare Gestaltung. Durch diese besondere Herangehensweise machen wir jedes Projekt zu einem Erlebnis und wecken Neugier beim Betrachter.

www.izaio.de

www.arminmorbach.de

Morbach

Hair & Make Up Artist, Producer,
Publisher TUSH Magazine

Contact . Piano on/off

Clients

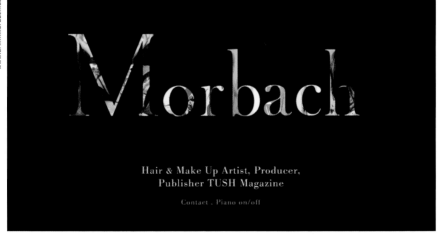

Hasselblad A/S, Hamburger Hochbahn AG, Squint Magazine, TUSH Magazine, found Fotografen, KLEIN PHOTOGRAPHEN, Izaio Models, Characters Models, HIGH-DEF Technology, Siemens, Armin Morbach, sticky jam.

Awards

ADC Berlin, Flash Film Festival New York (Winner), 2 Jahrbuch der Werbung, Germany Republic Design Prize (nomination), FWA.

SMILING WOLF

UK

www.smilingwolf.co.uk

since 2000

Mission

We are a team of problem solving designers. We don't really have a concise philosophy or snappy mission statement, and if we did we would probably change our mind next week... instead, we like to look at each project in a unique way, without the restriction of dogma – allowing us to be truly free to innovate.

www.baabar.co.uk

Location

Smiling Wolf
62 Hope Street
Liverpool, L1 9BZ
United Kingdom
<howl@smilingwolf.co.uk>

Team

1 Creative Director, 1 Graphic Designer/Illustrator, 1 Graphic Designer/Moving Image Designer, 1 Flash Programmer/Designer, 1 Digital Technologist/database/CMS Programmer.

Nous sommes une équipe de designers chargés de résoudre des problèmes. Nous n'avons pas vraiment de philosophie précise ni de phrase résumant notre mission avec du punch. Si nous en avions, nous changerions probablement d'avis chaque semaine. Nous nous consacrons plutôt à analyser chaque projet de façon unique, sans être limités par un dogme, et nous pouvons ainsi être totalement libres d'innover. ///

Unser Designerteam ist auf Problemlösungen spezialisiert. Wir haben keine in Stein gemeißelte Philosophie und auch kein prägnant formuliertes Mission Statement – und selbst wenn wir eins hätten, würden wir es wahrscheinlich schon nächste Woche wieder in den Papierkorb werfen... Stattdessen betrachten wir lieber jedes neues Projekt aus einer einzigartigen Perspektive, ohne uns durch Dogmen einschränken zu lassen – und das gibt uns die Freiheit, wirklich innovativ zu sein.

www.unionnorth.co.uk

UNION NORTH

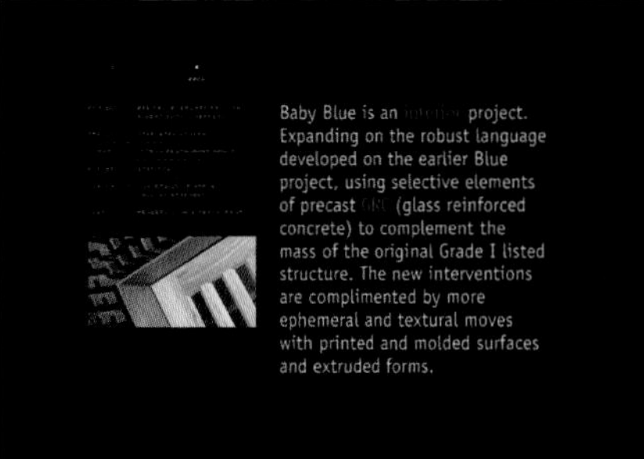

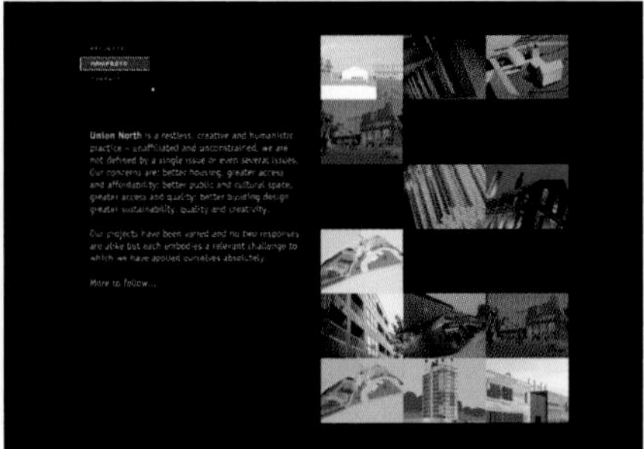

www.thekooks.co.uk

Clients

Virgin EMI, Sony/BMG/Red Ink Music, Union North, Baa Bar Ltd, Foundation for Art and Creative Technology (FACT), British Council – Brussels.

Awards

Roses Design Awards, Roses Advertising Awards, Best Website TBC, London International Advertising and Design Awards (Best interactive education).

SOAP CREATIVE

AUSTRALIA

www.soapcreative.com

since 2002

Mission

Our mission is to produce world class online creative work right here in Australia. /// Notre mission : faire un incomparable travail Internet créatif en Australie. /// Wir haben uns zum Ziel gesetzt, hier in Australien kreative Onlinelösungen von Weltklasseformat zu produzieren.

www.beerleaguethemovie.com/games/index.html

Location

Soap Creative
Suite 4.06, 22-36 Smail St
Ultimo, NSW 2007
Australia
<crew@soap.com.au>

Team

2 Creative Directors, 2 Art Directors, 4 Designers, 1 Technical Director, 5 Developers, 1 Executive Producer, 3 Producers.

http://therealaustralia.co.uk

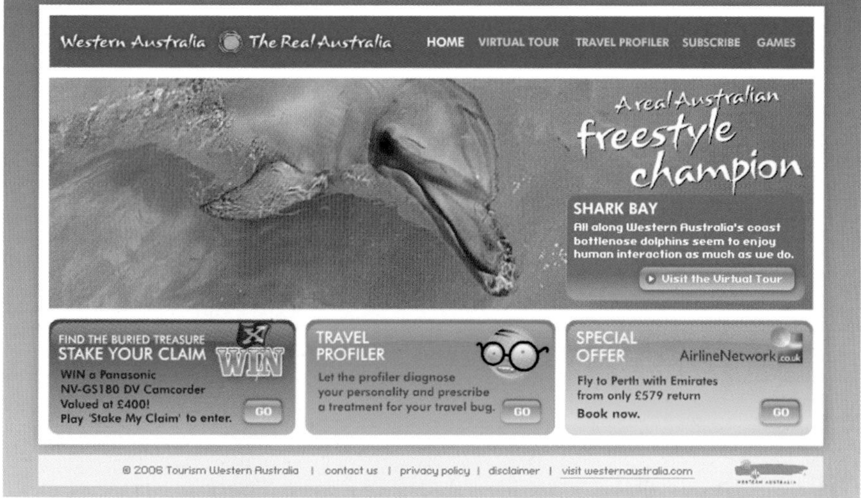

Clients

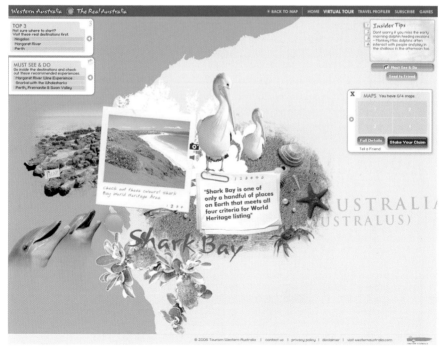

20th Century Fox, 3 Mobile UK, 3 Mobile AUS, Mambo, Austereo, EMI, Telstra, Foxtel, Yahoo! Australia.

Awards

Direct Marketing Awards, Internet Awards, AWARD (Australian Writers & Art Directors), Desktop Create Award, Golden Award of Montreaux, Horizon Interactive.

SOLEIL NOIR

FRANCE

www.soleilnoir.net

since 2000

Mission

Soleil Noir is an independent studio specialized in the creation of Internet websites with strong strategic and creative reflexions. Its business is to position, support and develop companies on the Internet.

www.soleilnoir.net

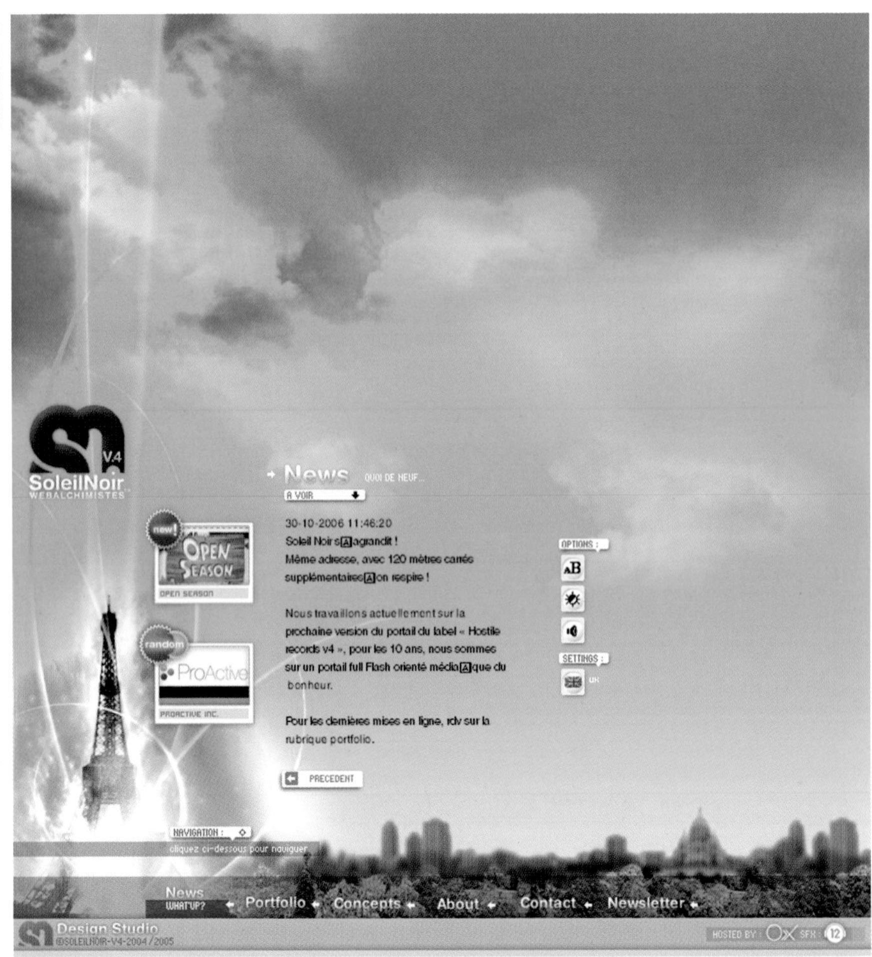

Location

Soleil Noir
13, rue Greneta
75003 Paris
France
<contact@soleilnoir.net>

Team

3 Projects Managers, 2 Art Directors, 3 Designers, 3 Programmers.

Soleil Noir est un studio indépendant spécialisé dans la création de sites Internet reflétant un univers stratégique et créatif. Son activité consiste à positionner, aider et développer des entreprises sur Internet. /// **Soleil Noir ist ein unabhängiges Studio, das auf die Produktion von Internetseiten mit Fokus auf kreativen und strategischen Gesichtspunkten spezialisiert ist. Unser Angebot umfasst die Positionierung, die Entwicklung und den Support von Internetpräsenzen für Unternehmen.**

www.girlattitude.com

www.splintercell.com

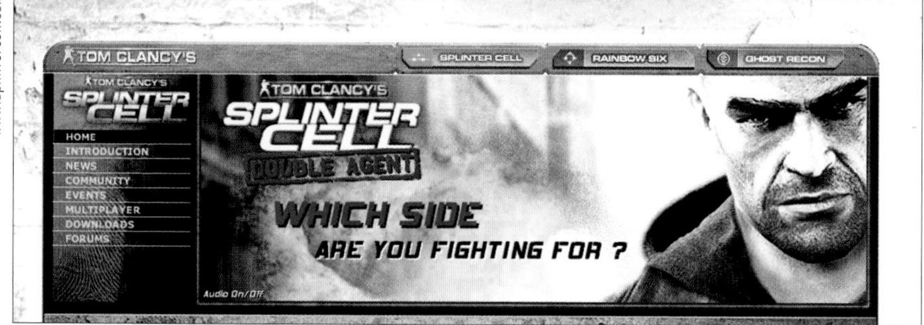

Clients

The Walt Disney Company, EMI Music, Ubisoft, Samsung, Laboratoire Vichy, France Télévisions, CanalSat, ...

Awards

FWA, Macromedia, Bombshock.

SONIC BOOM CREATIVE MEDIA CANADA

www.sonicboom.com since 1998

Mission

Sonic Boom is comprised of people who have a passion for ideas. We are a diverse and experienced team of clear-thinking, creative individuals who share an immense enthusiasm for the work we do. We deliver innovative interactive programs by providing smart strategy, creativity and technology – all providing measurable results for our clients.

www.siriuscanada.ca

Location

Sonic Boom Creative Media Inc.
67 Mowat Avenue, Suite 335
Toronto, Ontario, M6K3E3
Canada
Alex Pejcic, President, Co-Founder <a.pejcic@sonicboom.com>

Team

1 Creative Director, 1 Art Director, 2 Designers, 1 Flash Developer, 3 Interactive Developers, 1 Information Architect, 3 Programmers, 1 Strategist, 02 Project Managers.

Sonic Boom emploie des personnes passionnées par les idées. Les membres de notre équipe diverse et expérimentée, qui sont lucides et créatifs, partagent leur enthousiasme pour le travail. Nous fournissons des programmes interactifs originaux au moyen d'une stratégie intelligente, de créativité et de technologie, et nos clients obtiennent ainsi des résultats mesurables. /// **Sonic Boom besteht aus Leuten mit einer gemeinsamen Leidenschaft für Ideen. Wir sind ein erfahrenes und sehr vielseitiges Team aus kreativen Denkern, und was uns verbindet, ist die große Begeisterung für unsere gemeinsame Arbeit. Wir liefern innovative interaktive Lösungen, die sich durch smarte Strategie, Kreativität und Technologie auszeichnen und unseren Kunden messbare Resultate liefern.**

www.theadcc.ca

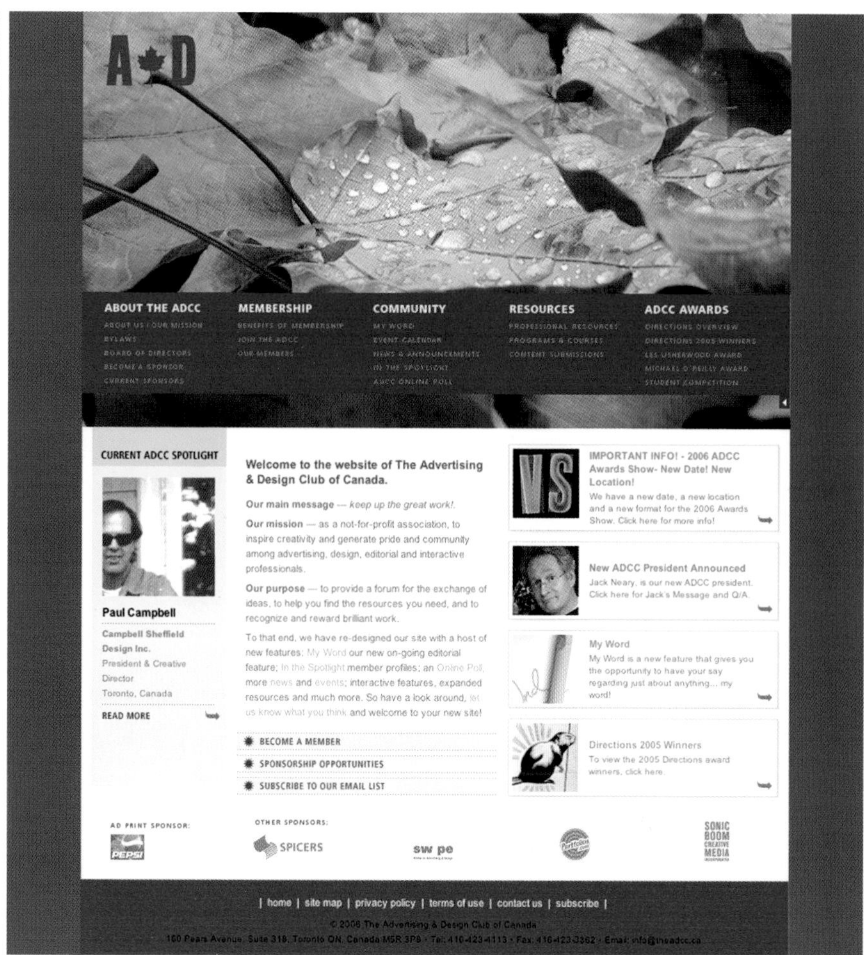

Clients

Bell Mobility, Citibank, Gillette, Harry Rosen, Honda, RBC Dexia, Sirius Satellite, Unilever.

Awards

Advertising & Design Club of Canada, Applied Arts, Communication Arts.

STARRING

SWEDEN

www.starring.se

since 1996

Mission

Starring is an interactive advertising agency. We offer trendsetting solutions in interactive communication. Our business concept is to help companies do things that give them something interesting to say. Our first aim is always to get the product/service to communicate with the target group, rather than having to communicate for the product or service itself.

www.sverigessamstavagar.se

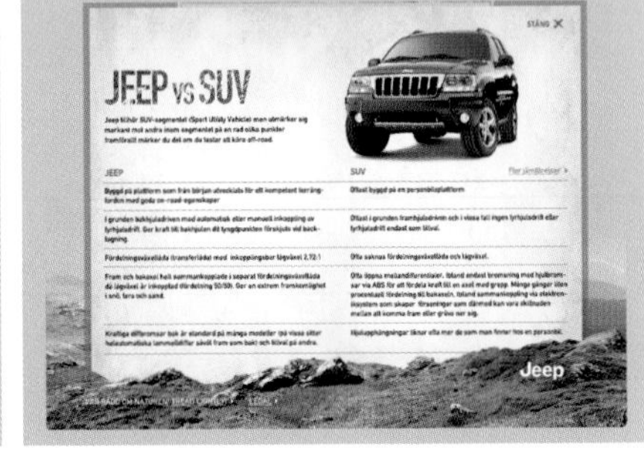

Location

Starring Ltd
Kungsgatan 6
111 43 Stockholm
Sweden
CG Neuman <cg@starring.se>

Team

1 CEO, 1 Creative Director, 6 Art Directors, 2 Designers, 4 Copywriters, 4 Flash Developers, 3 Web developers, 4 Account Managers, 5 Production Managers, 2 Technical Managers.

Starring est une agence de publicité interactive. Nous proposons des solutions innovatrices en matière de communication Web. Notre concept commercial consiste à aider les entreprises à réaliser des actions qui leur fournissent des éléments intéressants à transmettre. Notre principal objectif est de permettre la communication entre le produit/service et le groupe ciblé au lieu de nous charger directement de la communication du produit ou du service. /// **Starring ist eine Agentur für interaktive Werbung. Wir bieten Trend setzende Lösungen für interaktive Kommunikation. Unser Konzept: Wir helfen Unternehmen dabei, wirklich interessante Botschaften zu entwickeln und zu vermitteln. Unser vorrangiges Ziel besteht immer darin, zwischen dem Produkt/der Dienstleitung und der Zielgruppe eine Zwei-Wege-Kommunikation zu etablieren, statt für das Produkt oder die Dienstleistung direkt Werbung über die traditionelle Einweg-Kommunikation zu machen.**

www.hm.com

http://campaign.scania.com/v8

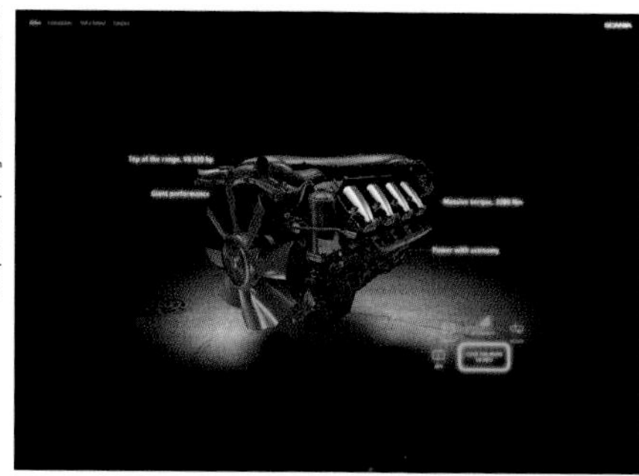

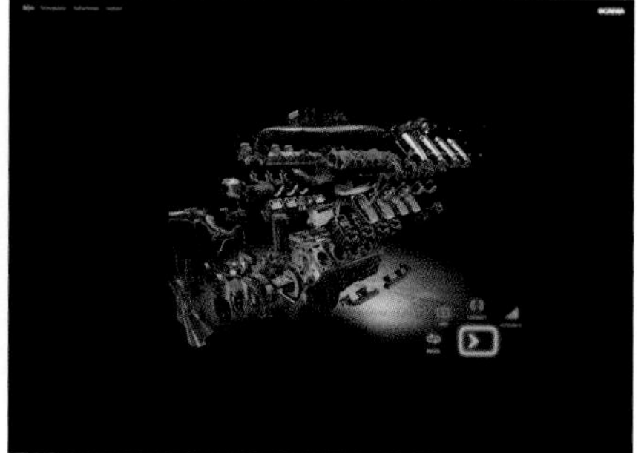

Clients

H&M, Jeep, Metro, ICA, Swedbank, Chrysler, Svenska Spel, Mercedes Benz, Spray, Durex, Björn Borg, Stadium, Allers Förlag, Scania, ...

Awards

Golden Egg (Golden/Silver), Silver Eurobest, Excellent Swedish Design Award, etc.

STRANGE CORPORATION

UK

www.strangecorp.com

since 2000

Mission

STRANGE is an award winning full service digital agency. We blend great creative with strong technical know-how to deliver campaigns that exceed our client's expectations. We work across all digital media to deliver the best results for our clients, putting their goals at the heart of our relationship.

www.punkyfish.com

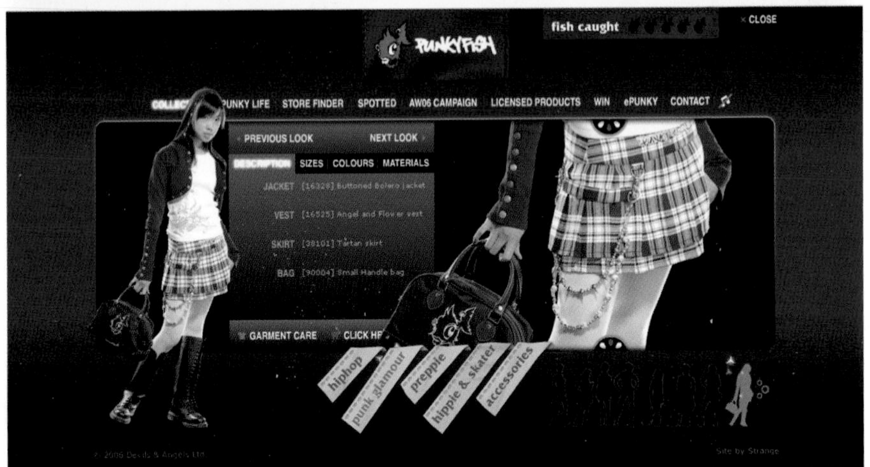

Location

STRANGE Corporation Ltd
11-15 Betterton Street, Covent Garden, London WC2H 9BP
Unit 4, The Old Generator House, Bourne Valley Road
Poole BH12 1DZ – United Kingdom
<results@strangecorp.com>

Team

1 Managing Director, 1 Creative Director, 1 Technical Director, 1 Business Director, 2 Account Managers, 1 Communications manager, 1 Marketing Manager, 2 Copywriters, 3 Designers, 3 Software Engineers, 3 Production Staff, 1 Music Production.

STRANGE est une agence numérique primée à service complet, qui mêle la créativité à un solide savoir-faire technique pour élaborer des campagnes répondant aux attentes de nos clients. Nous travaillons sur tous les médias numériques pour obtenir les meilleurs résultats pour nos clients et plaçons leurs objectifs au centre de nos actions. /// **STRANGE ist eine preisgekrönte Full-Service-Agentur für digitale Medien. Wir kombinieren immense Kreativität mit neuestem technischem Know-how, um Kampagnen zu liefern, die die Erwartungen unserer Kunden weit übertreffen. Wir arbeiten mit sämtlichen digitalen Medien, um unseren Kunden optimale Ergebnisse zu bieten, wobei die Ziele unserer Kunden im Mittelpunkt unserer Beziehung stehen.**

www.gear4.com

www.criminalclothing.com

Clients

PunkyFish, Criminal, Universal Music, Department of Health, Brittany Ferries, Kumala Wine, MKA-NYC, Gear4.

Awards

FWA, DOPE, lounge72.com, e-Creative, Website Design Awards, NewWebPick, PixelMakers, Bentley Awards.

STRUCK

USA

www.struckdesign.com

since 2003

Mission

When it comes to our interactive design, or any other design for that matter, our mantra comes down to two ideas. First, concept is king. Only on a firm conceptual foundation can exceptional design be built. Second, good relationships in turn produce good design.

www.shaveeverywhere.com

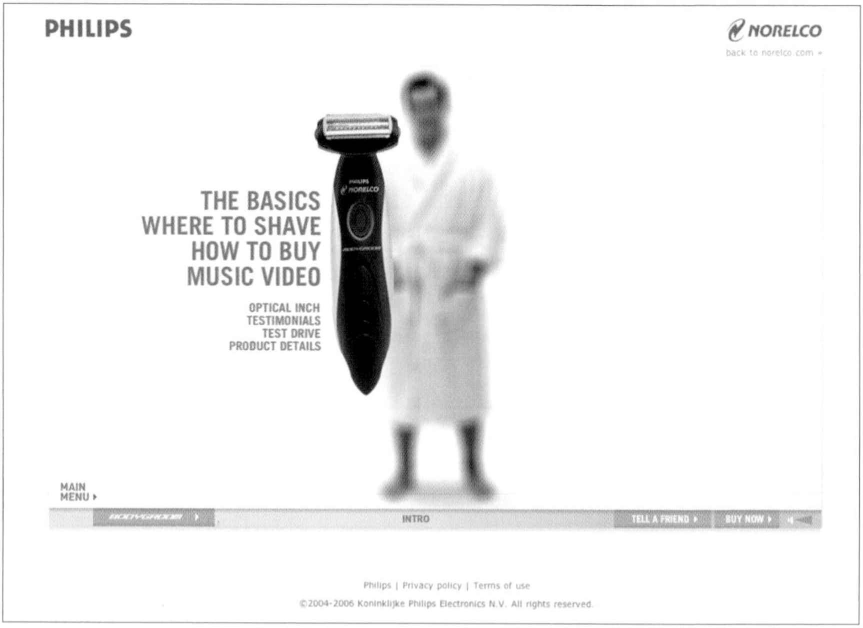

PHILIPS
NORELCO
back to norelco.com »
THE BASICS
WHERE TO SHAVE
HOW TO BUY
MUSIC VIDEO
OPTICAL INCH
TESTIMONIALS
TEST DRIVE
PRODUCT DETAILS
MAIN MENU ›
INTRO
TELL A FRIEND ›
BUY NOW ›
Philips | Privacy policy | Terms of use
©2004-2006 Koninklijke Philips Electronics N.V. All rights reserved.

PHILIPS
NORELCO
MAIN MENU ›
THE BASICS

PHILIPS
NORELCO
UNDERARMS
MAIN MENU ›
WHERE TO SHAVE

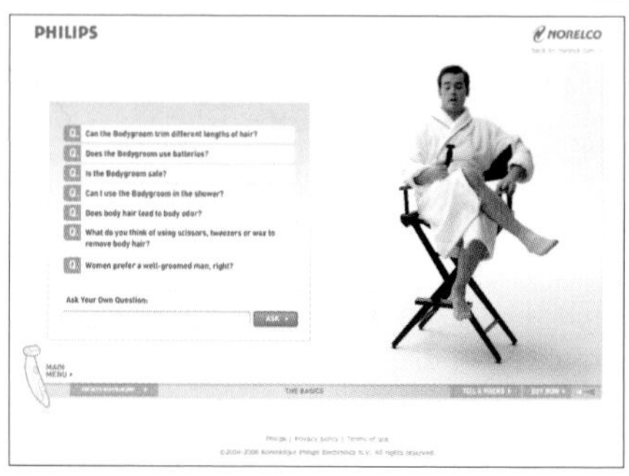

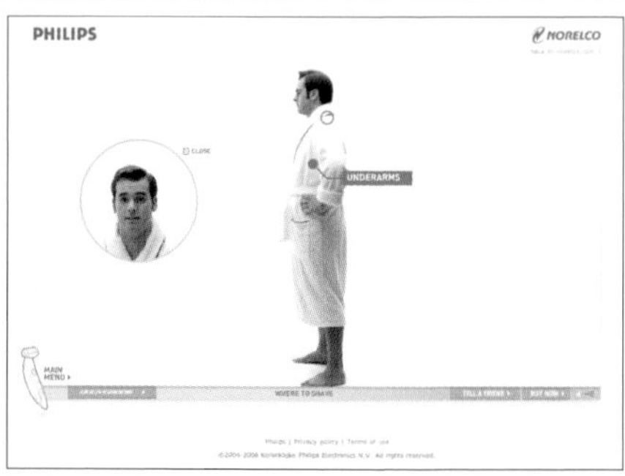

Location

Struck
157 Pierpont Avenue
Salt Lake City, UT 84101
USA
<info@struckdesign.com>

Team

1 Executive Design Director, 2 Design Directors, 7 Designers
4 Programmers, 4 Account Reps.

En matière de design Web ou de design de ce qui est important, notre leitmotiv se résume en deux idées. La première : le concept est roi, car seul un design exceptionnel peut être réalisé sur les fondements conceptuels d'une société. La seconde : de bonnes relations produisent à leur tour un bon design. /// Wenn es um interaktives Design geht – oder auch um andere Designarten – haben wir ein Mantra, das um zwei Ideen kreist. Erstens: Das Konzept ist König. Ein gut durchdachtes Konzept ist das Fundament für jedes herausragende Design. Zweitens: Der Kunde ist König. Denn gute Kundenbeziehungen fördern gutes Design.

http://10061.com

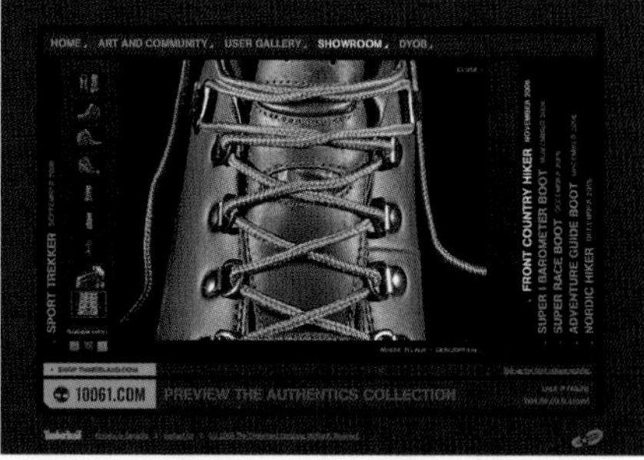

www.skylarnielsen.com

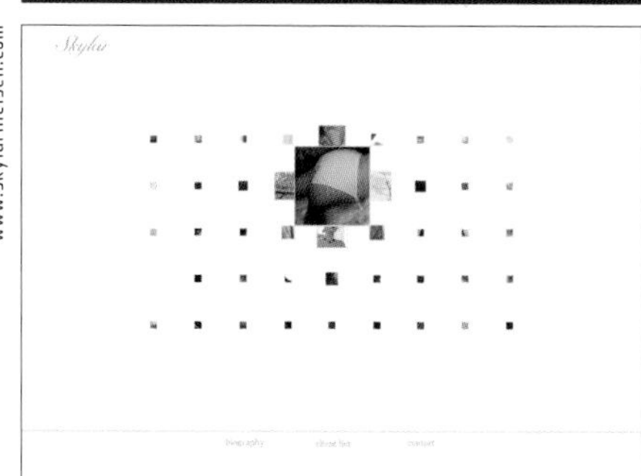

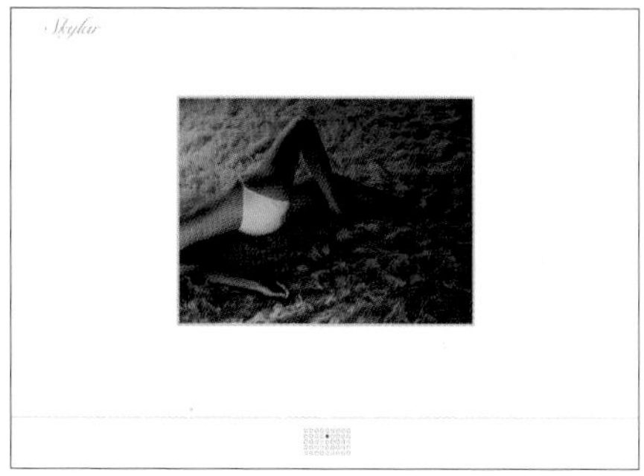

Clients Philips Norelco, Timberland, VW, Durex, Unisys, Microsoft, XanGo, Tribal DDB, DotGlu, Crispin Porter + Bogusky, Arnold Worldwide, Strawbery Frog.

Awards HOW Interactive Design Annual, AIGA, FWA (Site of the Day/Site of the Month), Digital Campaign of the Year, Cannes Cyber Lions (Gold).

STUDIO FM MILANO

ITALY

www.studiofmmilano.it

since 1996

Mission

Usability. /// Convivialité. /// Benutzerfreundlichkeit.

www.studiofmmilano.it

Location

studio FM milano
via Manfredini, 6
20154 Milano
Italy
<info@studiofmmilano.it>

Team

studio FM milano/Art Direction and Graphic Design, Parkmedia/Programming.

www.tecnospa.com/IT/index.htm

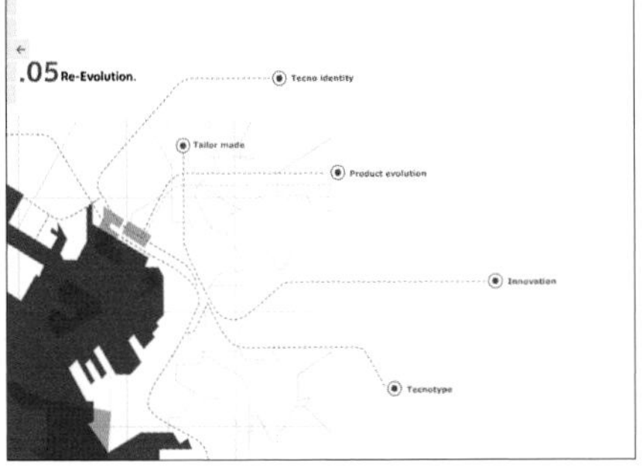

Clients

Boffi, Marni, Tecno, Living Divani, m&a architects, Central Groucho Pictures, Versace, Cesanamedia.

TANKA DESIGN

USA

www.tankadesign.com

since 2002

Mission

Tanka Design combines creativity, precision and a deep understanding of interactive media to build positive user experiences. /// Tanka Design associe la créativité, la précision et une profonde compréhension du média interactif pour construire des expériences positives pour les utilisateurs. /// Tanka Design verbindet Kreativität mit Präzision und umfassendem Know-how über interaktive Medien, um Usern positive Onlineerlebnisse zu vermitteln.

www.tankadesign.com

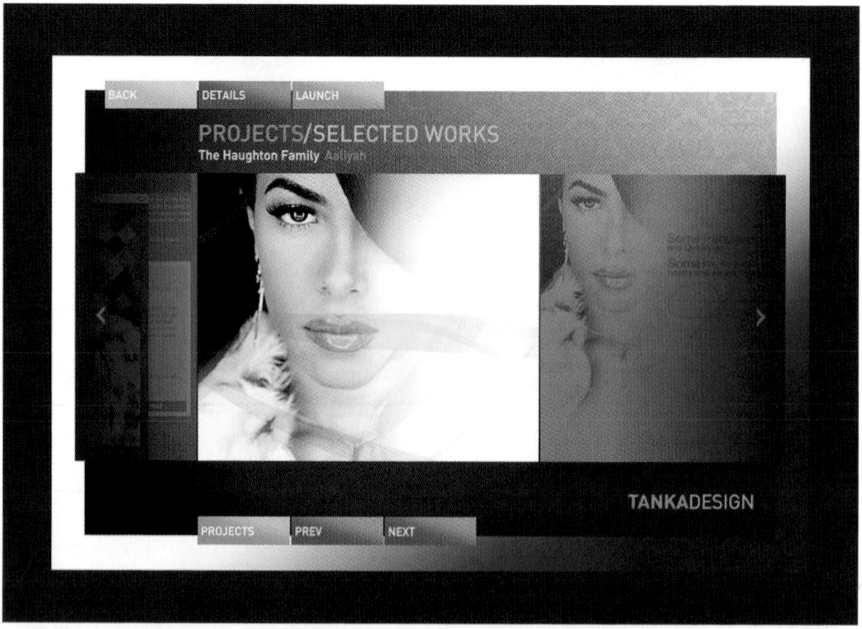

BACK
DETAILS
LAUNCH
PROJECTS/SELECTED WORKS
The Haughton Family Aaliyah
TANKADESIGN
PROJECTS
PREV
NEXT

PROJECTS/SELECTED WORKS
CNBC
TANKADESIGN

PROJECTS/SELECTED WORKS
OUTZONETV.com
TANKADESIGN

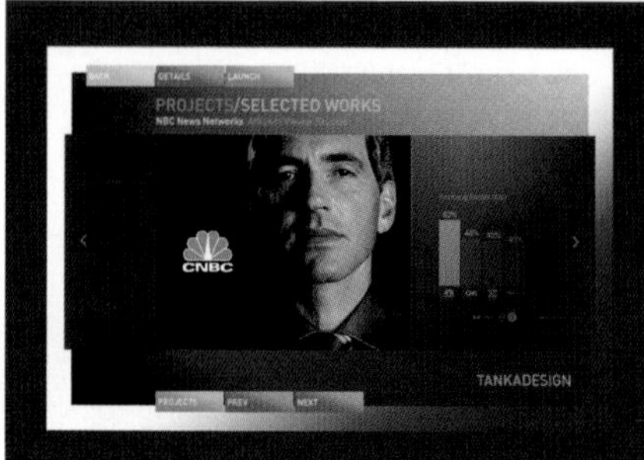

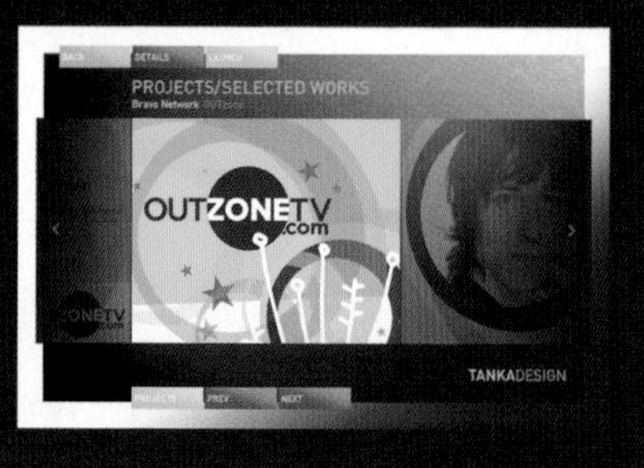

Location

Tanka Design
185 Varick Street Suite 508
New York, NY 10014
USA
<contact@tankadesign.com>

Team

1 Creative Director, 1 Flash/Web Developer.

www.udirectnyc.com

www.thelodge.com/musicproduction

Clients

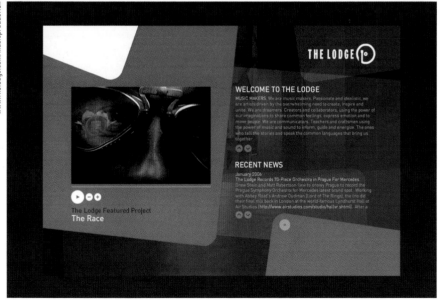

Bravo Network, USA Network, NBC News Networks, PBS, AtmosphereBBDO, VSA Partners, Aaliyah, The Lodge, etc.

TAXI

CANADA

www.taxi.ca

since 1992

Mission

We don't see interactive as a discipline or as a medium; it's a philosophy that has to penetrate everything we do. Whether it's a transit ad, a TV spot, or a micro site; interactivity is simply the best way to engage an audience and tell a compelling story.

Mini Canada

Location

TAXI
Calgary, Montreal, New York, Toronto, TAXI 2 (Toronto)
<hoxford@taxi.ca>

Team

1 Creative Director, 2 ACDs, 11 Designers, 4 Writers, 3 Interactive Producers.

Nous ne considérons pas le Web comme une discipline ni un média, mais comme une philosophie qui doit imprégner tout ce que nous faisons. Qu'il s'agisse d'un affichage transport, d'un spot télévisé ou d'un microsite, l'interactivité est la meilleure façon d'impliquer un public et de raconter une histoire intéressante. /// In unseren Augen steht der Begriff interaktiv nicht für eine Disziplin oder ein Medium, sondern für eine Philosophie, die unsere gesamte Arbeit durchdringt. Ob Transit-Ad, TV-Spot oder Mikroseite – Interaktivität ist einfach der beste Weg, um ein Publikum zu fesseln und spannende Geschichten zu erzählen.

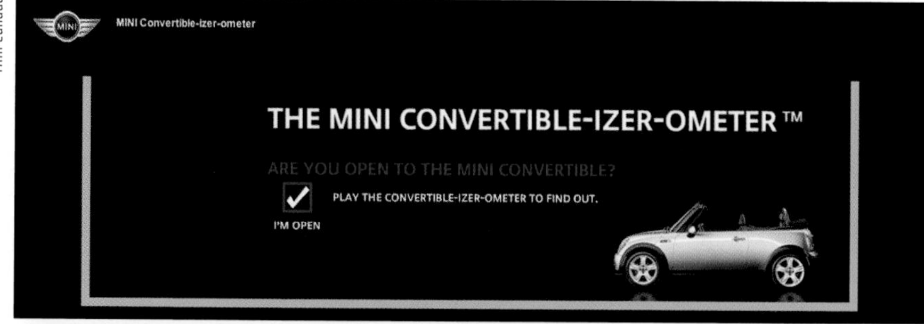

Clients

Amp'd Mobile, Canadian Tire, CNW Group, MINI Canada, Molson Canada, Nike Canada, TELUS Mobility and WestJet.

Awards

Cannes Cyber Lions (2 Gold/2 Bronze), One Show (Gold/Bronze), ADC (2 Gold/Silver), D&AD, CLIOs, How Magazine, New York Festivals, Advertising & Design Club of Canada, Webby Awards.

TEN4 DESIGN

UK

www.ten4design.co.uk

since 2001

Mission

Our award-winning studio designs and builds sites for a diverse range of clients. We have developed custom built Content Management Systems for HTML and Flash sites, a high-end social networking site structure and technology, mobile-to-web blogging, digital viral campaigns and often shoot specific film footage to integrate into sites.

www.meetjohnlegend.com

Location

Ten4 Design Ltd
Ground Floor – Back Building, 148 – 150 Curtain Road
London, EC2A 3AR
United Kingdom
<mail@ten4design.co.uk>

Team

3 Creative Directors, 1 Designer, 2 Programmers.

Notre studio primé conçoit et construit des sites pour divers types de clients. Nous avons développé des systèmes de gestion des contenus pour les sites HTML et Flash, une structure de mise en réseau sociale et une technologie d'excellente qualité, le blogage de portable à site Web, des campagnes numériques et fréquemment le métrage de films à intégrer aux sites. /// **Unser preisgekröntes Studio gestaltet und produziert Webseiten für Kunden aus den unterschiedlichsten Bereichen. Zu unseren Arbeiten zählen maßgeschneiderte Content-Management-Systeme für HTML- und Flash-Seiten, die Entwicklung der Struktur und Technologie für eine hochwertige Social Networking Webseite, Mobile-to-Web-Blogging und digitales Viral-Marketing; zudem produzieren wir häufig spezielles Filmmaterial, das auf Webseiten integriert wird.**

www.lemar-online.com

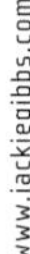

Clients

Columbia Records, Epic Records, RCA Label Group, 19 Management, Vince Power Music Group and Jackie Gibbs Photographic Agency.

Awards

Digital Music Awards (Best Electronic Artist/Best Urban Artist).

THE PHARMACY

THE NETHERLANDS

www.thepharmacy-media.com

since 2000

Mission

thePharmacy is constantly pushing the boundaries of what the web can be. Through the use of killer motion graphics, intelligent development, and a no-nonsense approach thePharmacy is pushing forward the way our clients communicate their message and achieve their goals.

www.hethuisanubis.nl

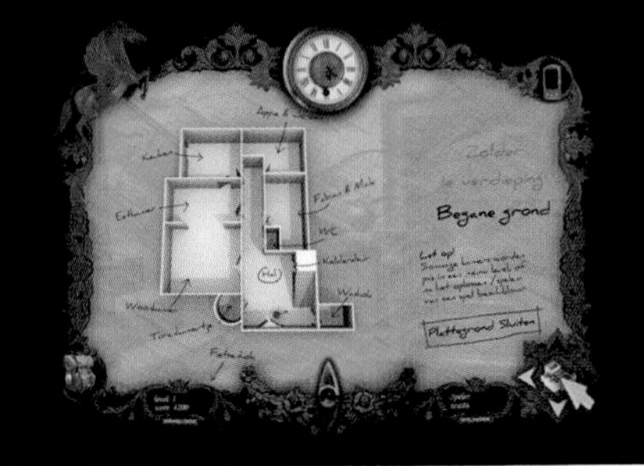

Location

thePharmacy
Julianastraat 7a
5401 HC Uden
The Netherlands
<frank@thepharmacy-media.com>

Team

1 Managing Director, 1 Creative Director, 1 Sales Director, 3 3d Artists, 2 Flash Developers, 2 PHP Programmers, 1 Audio & Sound FX.

L'agence thePharmacy repousse toujours les limites du Web. En utilisant des graphiques en mouvement, un développement intelligent et une méthode logique, thePharmacy enrichit la façon dont nos clients transmettent leurs messages et atteignent leurs objectifs. /// **thePharmacy** testet die Grenzen und Möglichkeiten der Internetnutzung ständig aus. Mit ansteckenden Motion Graphics, intelligenter Entwicklung und einem schnell wirkenden Ansatz macht thePharmacy seine Kunden fit für neue Kommunikationskanäle, damit sie ihre Botschaften wirkungsvoll verbreiten und ihre Ziele erreichen können.

www.shimano-xtr.com

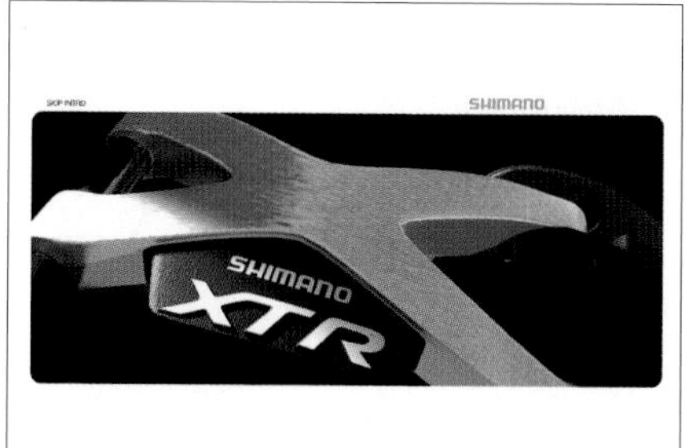

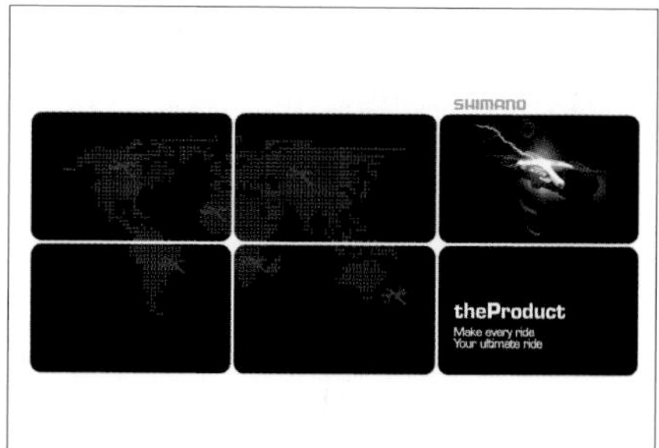

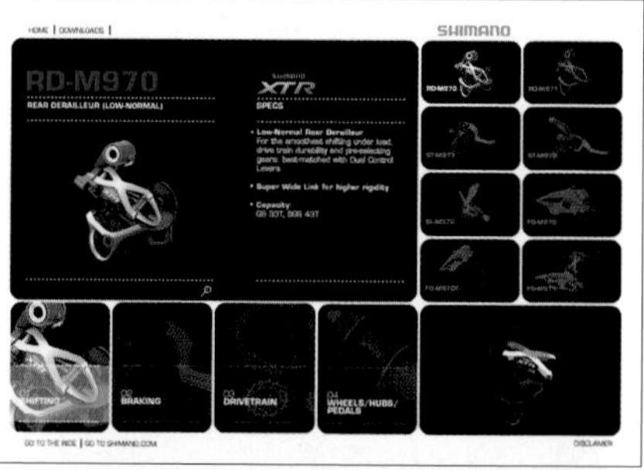

http://www.b2s.nl/hardbass

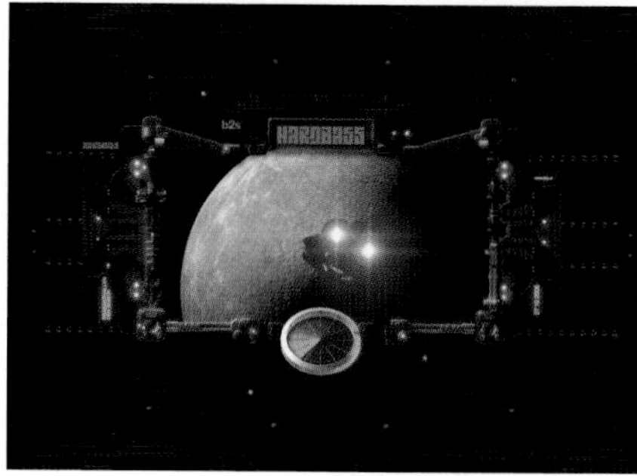

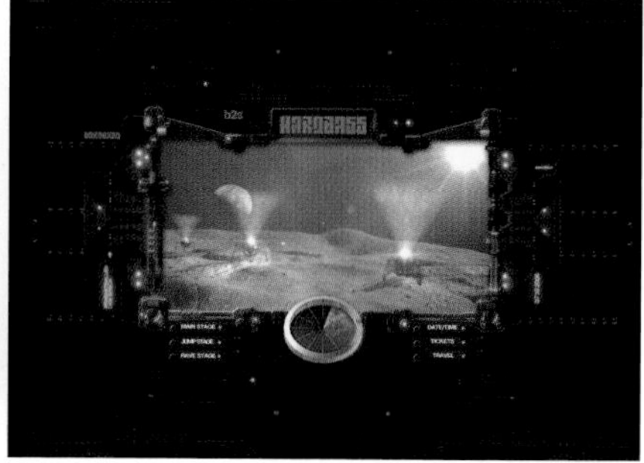

Clients

LG, Nickelodeon, Artis, ID&T, Unibet, Shimano, Altran.

Awards

FWA.

TRIWORKS.NET

PORTUGAL

www.triworks.net

since 2001

Mission

We are a team of professionals creating projects for International and National clients, striving to push the limits in web development using 3D animation and Flash interactive interfaces. We work with almost all available technologies for Internet Development in order to meet all of our client's desires with regard to their projects.

www.collegepokerassociation.com

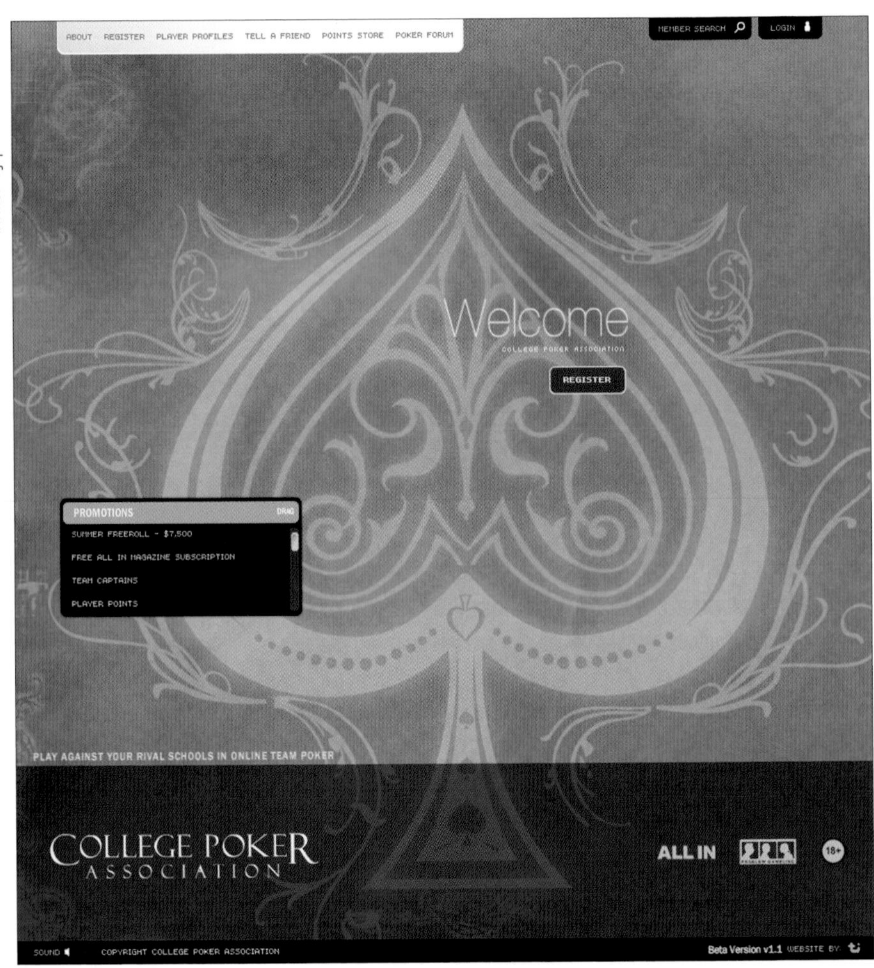

Location

Triworks.net
R. Sao Martinho 31
3810-185 Aveiro
Portugal
<commercial@triworks.net>

Team

1 Creative Director/Art Director, 3 Designers/Programmers, 1 3d Modeller.

Équipe de professionnels qui crée des projets pour des clients nationaux et internationaux et s'efforce de repousser les limites du développement Web au moyen de l'animation en 3D et d'interfaces interactives Flash. Nous utilisons pratiquement toutes les technologies disponibles pour le développement Internet afin de satisfaire les besoins de nos clients dans le cadre de leurs projets. /// **Wir sind ein professionelles Kreativ-Team, das unter Einsatz von 3D-Animationen und interaktiven Flash-Interfaces noch nie da gewesene Weblösungen für nationale und internationale Kunden entwickelt. Wir nutzen nahezu alle Technologien, die für Webdesign zur Verfügung stehen, um alle Wünsche unserer Kunden zu erfüllen.**

www.podmedialtd.com

Welcome to PodMedia website

We are ones to watch out for. From bustling urban cities such as London, New York and Dubai, to timeless resorts like Waikiki Beach, Cancun and Montego Bay we bring you the latest passions in architecture, design and lifestyle. A snoop around world-class real estate, unmissable living spaces, chilled out paradises to cutting edge luxuries. It's all here for those seeking escapesisim to a modern refuge from the big city traffic and noise. The concept is to create a hospitality lounge a magical spot where stylish people get to experience individualism, simplicity and exhibitionism all in one place.

Pod media is a dynamic collection of video features dedicated to an entirely new definition of a stylish, contemporary society. Unique in approach, we embrace the vibrant energy and spirit of each of our covered destinations and their individual design philosophy.

pod MEDIA

Myth Makers

n the past, well-known contemporary architects had a signature style, a series of coded responses to the task of design...

Urban Roof Gardens

Plants are blossoming on high as cities turn the rooftops of their homes and office blocks into little green paradises.

REIT's

Real Estate Investment Trusts, more commonly known as REITs, were first created in the US in the 1880s.

NAVIGATION MENU

LEGAL DISCLAIMER | PRIVACY POLICY

Clients

Sifrina, Drepelimp, Funel Design Group, NewWalk, PodMedia, College Poker Association, Atlanticopress, Fotobanco, 8Mais, Space, Ornel, C.M. Oliveira do Bairo, Tiberio e Cesar, Traço e Ambiente, Choque Virtual.

Awards

FWA (Site of the Day), Fcukstar (Site of the Day), e-Creative (Site of the Day), PixelMakers (Site of the Week), Webcreme (Site of the Day), BIGMAG (Site of the Day), Phirebrush (Site of the Day), Style-Awards (Site of the Day), GOUW (Site of the Day), Website Design Awards (Site of the Day), etc.

VANGOGH CREATIVE

ITALY

www.vangogh-creative.it

since 2004

Mission

Sometimes you need to break with your past in order to give more. It's a clean break away from pre-packed patterns, spreading globalization and artificial communication that makes all customers the same in front of the target. It's tough action that's needed and along with expressing passion and a will to make changes and innovations.

www.vangogh-creative.it

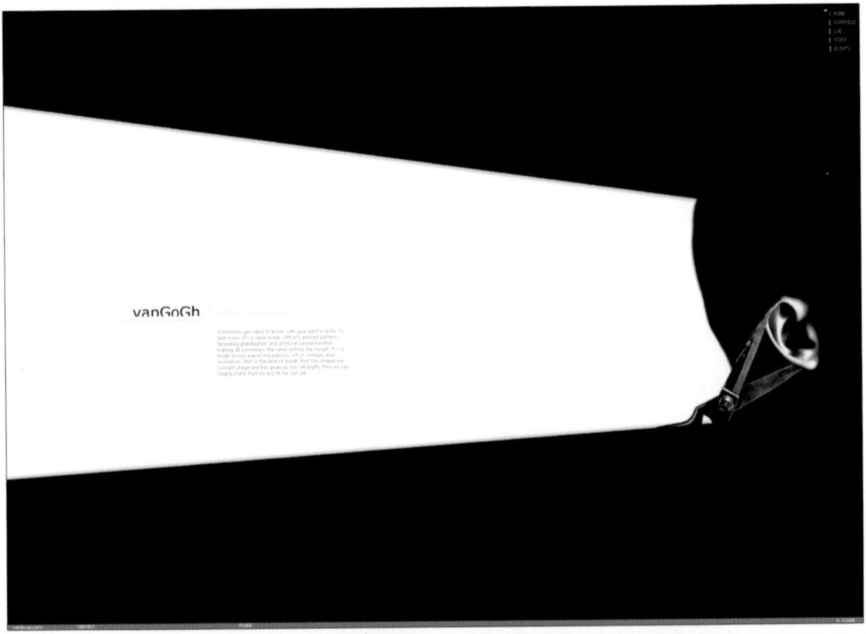

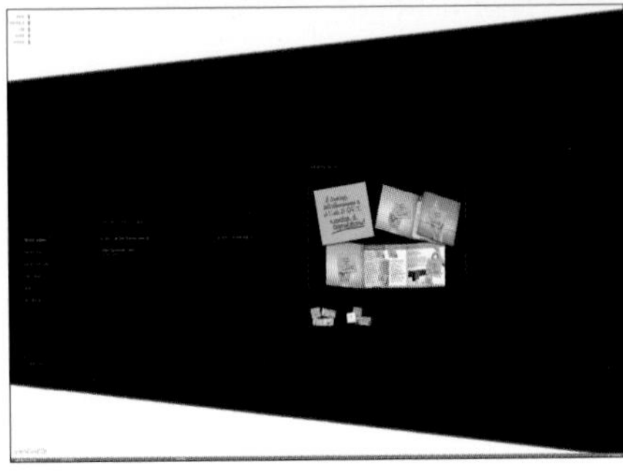

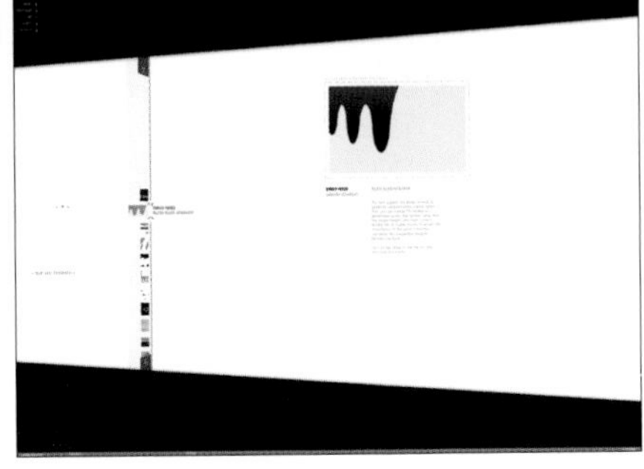

Location

vanGoGh
via Mariani, 1
20063 Cernusco s/N – Milano
Italy
<enrico@vangogh-creative.it>

Team

2 Creative Directors, 2 Art Directors, 4 Designers, 2 Programmers, 2 Copywriters.

Pour être capable de donner davantage, il est parfois nécessaire de rompre avec le passé. Rien à voir avec les modèles préconditionnés, l'extension de la mondialisation et la communication artificielle qui uniformisent tous les clients. Il faut une action énergique, une passion pour l'expression et la volonté d'apporter des changements et d'innover. /// **Wer vorwärts kommen will, muss manchmal die Vergangenheit hinter sich lassen. Wer seine Zielgruppe im Zeitalter der globalen Kommunikation noch erreichen will, muss bereit sein, sich von den allgegenwärtigen vorgefertigten Schemata von Internetauftritten zu lösen, die alle Produkte und Dienstleistungen auf fast identische Weise präsentieren. Das erfordert entschlossene Maßnahmen und den leidenschaftlichen Mut zu innovativen Änderungen.**

www.beboard.net

www.bodiocenter.com

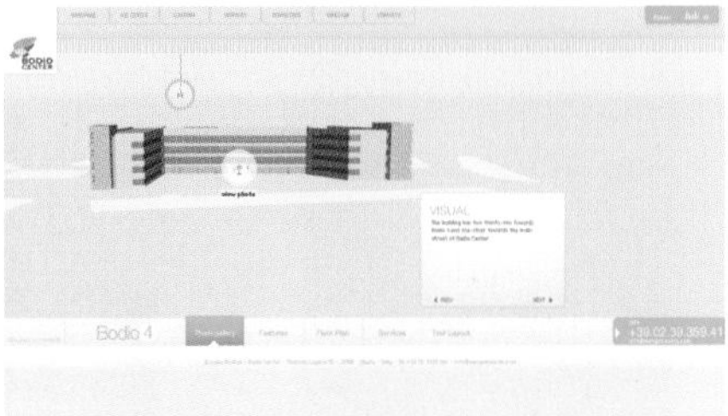

Clients IBM, BMG, Hotelplan, Sperling & Kupfer.

Awards FWA (Site of the Day), Internet TINY Awards.

VISUAL JAZZ

AUSTRALIA

www.visualjazz.com.au

since 2000

Mission

To create a dynamic web presence that embraces the latest technologies, we use practical functionality and cut through design to exceed industry and client expectations. And to take over the world... one web site at a time.

http://navylifestyle.defencejobs.gov.au

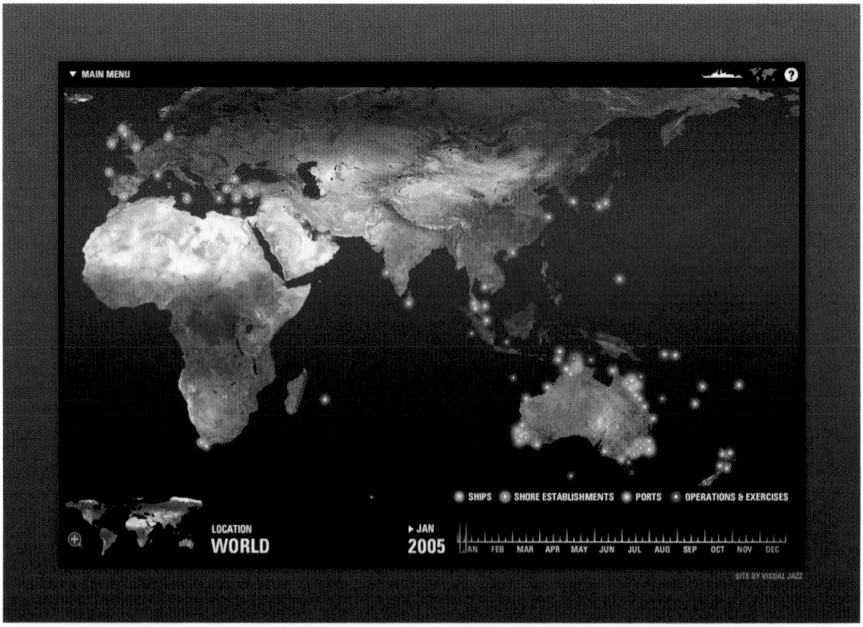

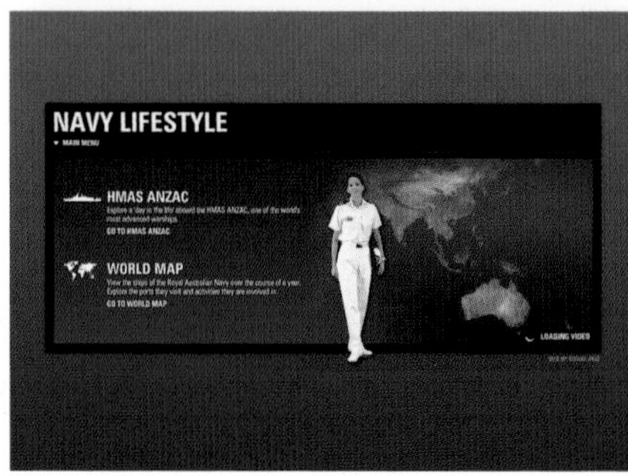

Location

Visual Jazz
Head Office: Level 1, 129 York Street, South Melbourne, VIC 3205
Canberra: Level 1, 44 Sydney Avenue, Barton ACT 2006
Australia
<jazz@visualjazz.com.au>

Team

1 Creative Director, 3 Interactive Art Directors, 6 Interactive Designers, 2 Interactive Producers, 2 Action Scripters, 2 3d Animators, 4 Asp Developers, 5 Account Managers, 1 Account Director, 1 General Manager.

Pour créer une présence Web dynamique qui englobe les technologies les plus récentes, nous utilisons des fonctions pratiques et le design pour répondre aux attentes de l'industrie et de nos clients. Et pour conquérir le monde... un site Internet à la fois. /// **Unsere Spezialität sind dynamische und hochfunktionale Internetlösungen mit durchschlagendem Design und neuesten Technologien, die immer wieder die Erwartungen unserer Kunden und Konkurrenten übertrumpfen. Wir erobern die Welt... von einer Webseite zur nächsten.**

http://porterdavis.com.au

Clients

Australian Defence Force, Holden Australia, Figgins Holdings, Gandel Retail Management, Care Australia, National Australia Bank, MAB Corporation, Acer Arena, BRW, Porter Davis Homes, Fremantle Media.

Awards

FWA (Site of the Day), Macromedia (Site of the Day), DOPE, Internet TINY Award, and the Internet Awards we stole back from GPYR by putting it down our pants.

W3HAUS

BRAZIL/UK

www.w3haus.com.br

since 2000

Mission

To create digital relations. /// Création de relations numériques. /// Wir erschaffen digitale Beziehungen.

www.rider.com.br

Location

W3Haus
Rua Mostardeiro, 780 sala 801, Porto Alegre, RS, Brasil
W3Haus - UK
35a Britannia Row, London, N1 8QH, United Kingdom
<contato@w3haus.com.br>

Team

2 Creative Directors, 3 Art Directors, 4 Designers, 9 Programmers.

www.ipanemagiselebundchen.com.br

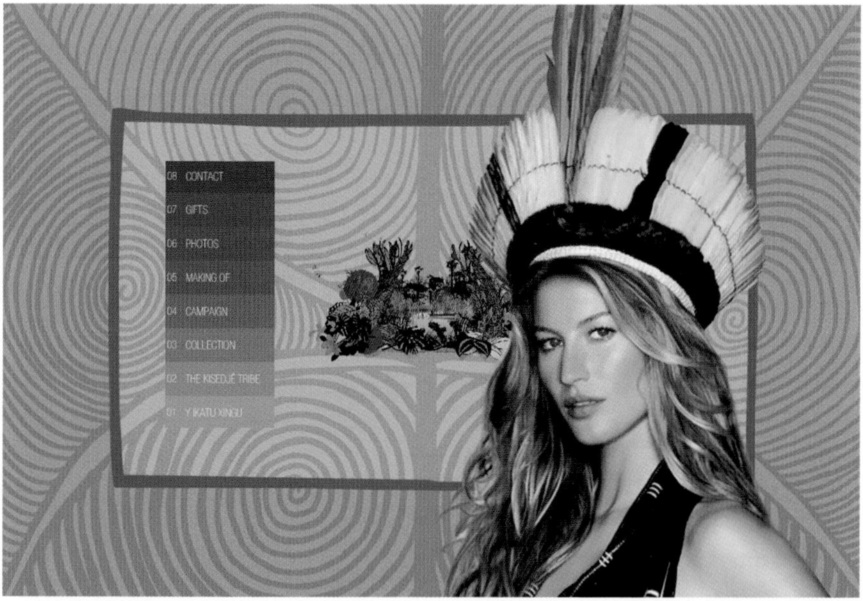

Clients

Amnesty UK, Converse Brasil, C&A Brasil, Tramontina, Grendene.

Awards

Peixe Grande 2005, Plug-in Website Awards.

WEBSHOCKER

SLOVENIA

www.webshocker.net

since 2004

Mission

Drawing on skills and talent from both an IT and design background, Webshocker develops modern internet communication portals. Client satisfaction, creativity and attention to detail, drives Webshocker on a constant mission - to push the boundaries of new media to the limit.

http://speedwave.elanskis.com

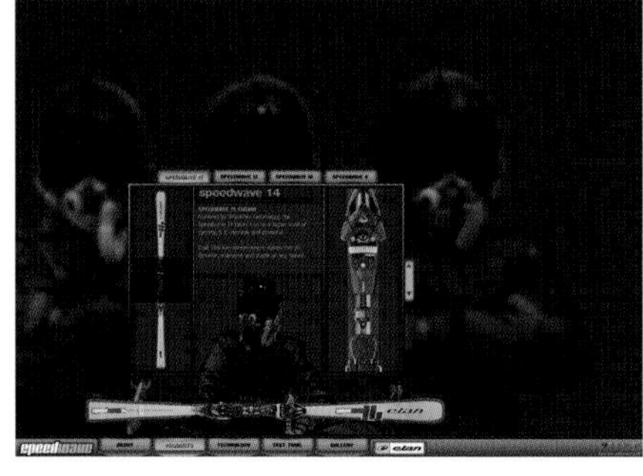

Location

Webshocker
Breznica 48/a
4274 Zirovnica
Slovenia
<info@webshocker.net>

Team

2 Designers, 2 Programmers.

Grâce à une équipe IT et de design compétente et talentueuse, l'agence Webshocker développe des portails de communication Internet très modernes. La satisfaction des clients, la créativité et le souci du détail sont la base de la mission de Webshocker : repousser les limites du nouveau média. /// **Webshocker entwickelt moderne Internet-Kommunikationsportale. Unser talentiertes Team verfügt über jede Menge Know-how in punkto Design und IT. Kundenzufriedenheit, Kreativität und Liebe zum Detail sind die Antriebsmotoren, die Webshocker immer wieder neu auf Touren bringen auf seiner Mission, an die Grenzen der neuen Medien vorzustoßen.**

http://skiselector.elanskis.com

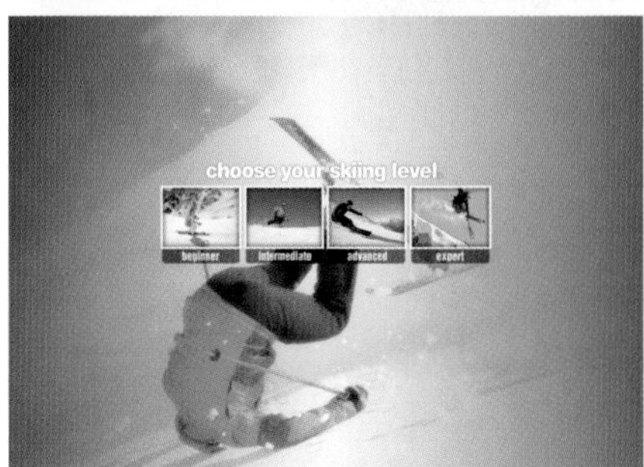

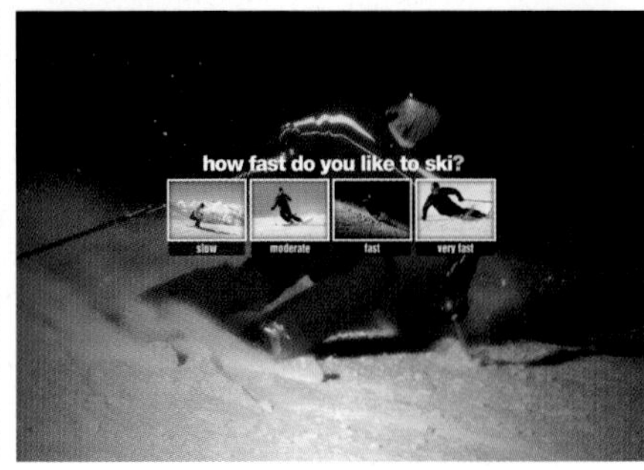

www.fletch.com

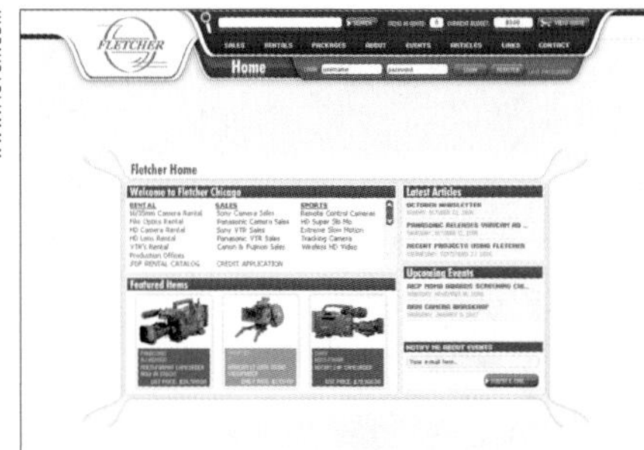

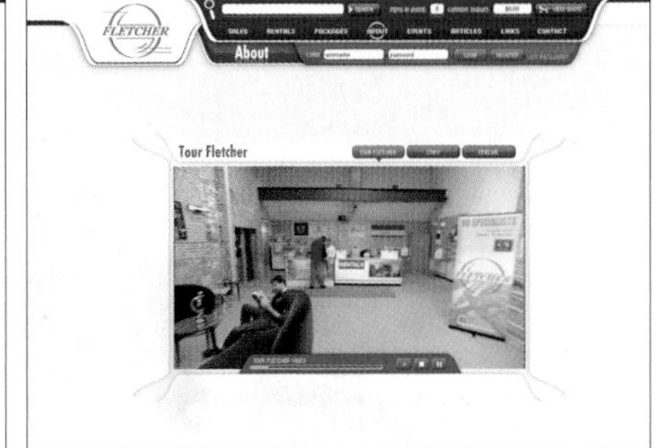

Clients

Fletcher Chicago, Elan Skis, Elan Yachting, Elan Marine, Fructal, Carousel Games, Triumph International, Db Recordings, Onlysamo Photo Agency, Ski&Fun...

Awards

FWA, DOPE, Internet TINY Awards, e-Creative, King for a week, Crossmind.

WEFAIL

USA/UK

www.wefail.com

since 2003

Mission

To make flash websites that only we could make. /// Nous sommes les seuls à pouvoir créer des sites Web Flash de ce type. /// Unser Markenzeichen sind unverwechselbare Flash-Webseiten.

www.matthewmahon.com

Location

WEFAIL
Wilmslow, Cheshire, United Kingdom
Austin, Texas, USA
<fail@wefail.com>

Team

2 Designers.

www.eminem.com

www.dixiechicks.com/underground

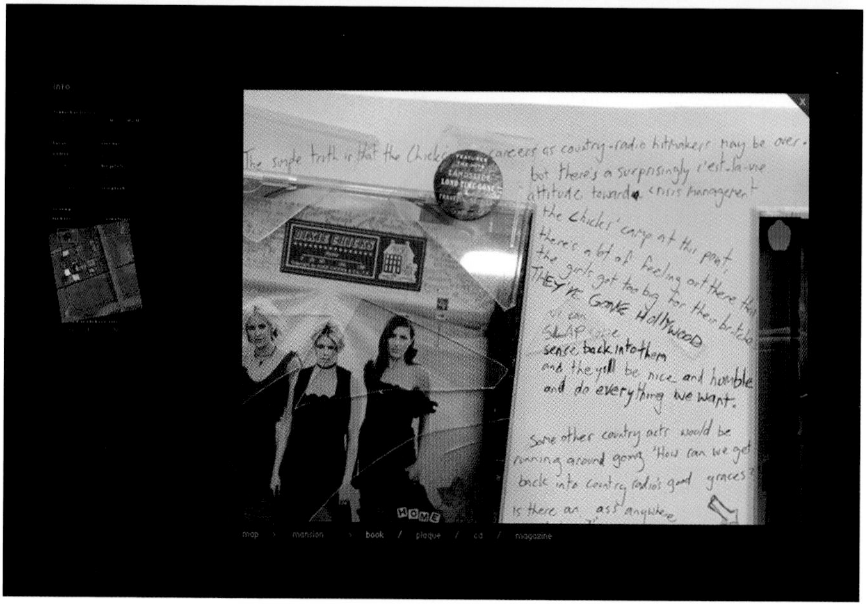

Clients BBDO, Eminem, Dixie Chicks, MTV, Cartoon Network, Christian Aid.

Awards Flashforward (Technical Merit), SXSW (Best Music Site), Communication Arts, FWA (People's Choice Award).

WORKROCKS

UKRAINE

www.workrocks.com

since 2003

Mission

Our company provides clients with everything they could possibly need in the fields of internet, design and new media. We help clients to make key decisions with regard to brand identity. In announcing the high level of performance and success of our work, we would like to call special attention to our production debugging system, and our company's great teamwork.

http://style.dp.ua

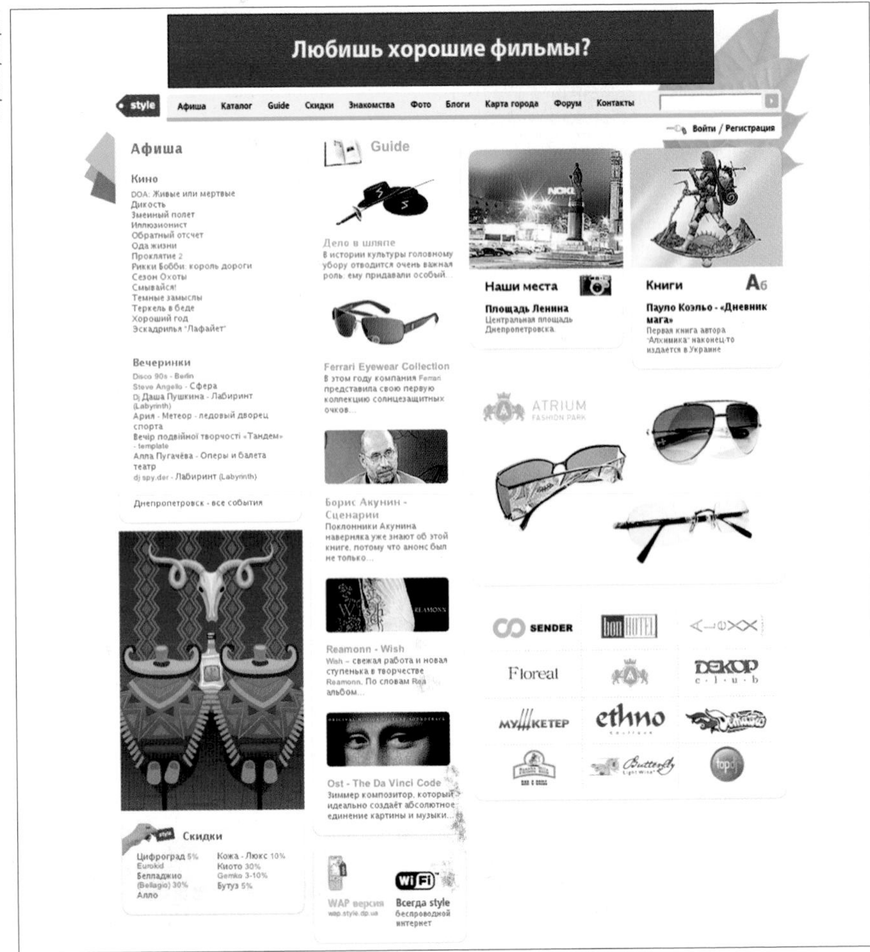

Location

Workrocks
Ukraine
Naberezhnaya Lenina str. 15a
<info@workrocks.com>

Team

1 Creative Director, 3 Art Directors, 5 Designers, 5 Programmers.

Nous offrons aux clients tout ce dont ils peuvent avoir besoin dans le domaine d'Internet, du design et du nouveau média. Nous aidons les clients à prendre des décisions importantes concernant l'identité de leur marque. Nous réalisons un travail très efficace et performant et nous disposons d'un système de débogage de la production et d'une équipe fantastique. /// **Wir versorgen Kunden mit allem, was sie in Sachen Internet, Design und neue Medien benötigen. Wir unterstützen unsere Kunden dabei, elementare Entscheidungen hinsichtlich ihrer Markenidentität zu fällen. Top-Leistungen mit einem Top-Team sind der Schlüssel zu unserem Erfolg. Zudem bieten wir unseren Kunden mit unserem Production Debugging System ein besonderes Plus.**

http://meladze.ru

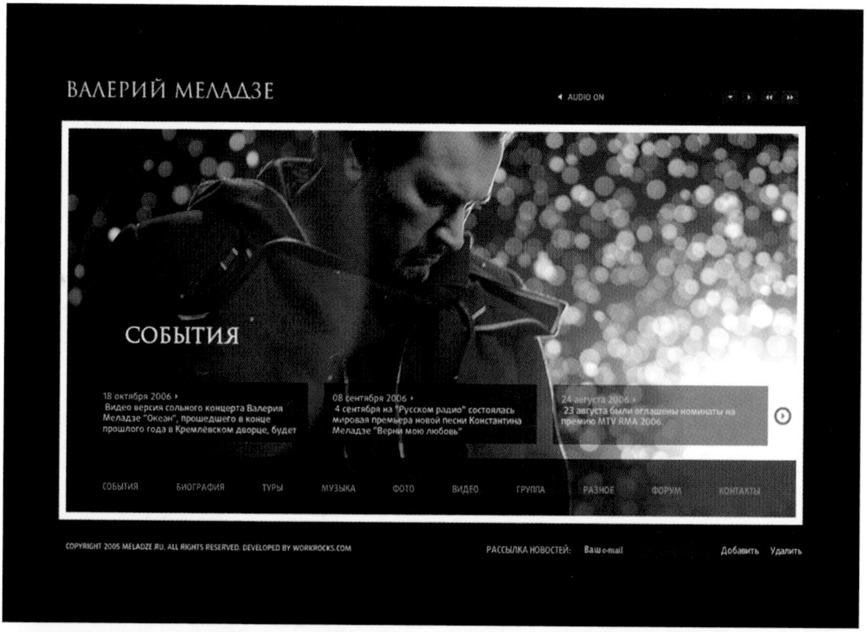

ВАЛЕРИЙ МЕЛАДЗЕ
AUDIO ON
СОБЫТИЯ
18 октября 2006
Видео версия сольного концерта Валерия Меладзе "Океан", прошедшего в конце прошлого года в Кремлёвском дворце, будет
08 сентября 2006
4 сентября на "Русском радио" состоялась мировая премьера новой песни Константина Меладзе "Верни мою любовь"
24 августа 2006
23 августа были оглашены номинаты на премию MTV RMA 2006.
СОБЫТИЯ БИОГРАФИЯ ТУРЫ МУЗЫКА ФОТО ВИДЕО ГРУППА РАЗНОЕ ФОРУМ КОНТАКТЫ
COPYRIGHT 2005 MELADZE.RU. ALL RIGHTS RESERVED. DEVELOPED BY WORKROCKS.COM
РАССЫЛКА НОВОСТЕЙ: Ваш e-mail
Добавить Удалить

ВАЛЕРИЙ МЕЛАДЗЕ

ВАЛЕРИЙ МЕЛАДЗЕ
МУЗЫКА

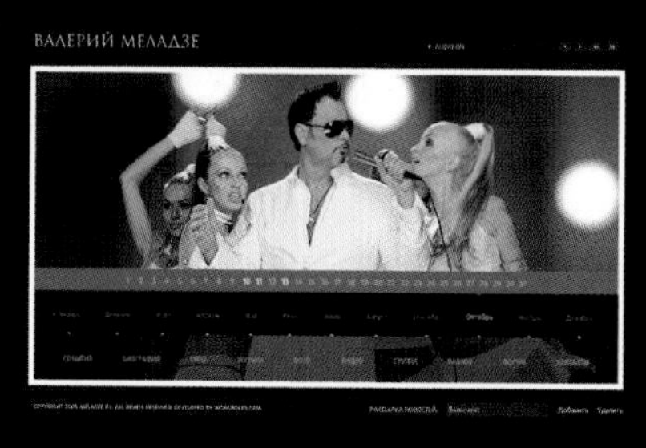

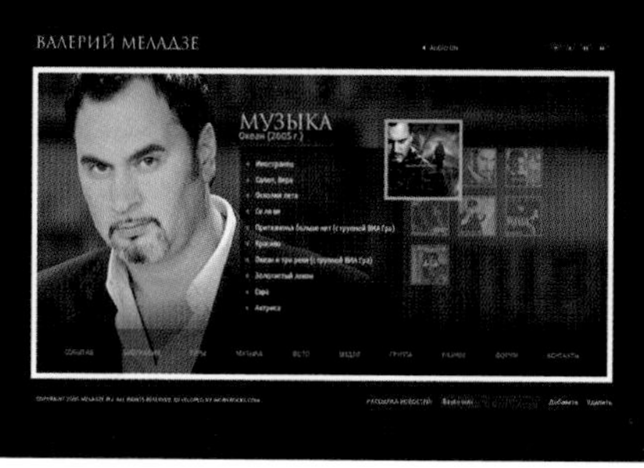

Clients

Valeriy Meladze, Honda Russia, DJ Joss, Juzmin Media, Party Salon Agency, TM Mushketer, TOP DJ, style.dp.ua.

Awards

Kiev International Advertising Festival, FWA, NewWebPick.

ZUM KUCKUCK

GERMANY

www.zumkuckuck.com

since 2002

Mission

A design studio focused on corporate design, interface design and interactive media. Founded in 2002, the studio works with traditional agencies and medium-sized businesses. By combining the traditional design process with technology, research and prototyping, the studio is able to develop innovative experiences in interactive media.

www.reisenthel.de

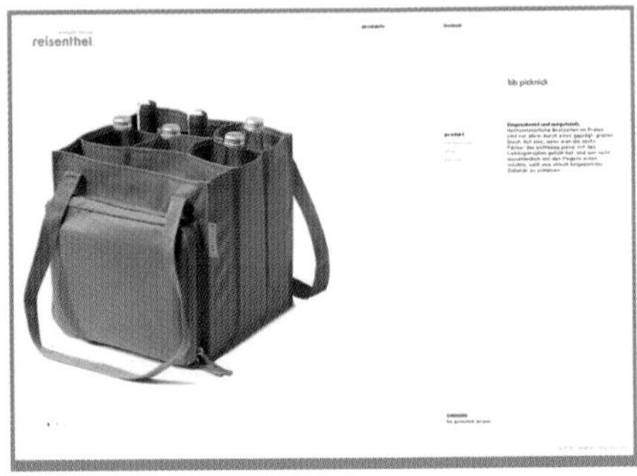

Location

ZUM KUCKUCK
Burkarderstr. 36
D-97082 Würzburg
Germany
<info@zumkuckuck.com>

Team

4 Designers, 4 Programmers, 1 Contacter.

Studio de design centré sur le design d'entreprises et d'interfaces et les médias interactifs. Fondé en 2002, ZUM KUCKUCK collabore avec des agences traditionnelles et des moyennes entreprises. En associant le processus de design traditionnel et la technologie, la recherche et le prototypage, le studio peut développer des expériences nouvelles sur le Web. /// **Das Designbüro ZUM KUCKUCK ist auf Corporate Design, User Interface Design und Interaction Design spezialisiert. Das Büro wurde 2002 gegründet und zählt neben klassischen Agenturen auch mittelständische Unternehmen zu seinen Kunden. Das Studio kombiniert den traditionellen Designprozess mit Technologie, Forschung und Prototyping, um innovative und erlebnisorientierte Lösungen für interaktive Medien zu entwickeln.**

Volkswagen FOX

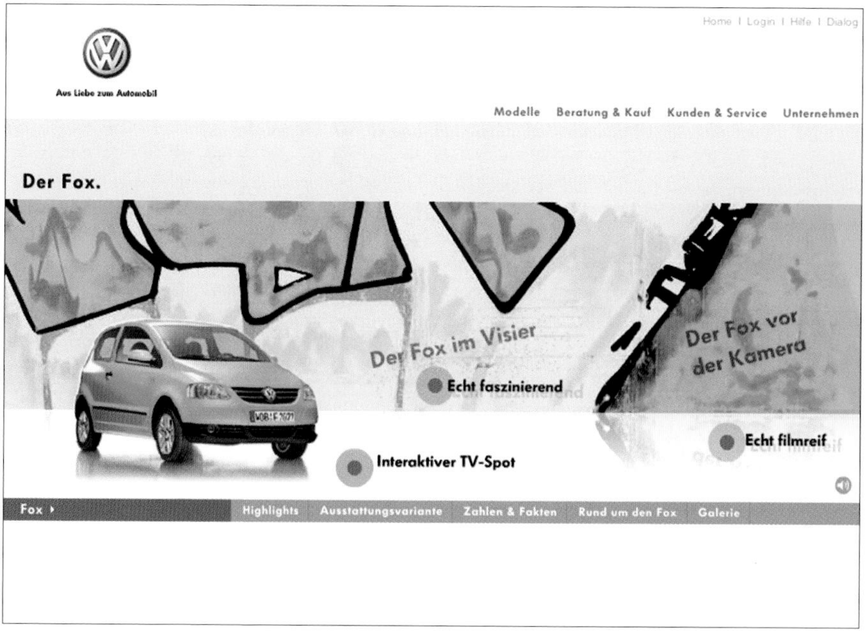

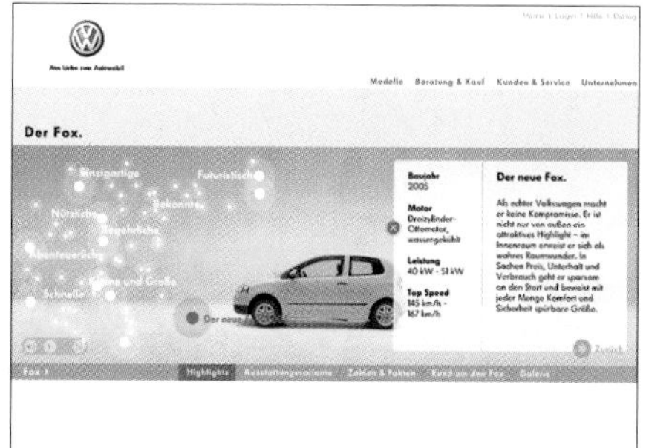

Clients

Audi, Bayern Design, Buena la Vista AG, byteconsult, DDB Berlin, Drykorn, Huth+Wenzel Werbeagentur, Ingo Peters Photography, IWA, iWelt AG, krick, McCann-Erickson B.C.A, neckermann.de, Patisserie, Reisenthel Accessoires, Schitto Schmodde Waack Werbeagentur, Tribal DDB Hamburg.

Awards

Flashforward (Flash Film Festival: Commerce), red dot award (Best of the Best), iF communication design award, Output 08, ADC New York (Distinctive Merit), Communication Arts Network (Site of the Week), Macromedia (Site of the Week/Site of the Day).

CREDITS

Dear readers, here comes the second, but not renewed. They are all new. This book is a continuation of the first **Web Design: Studios** book, published in the end of 2004. After a little over two years we bring to you a completely new selection of studios that do outstanding interactive work.

It has been once more a hard time to decide which offices we had to leave out. The internet is not only growing bigger, it is growing better. The quality of the work and the availability of resources are now reaching a point where creators have almost all the freedom they always hoped to have. It is of course also growing more complex, as designers and corporations push the resources to their limits, demanding a whole new thinking for the web. In this direction, we have seen an astonish increase in the pre-production for materials to be used on the net. The time when someone would step into a design office with some images in a folder and text on a CD, and then as for a website, is almost gone. Websites require now briefing, strategy, conceptual development phase, casting, video production, special shooting sections, special effects, soundtrack, illustration, customized content management, and there it goes. It is an-precedent.

This book should serve as a reference for anyone willing to work in the highest levels online. Today almost a necessity to any businesses and professionals. The portfolios of these studios, the complexity of the work they execute and the demanding clients they handle will leave no doubt that the featured works in this book are a reference to what has been done these days.

We had the luck to have great contributors in this book, starting with **Jonathan Hills**, from **Domani Studios**, who wrote the inspiring Intro for the publication. Domani was published in the first edition and now Jonathan introduces the new published interactive design studios. We also have a pleasure to count with other three guys that have written really insightful essays. These are **Hideki Ogino**, from **FICC** in Tokyo, Fred Flade from **de-construct** in London and **Roger Stighäll** from **North Kingdom** in Sweden. The only things I can say about them in thank you, and that they know what they are talking about.

I would like to thank all the studios for submitting material and collaborating in the book. Also to those which were not selected this time. The work you do led as to ask you for submission. Was not this time, but the series will move on and new titles will come. Also many thanks to Daniel Siciliano Brêtas for making the whole process very smooth. To our production man Stefan Klatte for making this series always looking better and working in the speed of light. Have a nice read!

Julius Wiedemann

IMPRINT

Web Design: Studios 2

To stay informed about upcoming TASCHEN titles, please request our magazine at www.taschen.com/magazine or write to TASCHEN, Hohenzollernring 53, D-50672 Cologne, Germany, contact@taschen.com, Fax: +49-221-254919. We will be happy to send you a free copy of our magazine which is filled with information about all of our books.

Design & layout: Daniel Siciliano Brêtas
Production: Stefan Klatte
Editor: Julius Wiedemann
Editorial coordination: Daniel Siciliano Brêtas

French translation: Valérie Espinasse
German translation: Heike Reissig
Spanish translation: Mar Portillo
Italian translation: Marco Barberi
Portuguese translation: Alcides Murtinheira

Printed in Italy
ISBN: 978-3-8228-3010-9

Web Design: E-Commerce
Ed. Julius Wiedemann /
Flexi-cover, 192 pp. / € 6.99 /
$ 9.99 / £ 5.99 / ¥ 1.500

Web Design: Flash Sites
Ed. Julius Wiedemann /
Flexi-cover, 192 pp. / € 6.99 /
$ 9.99 / £ 5.99 / ¥ 1.500

Web Design: Music Sites
Ed. Julius Wiedemann /
Flexi-cover, 192 pp. / € 6.99 /
$ 9.99 / £ 5.99 / ¥ 1.500

"These books are beautiful objects, well-designed and lucid." —*Le Monde*, Paris, on the ICONS series

---

" Buy them all and add some pleasure to your life."

African Style
Ed. Angelika Taschen
Alchemy & Mysticism
Alexander Roob
American Indian
Dr. Sonja Schierle
Angels
Gilles Néret
Architecture Now!
Ed. Philip Jodidio
Art Now
Eds. Burkhard Riemschneider, Uta Grosenick
Atget's Paris
Ed. Hans Christian Adam
Audrey Hepburn
Ed. Paul Duncan
Bamboo Style
Ed. Angelika Taschen
Berlin Style
Ed. Angelika Taschen
Brussels Style
Ed. Angelika Taschen
Cars of the 50s
Ed. Jim Heimann, Tony Thacker
Cars of the 60s
Ed. Jim Heimann, Tony Thacker
Cars of the 70s
Ed. Jim Heimann, Tony Thacker
Chairs
Eds. Charlotte & Peter Fiell
Charlie Chaplin
Ed. Paul Duncan
China Style
Ed. Angelika Taschen
Christmas
Ed. Jim Heimann, Steven Heller
Classic Rock Covers
Ed. Michael Ochs
Clint Eastwood
Ed. Paul Duncan
Design Handbook
Eds. Charlotte & Peter Fiell
Design of the 20th Century
Eds. Charlotte & Peter Fiell
Design for the 21st Century
Eds. Charlotte & Peter Fiell
Devils
Gilles Néret
Digital Beauties
Ed. Julius Wiedemann
Robert Doisneau
Ed. Jean-Claude Gautrand
East German Design
Ralf Ulrich / Photos: Ernst Hedler
Egypt Style
Ed. Angelika Taschen
Encyclopaedia Anatomica
Ed. Museo La Specola Florence
M.C. Escher
Fashion
Ed. The Kyoto Costume Institute
Fashion Now!
Eds. Terry Jones, Susie Rushton
Fruit
Ed. George Brookshaw, Uta Pellgrü-Gagel
HR Giger
HR Giger
Grand Tour
Harry Seidler
Graphic Design
Eds. Charlotte & Peter Fiell
Greece Style
Ed. Angelika Taschen
Halloween
Ed. Jim Heimann, Steven Heller
Havana Style
Ed. Angelika Taschen
Homo Art
Gilles Néret
Hot Rods
Ed. Coco Shinomiya, Tony Thacker
Hula
Ed. Jim Heimann
Indian Style
Ed. Angelika Taschen
India Bazaar
Samantha Harrison, Bari Kumar
Industrial Design
Eds. Charlotte & Peter Fiell
Japanese Beauties
Ed. Alex Gross
Las Vegas
Ed. Jim Heimann, W. R. Wilkerson III
London Style
Ed. Angelika Taschen
Marilyn Monroe
Ed. Paul Duncan
Marlon Brando
Ed. Paul Duncan
Mexico Style
Ed. Angelika Taschen
Miami Style
Ed. Angelika Taschen
Minimal Style
Ed. Angelika Taschen
Morocco Style
Ed. Angelika Taschen
New York Style
Ed. Angelika Taschen
Orson Welles
Ed. Paul Duncan
Paris Style
Ed. Angelika Taschen
Penguin
Frans Lanting
20th Century Photography
Museum Ludwig Cologne
Photo Icons I
Hans-Michael Koetzle
Photo Icons II
Hans-Michael Koetzle
Pierre et Gilles
Eric Troncy
Provence Style
Ed. Angelika Taschen
Robots & Spaceships
Ed. Teruhisa Kitahara
Safari Style
Ed. Angelika Taschen
Seaside Style
Ed. Angelika Taschen
Signs
Ed. Julius Wiedeman
South African Style
Ed. Angelika Taschen
Starck
Philippe Starck
Surfing
Ed. Jim Heimann
Sweden Style
Ed. Angelika Taschen
Sydney Style
Ed. Angelika Taschen
Tattoos
Ed. Henk Schiffmacher
Tiffany
Jacob Baal-Teshuva
Tiki Style
Sven Kirsten
Tokyo Style
Ed. Angelika Taschen
Tuscany Style
Ed. Angelika Taschen
Valentines
Ed. Jim Heimann, Steven Heller
Web Design: Best Studios
Ed. Julius Wiedemann
Web Design: E-Commerce
Ed. Julius Wiedemann
Web Design: Flash Sites
Ed. Julius Wiedemann
Web Design: Music Sites
Ed. Julius Wiedemann
Web Design: Portfolios
Ed. Julius Wiedemann
Women Artists in the 20th and 21st Century
Ed. Uta Grosenick
70s Fashion
Ed. Jim Heimann

ICONS